THE
BOOK
OF
PRIDE

THE
BOOK
OF
PRIDE

LGBTQ HEROES
WHO CHANGED THE WORLD

MASON FUNK

HarperOne
An Imprint of HarperCollinsPublishers

HarperOne

HarperCollins books may be purchased for educational, business, or sales promotional use. For information, please email the Special Markets Department at SPsales@harpercollins.com.

FIRST EDITION

Designed by Yvonne Chan

Library of Congress Cataloging-in-Publication Data

Names: Funk, Mason, author.
Title: The book of pride : LGBTQ heroes who changed the world / Mason Funk.
Description: First edition. | New York, NY : HarperOne, [2019]
Identifiers: LCCN 2019006758 | ISBN 9780062571700 (trade pbk)
Subjects: LCSH: Sexual minorities—United States—Biography. | Gays—United States—Biography. | Gay rights.
Classification: LCC HQ73.3.U6 F86 2019 | DDC 920.0086/6—dc23
LC record available at https://lccn.loc.gov/2019006758

22 23 24 25 26 LBC 9 8 7 6 5

CONTENTS

INTRODUCTION

BY MASON FUNK

Once upon a time, nearly thirty years ago, I embarked on a daring trip. I joined an expedition of seventy-five people traveling by jeep and motorcycle from Portugal, in southern Europe, to the country of Angola in southern Africa, a distance of around forty-two hundred miles. After months of planning and preparation, vaccinations, and obtaining visas for thirteen countries, we set out in April 1992. But just after we'd crossed the border from Algeria into Mali on the southern flank of the Sahara Desert, our trip took a very bad turn. As we drove through a narrow valley with sandy hills on either side, six men emerged from the scrub brush, their faces wrapped in scarves, and raised Kalashnikov submachine guns over their heads. They stopped us in our tracks, and over the next hour, they went from jeep to jeep, stripping us of cash, cameras, and anything else they wanted. Meanwhile, other people came and started driving our jeeps away.

Among our possessions, there was one item we absolutely needed to hold on to: our satellite phone. If the bandits took that phone from us, we would be stranded. It was our lifeline.

Somehow, we hatched a plan. Working in coordination with one another, communicating entirely by glances and head tilts, we managed to smuggle the satellite phone, wrapped in a sleeping bag, from jeep to jeep ahead of the bandits. Then, at a critical moment, we snuck it around and past them into a jeep they had already searched. No small feat, given that the satellite dish was the size of a small coffee table.

When the bandits finally departed, we used the phone to call for help. Days later, the Portuguese government came and airlifted us to safety.

So why introduce *The Book of Pride*, a collection of interviews with LGBTQ heroes, with this story? Because as this book came together, I often thought of that satellite phone and that terrifying moment in the desert. That phone was the most precious thing in the universe. Hidden inside a sleeping bag, it was like a treasure (with lifesaving ramifications) that needed to be salvaged, protected, and moved from one location to another.

So, also, are the stories in *The Book of Pride*. The people who have lived these stories are mortal. The force advancing on them is not desert outlaws, but time. Now, as never before, their stories need to be saved, protected, and moved to a new location: the hearts and minds of people who will carry their legacies and their mission forward.

In 2016, I created a project called OUTWORDS to collect, treasure, and share these stories. And this book is our first transmission device.

As I type these words, a thin gold band encircles my left ring finger. Six years ago, my husband, Jay, and I got legally married in our home state of California. Two years later, the US Supreme Court made marriage equality the law of the land. The morning after that historic decision, I picked the *Los Angeles Times* up off our driveway and went to breakfast at a local café. I ordered coffee, opened the newspaper, read the headlines, and started crying. I was so happy. Glancing around, a little embarrassed, I saw a man and woman watching me. They could see the headlines. They were smiling. They were happy too. Love is love.

That couple might have been surprised to know that within the American LGBTQ community, the campaign for marriage equality was and is hotly debated. A lot of queer people see marriage as a betrayal of who we are and who we should be. They point to marriage's deeply flawed history as a system for men to effectively own women, and they note that today, a majority of marriages end in divorce. Why would we want to buy into such an institution?

That debate reflects a fundamental truth—perhaps obvious, perhaps not—about the queer community. On marriage and a thousand other topics (including the word "queer," which I like and use interchangeably with "LGBTQ"), we are not united, and we are not monolithic. We cross boundaries and transcend definition, encompassing every facet of America's richly pluralistic population.

So why even call us a community? What unites and defines us, in my opinion, is that we are all rule-breakers in one of mainstream society's most deeply entrenched and ferociously protected systems: the roles of women and men. Simply put, we refuse to conform to expectations based on gender, declaring with varying degrees of openness and defiance that who we are, who we love and who we have sex with isn't defined by our anatomy, our appearance, or how others perceive us. Frequently, we take things a step further, asserting that the basic rules of engagement—the either/or, fixed notion of gender and gendered behavior—are flawed.

We refuse to play by the rules. And if our own community's rules don't feel right, we reject them too. Take Lani Ka'ahumanu (p. 207). In the early 1970s, Lani came out as a lesbian in San Francisco. A few years later, she surprised herself by falling in love with a man. ("Whoops!") Facing condemnation from virtually every side, including many of her lesbian friends, Lani stood her ground. Today, she's one of America's most honored and cherished bisexual leaders.

Marcus Arana (p. 192) is another person who has truly carved his own path. At birth, Marcus was designated female and given the name Mary. When Mary transitioned and became Marcus, he took the middle name DeMaria—"from Mary"—because he didn't want to buy into the narrative that his former gender identity was "wrong." Along the way, Marcus discovered that he's attracted to both men and women, so today he identifies as a bisexual man. He'll take complexity over categories any day.

Lani, Marcus, and everyone else in this book represent where I hope the human race is headed. In moving toward more freedom, openness, and transparency, they are also moving toward more integrity. In living by their own rules and being exactly and un-apologetically who they are, they are helping create a world where other people can do the same.

Our elders didn't necessarily choose this leadership role. I didn't. But when it was offered to me, I accepted it. I accepted it when I came out as gay, and I continue to accept it every time I make the effort to honestly be and express who I am. Every time I do that, I hope and believe I make it a little easier for someone else to do the same.

That's why this book is called *The Book of Pride*, and that's why I am deeply proud and grateful to be part of the community it reflects.

I wasn't always proud.

In December 2014, I ran a marathon in Death Valley. Although this was my twelfth marathon, this race was particularly brutal for me. Around mile 14, I hit the wall (yes, it's a thing), and the final twelve miles were sheer agony.

When I finally crossed the finish line, I somehow managed to smile. Jay captured the moment in a photo, which I posted to Facebook. The caption read, "Smiling now, but that was some hard shit."

That pretty much sums up my story as a gay man. Smiling now—but that was some hard shit.

Lots of loneliness. Lots of shame. Lots of praying for God to make me straight. Lots of confusingly brief sexual encounters with both men and women. End result: lots of self-hate. To this day, it is sometimes hard to believe that anyone, including Jay, loves me for exactly who I am.

As a result, up until around five years ago, I'd say my sense of connection to the LGBTQ community was pretty thin. Sure, I was living as an openly gay man in Los Angeles. I was out to my family and my friends and at work. I rarely hid my sexuality in any active way.

But was I proud? Not really. And I certainly had no idea of how my journey as a gay man, and my connection to the LGBTQ community, might suddenly undergo a radical shift.

One night in June 2014, I fell asleep next to Jay as usual; but then I woke up, and couldn't get back to sleep. For some reason, lying there in the darkness, I looked back over my life, from the first terrifying moments in high school when I knew I was gay, up to my present life—a life overflowing with good things. A life where I was no longer afraid.

Something clicked in me. As I contemplated how much life had changed for me,

I felt connected in an entirely new way to something much larger than myself: a *movement*. A profound societal shift that I had witnessed, been part of, and benefited from. I myself had not done much to bring that shift about. But other people had.

In that moment, in that darkness, I was seized by the desire to find those people, wherever they were, and interview them.

This idea didn't come completely out of the blue. For about twenty years, I had been a writer and producer of nonfiction TV programs for networks like the Discovery Channel, A&E, FOX Sports, and others. Part of my job had been to find and interview people in countless obscure locations, from a professional baseball scout in Anchorage, Alaska, to a petroleum engineer in the Gulf of Mexico. I absolutely loved this work. I loved carefully preparing for each interview. And I loved how, in the blink of an eye, the interview could take off in a completely unexpected direction, fueled by elements in the subject's life that I had no idea about.

At some point in my career, I had also learned of a project called the Shoah Foundation, a collection of fifty-two thousand interviews from around the world with witnesses and survivors of the Holocaust. I found this project deeply moving and inspiring—the idea that people traveled all over the world to document this profound, seminal, horrific historical event.

In simple terms, on that night in June 2014, I realized that's what I wanted to do. Crisscross America (I would tackle the world later) with a camera, interviewing the people

who were responsible for, participated in, or simply witnessed the movement that gave rise to the LGBTQ community.

For the next six months, I sat on the idea. I didn't know what to do with it—or how to do it. My initial excitement faded. I got caught up in a new TV project. I was training for a marathon. And my mom was dying.

Then, one Sunday morning in January 2015, I read an article in the *Los Angeles Times* about a man named Eric Julber (p. 126). In the 1950s, Eric was a freshly minted lawyer looking to do some pro bono civil rights work on the side. He got connected with a small "homosexual magazine" called *ONE*, which the US Postal Service was refusing to deliver because they deemed it obscene. Eric took that case all the way to the US Supreme Court—and won.

This was it! Eric Julber wasn't a member of the LGBTQ community; he was an ally. But his story was exactly the kind of story that I had envisioned capturing.

Two weeks later, I was on Eric's doorstep in Carmel, California, cameraman in tow. At ninety years old, Eric only had enough energy for a forty-five minute interview. But those forty-five minutes were electrifying. I had captured a small, almost-forgotten, undeniably pivotal chapter in queer history. This was OUTWORDS. And OUTWORDS had to go forward.

People often ask, How do you find your subjects? The answer is every which way under the sun. My first major subject source was a history of the LGBTQ movement called

The Gay Revolution, by Lillian Faderman. Lillian's book became my bible, and Lillian became an invaluable adviser. So did Gautam Raghavan, who worked as one of President Obama's liaisons to the LGBTQ community. Gautam and I met through Stanford University, our alma mater, and Gautam helped me connect with important OUTWORDS subjects all over America.

Another obvious source for compelling subjects was the internet. In early 2018, I was putting together OUTWORDS' first trip to the Upper Midwest, including Minnesota and Wisconsin. Researching the trip, I came across a wonderful website called WisconsinGayHistory.org. A tragic number of the LGBTQ pioneers listed there had passed from HIV/AIDS. Others had died of natural causes. Others were still pretty young. We wanted to find people in their seventies and eighties, those who had seen and done

We interviewed the irrepressible Mark Segal on a Sunday night—the only free time in his busy schedule

the most and who had limited time left to share their stories.

Then I saw the name Donna Burkett (p. 92). Clicking on Donna's name, I discovered an African-American woman who had applied for a license to marry her then-girlfriend, Manonia Evans, all the way back in *1971*.

Donna wasn't easy to find. I made phone calls and sent out emails. People had either never heard of Donna or didn't know where she was. Increasingly stymied, and with our trip looming, I finally tried the most obvious solution: google her. Up came Donna's name and phone number. She picked up on the fourth ring.

I learned that Donna had suffered a stroke some fifteen years earlier, lives in public housing, and gets around in a motorized wheelchair. It took a while to earn her trust. Frankly, she felt pretty forgotten up there in Milwaukee. Over the course of several phone calls, we formed a bond. At the end of every call, Donna said, "Bye . . . for now." Her courage and strength were tangible. And her story was inspiring.

I know how much it means to Donna that we found her. She matters. She hasn't been forgotten. And now she's in *The Book of Pride*.

One of my recurring concerns about publishing this book now is that you will think OUTWORDS is finished, complete. Nothing could be farther from the truth. *The Book of Pride* is only a sample, a suggestion, the tip of the proverbial iceberg. You can catch a glimmer of how incredible our LGBTQ elders are by diving into this book—but only in the same way that you can gain an idea of the mighty Pacific Ocean by taking a swim in California or Chile or Japan. You'd be crazy to mistake that one dip for the whole ocean.

To do justice to the long, complex journey that our community has traveled, there are countless more stories we need to record. The agonizing reality, however, is that with each passing day, there are fewer of our elders around to interview. In demographic terms, the majority of queer pioneers are baby boomers. Born just after World War II, they came of age in the 1960s, when America was splitting apart at the seams and the air was churning with the winds of change. By the year 2025, the first baby boomers will be eighty years old. That's why, if ever there was a critical time to mount a massive effort to crisscross America from north to south and

Dick Leitsch's apartment was a treasure trove of queer memorabilia.

east to west, recording our LGBTQ elders' stories, it's now.

And why is that important? To begin with, recording our elders' stories will serve as a critically important bulwark against the "fake news" crowd. To this day, there are people who deny the Holocaust ever took place. What's to prevent people fifty or one hundred years from now from denying the queer community's collective journey, our vitality, our very existence? OUTWORDS alone won't prevent this—but we can help.

Beyond safeguarding our story, OUT-WORDS will empower generations to come. Our elders' courage will inspire young people to be courageous as well, and will help them to know they are not alone. Our elders' ingenuity will inspire future generations of queer youth to be bold and inventive as they tackle challenges in their own lives, and, even more importantly, as they work to make their communities more just and equitable. Last but not least, our elders' sacrifices will help protect against any tendency on the part of young people to take their freedoms for granted.

And there's still more. Apart from its educational and inspirational value, we must build this archive as a permanent place of honor for the people who found the courage, strength, and conviction to picture something better for themselves and who set out on the long, tumultuous, chaotic, unmapped journey to transform their vision into reality. They were tired, and rightly so, of being treated like refuse. They were tired of being arrested. They were tired of being told they were mentally ill, of being called perverts and much, much worse. They were tired of the shame that took hold in their beings, in spite of their best efforts to slough it off. Out of the depths of that shame, something kicked in. A spark, a flame, a cry of rage. It simply said, no more. *No más.* We are humans. We are people. We deserve to be treated with dignity. And not just dignity. We deserve to be celebrated. When society as a whole moves beyond treating us "nicely" to welcoming us with open arms, when we can live openly and fully as who we are, when we can bring our entire grab bag of perspectives, talents, and sensibilities, our slightly jaded, salty sense of humor, our exaggerated mannerisms, our pumping hearts, and our outlaw sexualities—when we can bring all of who we are to the altar of the world, the world will be a better place. It will be a more *interesting* place. Thanks to us.

In the pages of this book, you'll get a sense of the different ways that our pioneers and elders laid claim to our rightful space in thoughts, words, and actions. Some wielded signs (John James, p. 168). Some wielded hoes (Diana Rivers, p. 78). Some wielded a light switch (Karla Jay, p. 180). Some wielded pieces of chalk (Mark Segal, p. 225). Some wielded a beer tap (Gene La Pietra, p. 6; Jack Myers, p. 20). Some wielded the Bible (Troy Perry, p. 135). And some wielded the power of the US Constitution (Grethe Cammermeyer, p. 46).

Others wielded pens, tattoo guns, paintbrushes, and mascara brushes. Some enlisted the power of the open ocean to make their point (Diana Nyad, p. 177). And some relied

I was thrilled to interview retired English teacher Betsy Parsons in Portland, Maine, where I came out in the 1980s.

on the love of a family (Gary and Millie Watts, p. 156) to fight back and drive a stake through the shame that has driven so many precious, honorable people to lives of dishonesty, despair, and early death.

These are the men, the women, the gender fluids, and the decline-to-states who carved a road through the wilderness, and then out of the wilderness, for those of us who came after. If OUTWORDS accomplishes nothing else, it will lay a wreath of tribute and gratitude at the feet of these determined souls. And if we hurry, we can record many more stories—and thank our pioneers in person.

In putting this book together, I faced some challenges—primarily, the happy challenge called "an abundance of riches." The average OUTWORDS interview runs around fifteen thousand words. This book contains around five hundred words, maybe a few more, from each subject. As Bob Seger sang, "What to leave in, what to leave out?" Some parts of each interview (like my occasionally long-winded questions) were easy to cut out. Beyond that, there were a lot of difficult decisions.

To begin, from each interview I pulled about three thousand words of what I felt were the strongest stories. On plenty of occasions, I tightened up and combined stories. I then turned my excerpts over to Sydney Rogers, my editor at HarperOne, who whittled my excerpts down to the stories she felt were most compelling, surprising, or simply unique. The end result, as you can imagine, is that dozens and dozens of important, profound, compelling stories ended up on the cutting room floor.

In addition to having to shorten each subject's story, we also didn't have room in *The Book of Pride* for every interview we recorded. Rather than giving a superficial rendering of more subjects, we preferred to go deeper with a smaller number. Thus, out of 131 OUTWORDS interviews recorded to date, *The Book of Pride* contains seventy-five subjects, grouped under themes like Community, Integrity, and Spirit. These themes are certainly not definitive, so take them with a grain of salt. I enjoy imagining the categories as dinner parties—as in, "Wow, this would be an interesting group of people with whom to share a pan of lasagna." Even the juxtaposition of specific individuals in the flow of the book is exciting to me. I love to imagine sitting between ABilly Jones-Hennin (p. 43) and Grethe Cammermeyer (p. 46) at

an Integrity dinner party, or plunking myself down between Kylar Broadus (p. 17) and Jack Myers (p. 20) at a Community meal. Examples like these abound—and I hope you will have as many interesting "conversations" with these extraordinary individuals as I have.

Regarding the OUTWORDS subjects not included in *The Book of Pride*, this is where the OUTWORDS digital platform comes in. Our platform (theoutwordsarchive.org) is where we will eventually share every interview we've collected (full-length video and transcripts, plus bios, portraits, and personal photos). The platform is and will always be completely free. Stay as long as you want, come back as many times as you want. Because it's free, and because it can be endlessly updated and expanded, the platform is actually the heart of OUTWORDS.

I take that back. The heart of OUTWORDS is the people who shared their stories. Let's meet them.

COMMUNITY

EMMA COLQUITT-SAYERS

BUSINESSWOMAN, COMMUNITY ORGANIZER

DALLAS–FORT WORTH, TEXAS

Emma Colquitt-Sayers was born in 1953 in Alabama and grew up mostly in Hastings, Florida, with her grandmother, a sharecropper who taught her the value of honest work. Emma moved to New Orleans with her first lover, and later to Texas, where she launched a variety of successful businesses, most recently a mobile cardiology company called Cardiac Dynamics. Emma has also been involved in a broad array of causes in the Dallas–Fort Worth area. One of her first community projects was Emma's Elves, which for eleven years provided holiday gifts and toys to needy kids. At the height of the AIDS epidemic, Emma became involved with Oak Lawn Community Services, serving as board president in 1992. Under her leadership, Oak Lawn created LifeWalk, a major ongoing AIDS services fundraiser for Dallas. Emma also served on the Committee of 30, an advisory board for Florida State University women's athletics. At the home she shares with her wife, Joan, there are FSU Seminole banners and flags everywhere.

When I was nine years old, I was riding my bike around the housing complex where my grandmother lived. A ten-year-old boy came out with a shotgun and he said, "Don't you believe I'll shoot you?" I gave him a typical nine-year-old answer, "No, because your mom might beat you good for doing that." My bike had fallen at his doorstep. I dropped down to my knee and reached over to get my bike, and that's when he shot. He actually shot my right elbow out.

I spent the next six years or so in and out of hospitals doing different procedures. The doctors said that under normal circumstances, they would immediately amputate it.

But they decided to try to put it back together. They put me in a cast for six months. When they took the cast off and they pulled the wires out, the arm had constricted. I didn't want for them to re-break the arm to try to put it back, so having thought at one point I may have to get it amputated, I thought keeping it this way was fine.

In my twenties, I went to New Orleans because of a relationship with a woman I met from the church. I also moved away to not embarrass my grandmother. She was well respected in town. I would never want to do anything to hurt her or to offend her. My aunt was also married to a minister and they had the biggest church in Hastings, and they were well respected.

I remember being out there in New Orleans, and it was a Saturday night, and I don't even drink, but I went and bought some Cokes. I bought some rum, and I remember, it was a one-bedroom apartment, and I remember squatting in a corner of my kitchen just crying. And I was so angry with God because I was very spiritual. I was raised by my grandmother. Very Baptist. But I remember squatting in my kitchen in the corner, so angry with God, and I was saying, "Look, I'm black, I'm a woman, I'm handicapped, and I'm gay. Can't you pick one or two things? You had to have all four of those things?"

What I was feeling at the time was that all four of those things were bad. Woman, black, gay, handicapped. They were all bad. But all

Emma and Joan at Trinity's college graduation

four of those things have defined who I am today, and if you took that away from me now, you would actually take away a part of me.

EMMA'S ELVES

Back in 1984, I was working at a hospital, and I heard the social services office talking about how they were going to get food and gifts for families at Christmas. I stopped into the office and asked, "What do you need?" So I went to the gay community right here in Dallas and got some people together to get some of these families taken care of for Christmas.

They called the project Emma's Elves. [*chuckling*] It ran for eleven years, and during that time Joan and I figured out we had bought presents and food and clothing for about two thousand people. I said, "In addition to presents, let's give them some food, because it's not good to be able to open all these presents and not have food in your kitchen."

It was really so cool—because here's a secret. There is no giving like the gay community giving. It's almost like, we know as gay people what it feels to not have, or to be without. Whether that be love, or emotions, or whatever. So the gay community really poured it out on these kids. I eventually had 250 volunteers, most of which were the gay community in Dallas.

The gay community is a very giving, loving community. I think for people who don't see that or who are trying to put that down, they are depriving themselves of the great opportunity to serve and to love each other and to help each other.

TRINITY

How we got to get custody of Trinity was a long process. We met her on her fourteenth birthday, July 31st, 2004. At the time, I thought I was just mentoring her as a basketball player. We did not know, but her father was just leaving her basically by herself on the weekends. Her mother had abandoned her. We went to the courts and got custody of her. She came to live with us. My wife, Joan, said, "Emma, I can't go to my maker knowing that this kid needs us, and we don't help her." So I said okay.

It was hard because Trinity's mother came back into the picture, and her father was saying that Child Protective Services in Dallas gave his daughter to two lesbians. He didn't think that was right. And because her mother was part Navajo, she got the Navajo Nation involved, and they said that they didn't want Trinity living with us.

It was difficult for Trinity once we got her, because keep in mind she was fourteen. And at fourteen, when you've been beat down like that, when people start pouring love at you, you kind of ask why. Is this short-lived, or am I gonna get this forever and ever? So she had some things she had to work through. There was a time when Trinity dropped out of school for about eighteen months. For me, that was one of the more difficult times, because I realized for the first time all I could do is pray. I fix stuff, I'm a fixer-upper, I'm an alpha cat. But there was nothing I could do, but let that kid go find herself, and hopefully come back.

Luckily for us, the time of love and sup-port that we had given her did sink in. About eighteen months later she called and asked for $25 to fill out an application to go back to school, and we said okay.

Before Trinity, I had a professional life, and I had a personal life, and I kept them separate. Trinity made me bring them together. We went through custody battles with her where we had to say that we were gay. There was a private school that didn't accept her, because we were gay. To have the Navajo Nation say we don't want her to be with two women. We had done nothing wrong. We had actually tried to save a kid that needed to be saved and deserved to be saved. But we were made to feel bad for doing that. So yeah, she did a lot for us.

GENE LA PIETRA

NIGHTCLUB OWNER

LOS ANGELES, CALIFORNIA

Gene La Pietra was born on Saint Patrick's Day in 1948, in Providence, Rhode Island. After getting tossed around in the foster-care system, Gene finally found a stable home with a couple named Alfred and Mary Patnaude. Gene lived with the Patnaudes until he was fourteen, then he struck out on his own, holding down a series of low-paying jobs under tough, caring bosses who taught him to exceed expectations, be honest, and not sweat the small stuff.

In 1969, Gene moved to Los Angeles with his lover at the time, Ed. Together they opened an adult bookstore called Book City News in the suburb of Hawaiian Gardens. Soon they had thirteen stores all over LA. Two years later, Gene and Ed opened their first gay nightclub, dubbed Disco 1985 because they thought it sounded futuristic. In 1974, they opened Circus, LA's first "all-inclusive" gay nightclub. Circus eventually expanded to thirty-six thousand square feet, becoming a key birthplace for Los Angeles's queer Latinx community. Civil rights and labor leader Cesar Chavez held a gathering there in 1983 to train gay and lesbian activists on how to organize boycotts and raise money. Seven years later, Gene and Ed opened a second club, Arena, next door to Circus.

While operating his clubs, Gene adopted two children, Alwin and Janay, and fostered many others. In January 2016, failing health forced Gene to close both Circus and Arena.

I was in five foster homes by the age of seven. We were packing all the time, and it was confusing, because you never get to know who your brother or sister was, because every time you've landed somewhere you had a new set of siblings, you had new parents.

I ended up joining the Coast Guard and, boy, was I happy. I had the time of my life there.

One day, we were up in Seattle and I got liberty. The cab was out front and I asked the cabbie to take me to a queer bar, because they didn't have the "gay" word then. I was twenty-one years old, looking good, handsome young kid, and in the military. What I saw when I opened the door was this kid standing against the jukebox, and I had never seen anybody look like that before. He had a bandana on, real dark long hair.

Gene with his family in front of Arena Nightclub. Above all else, he values love and community.

I walked over to the jukebox and said, "Let's go." He looked at me. He put his beer down. We both walked out. We went to his place, and of course we made crazy love and we had a great time.

Before I left, I said, "I'm going to take you to Los Angeles, and I'm going to make you a millionaire." He thought I was crazy. I went to the base and told my commanding officer I wanted to leave. He said, "Why do you want to leave?" I told him the story: I met the man of my life. He said, "But you're not queer." I said, "Yes, I am." I appealed to the base commander. I said, "I've never been in love. I'm not letting him get away. So, I'd appreciate it if you let me go." Ten days later, I had an honorable discharge with all the benefits.

Ed and I spent twenty-two of the happiest years of my life together. He was my man. We came to Los Angeles, and we worked very hard together. We had a little store selling pornography, and we were constantly getting arrested, constantly going to court, constantly going to jail. In those days, the police would hope they'd break you down. Most people

would give up. I don't know what it is to give up. I just don't know what it is. Why not just spit in their eye and keep going?

In no time, we had thirteen stores all over Los Angeles, and we're just going crazy. Everybody you could imagine came in. They were your school teachers, your doctors. One day I see a guy there and he was a pilot of the plane that I had just been on. Everybody in America was buying this, except Richard Nixon. Everybody else was buying it.

CIRCUS DISCO

The strategy with Circus was to have clean restrooms, which was not a high priority back then; give them their money's worth, treat them good, and anybody who wanted to come in could come in. Often you'll have people compare Studio 54 in New York to Circus, and I'm always offended by that because we were opened first.

At other clubs, they picked and chose who could come in, and the white power structure of the gay community were okay with that because they participated in it. They

let it happen. They knew outside that blacks weren't allowed in, that Puerto Ricans weren't allowed in, that Mexicans weren't allowed in, that certain women were not allowed in, and they participated in it.

The same as Studio One in West Hollywood. Women couldn't get in there. They couldn't wear open-toed shoes. Well, that's the only shoes that were made for women, were open-toed shoes. What were they supposed to do? Get dressed up and then put combat boots on? Blacks couldn't go in. Hispanics couldn't go in. But the white power structure in West Hollywood went along with it and supported it.

We did the opposite. Everybody could come in, and we became the focal point of the Latino community, a power base where they

could meet, where they could build a base, where eventually they were running for office left and right and winning. Cesar Chavez had a political organizing meeting at Circus. I read an article where it said a hundred people were there. There were twelve hundred people there, but that's how history is rewritten. I got to sit with Cesar for five hours on a couch and talk with him about his life. It was so inspiring. Every question I asked him, he answered. He was getting paid no more than a field worker. He lived in the same house he'd always lived in, had the same car. This man was the real deal.

A little while later, Cesar calls me up and says he wanted us to boycott Coors Beer. I didn't hesitate. Even though I was making a ton of money on Coors, I called them and told them, "Pick your stuff up. It's in the parking lot right now." That was it. Of course, the Coors' son offered me $100,000. Today's money, what's that, a million? And I said, "No, thank you," because that's not how you build alliances.

Those days, the cops ruled Hollywood. They could do what they want. We have a report that an officer is down, and all of a sudden you'd have fifty cops inside the club, helicopters, the whole thing, streets blocked off, because somebody reportedly called and said an officer was on the dance floor being beat up by customers. Of course it was all fake news, as we call it today, but what can you say? You can't say anything, until all of a sudden one night, we got lucky.

One night the cops came in with their billy clubs flying, fifty cops, helicopters, the whole nine yards. They told all the people to sit on the floor. "If you have your ID, sit on this side of the floor. If you don't have it, sit on this side," giving out commands just like Nazis.

The next day, my DJ comes over and says, "You're not going to like this because you told me not to do it." What he was doing was taping the music in the club and selling the tapes, and I didn't want that happening. But the result was, he taped everything the cops said that night. When I went to the station to make my complaint, they said it didn't happen. So I gave the tape to Channel 2 news. It went viral. It was on every news station. City Hall called a meeting for it and the cops denied it, but then they heard the tape, and it was over.

But the thing that made the biggest difference is this old lady up in Hollywood Hills had her house burglarized. She called the police. It took the cops several hours to get there. Then she read the article that said there were fifty police officers at my club on Halloween night. So she wrote a letter to the *LA Times*. "What do I have to do to get a cop? Call Circus Disco?" That one line shook the foundations at LAPD headquarters.

OUTWORDS interviewed Gene in April 2017 at his palatial home in the Los Feliz neighborhood of Los Angeles. In his blunt Rhode Island accent, Gene continues to insist that every single person's life is valuable, important, and interesting. And he continues to fret about the people society doesn't want—just as, once upon a time, Gene was a kid no one wanted.

K.C. POTTER

DEAN EMERITUS, VANDERBILT UNIVERSITY

NASHVILLE, TENNESSEE

K.C. Potter was born in 1939 in Fallsburg, Kentucky. He attended Berea College, then earned his law degree at Vanderbilt, graduating in 1964. But K.C. didn't think he'd be "worth a damn" as a lawyer; so when Vanderbilt offered him a job as assistant dean of men, he took it. He would stay at "Vandy" until his retirement some thirty-six years later.

Known to many as the Harvard of the South, Vanderbilt in the 1960s and '70s was deeply conservative and very hostile to any hint of gay activity. As AIDS emerged in the 1980s, it only got worse. Against this backdrop, in 1987, K.C. took the first steps to create safe places for gay students on campus. Later, when Vanderbilt's fledgling gay rights group began organizing in support of a formal university nondiscrimination policy, K.C. advocated for congressional-style hearings to develop a policy, bringing gay and lesbian students before the Board of Trustees to testify about their campus experiences. The students helped win the board over—and Vanderbilt was forever changed.

During his entire tenure at Vanderbilt, K.C. could not come out himself as a gay man. That would change, once he retired.

As the assistant dean of men at Vanderbilt, I was responsible for housing and discipline and the Vanderbilt Police Department.

Students would get in trouble for all kinds of things. They would get drunk. There was date rape. There was theft. There was making too much noise. There was beating up people. Anything that would happen in any city of five thousand young people. And I would try to figure out the reason behind it.

One case, a student was reported for being nasty, mean, and hateful to his professor. He said, "I know that I am smart as everybody else, but I can't make any good grades." I said, "Have you ever been tested for dyslexia?" "No." Sure enough, he's dyslexic. They have to teach him differently. He does well, you never see him again.

Occasionally it was just, "Now, the next time this happens, I'm going to write a letter to your parents, so you better straighten up and stop drinking too much." It could be serious enough that I would suspend them, but that was rare.

THE REASON HE JUMPED

The climate of Vanderbilt was very, very conservative. Most of the people were from fairly wealthy families. Very conservative wealth is what it amounted to.

In the late 1960s, a student came and told me that he needed to be changed to another room. He said, "My roommate is gay. I can't deal with that." So I authorized the room change.

There are four twelve-story towers on campus. About a year later, a student ran into my office and said, "Someone has jumped out of Tower Three." I ran to Tower

K.C. at the 1993 March on Washington for Lesbian, Gay, and Bi Equal Rights and Liberation, accompanied by students from the Vanderbilt Lambda Association, which K.C. helped found six years earlier

Three. And sure enough, there was this student lying on the sidewalk. He had jumped from the tenth floor. The color was gone in his eyes, and there was no pulse. About that time, the police arrived with blankets to put over him.

So I went up to his room, and there were medications from psychiatrists where they had been treating him and probably trying to change him. There were some girls who came up to me afterwards and were heartbroken because he wanted to date them and he was trying. They turned him down for whatever reason, and now they felt very guilty about it.

I didn't tell anybody. I didn't tell the parents that he was gay. I didn't do that. It was something that I knew was probably true and was probably the reason he jumped out of the tower. I couldn't get away from the idea that it was because he was gay and he was struggling, and he just couldn't see any way out.

In 1986 or 1987, there was an article that appeared in a campus publication. The article said something like, "You have to come out of Centennial Park," which is the park across the street from campus, "before dark, before the faggots come out."

There were three students that wrote a letter to the student newspaper protesting that. I went to the associate provost, to whom I reported at that time, and I said, "We need to reach out to these students. I'm going to call them and make an appointment for lunch with them." The first thing out of his mouth was, "Vanderbilt's not ready for this." And then, in the second breath, he said, "Yeah, do it." So I called up the students. It was right before the end of the school year, so it was too late to do anything that year. I said, "In the fall, as soon as you get back, you come and see me and we'll put an ad in the student newspaper, and we'll start a group." So they agreed.

We were afraid that people just wouldn't come to an open meeting. So the ad provided a box number. You write a note to this box number. And someone would then contact you and pick you up and take you to the meeting. We had to get it started, and that's the way we did it.

We started meeting at the off-campus apartment of these two young lesbians. Then the young ladies got tired of us. Finally I suggested we use my house on campus. I said, "No football players are going to come over there and crash my house." We started to use my house, and it worked really superbly well. But the kids would be very secretive about getting into my house. I remember one student. There's a knock at the door at my house, and I open the door, and there's this little tiny boy standing there. He's sure he's in the wrong place, because here's this big, powerful, ugly old man who's the one who kicks you out of school, standing in the doorway. And he starts to turn and make his apologies, and I say, "You're in the right place, come on in." That little fella, I remember well. He's a doctor now. He works with people with AIDS.

Shortly after K.C.'s retirement in 1998, he met his partner, Richard Patrick, and began his first real relationship. Today, they live together on a farm in Hickman County, Tennessee. But for K.C.'s interview, it only seemed fitting for him to return to Vanderbilt, to the Office of LGBTQI Life, which is housed in a stately brick building called the K.C. Potter Center.

ADA BELLO

CUBAN-AMERICAN ACTIVIST

PHILADELPHIA, PENNSYLVANIA

Ada Bello was born into a middle-class family in 1933 in Havana, Cuba. Aware from early on that she was attracted to girls, she also knew coming out in heavily Catholic, intensely *machista* Cuba would be impossible. In 1957, she crossed to the United States in search of freedom.

In 1967, Ada helped launch the Philadelphia chapter of the Daughters of Bilitis (DOB). Later, she helped found the Homophile Action League (HAL), possibly the first gay rights organization to seize on the idea of enlisting politicians as allies. For several years, Ada also participated in July 4th Reminder Day demonstrations in front of Philadelphia's Independence Hall, designed to draw a connection between lesbian and gay rights and the Constitution. [For more about the Reminder Day marches, see pp. 168–69.]

Over the decades, Ada has contributed to countless Philadelphia gay groups and initiatives. In 2015, Ada was honored by GALAEI, Philadelphia's queer Latino social justice organization, with their David Acosta Revolutionary Leadership Award.

I was aware of being different very early, even before I knew that there was a name for it. I didn't feel comfortable doing what I was supposed to do as a girl. I wasn't interested in dolls. I wasn't interested in playing house. I remember my father at some point brought me a police uniform. I loved it. Just to wear pants. My mother made it disappear in about a week.

In Cuba, in general, it was extremely difficult to be gay. It was a big small town, so it was difficult to have any kind of privacy. There was the *machista* tradition, and to a certain extent the Catholic Church was also influential, even if Cubans were not particularly religious. To be gay in Cuba was to be in the closet. It was very risky, especially for the middle class. The upper classes, they could either go into a marriage of convenience with separate houses, and they could leave the country for long vacations. My family was middle class, so we were stuck in the bourgeois limitations of behavior.

Even when I went to Havana to go to university, it was not much better than a small town. That is why I knew that I had to leave in order to live a full life.

In 1957, I transferred to Louisiana State

University in Baton Rouge. It wasn't an easy transition because although I could read English, I didn't understand English and I could not speak English. The first six months were the worst, but I did survive.

To my surprise, the situation at LSU in Baton Rouge was not particularly better than it was in Cuba. The university had some outrageous laws and regulations. You could be expelled from the university if they found you off campus wearing pants. You couldn't wear pants to the cafeteria. You can imagine any question of having a gay life at all. We would go to gay bars in New Orleans, in the French Quarter, but we were always fearful that somebody from the university was going to be there.

When I came to Philadelphia, I thought, oh my God, this is El Dorado. This is the anonymity of a big city, and the fact that nobody knew me, and I was working at the University of Pennsylvania, and they had more liberal standards. But when I started looking for a gay community, the way to find the gay community was going to bars. To go to a bar, you had to go down some dark alley and then you

Ada at the 1990 Philadelphia Pride March

knock on the door of an unmarked address, and then once you were in, the police could come in and raid the place. It didn't take too long to disabuse me of the notion that this was a perfectly free environment.

DRIVING THE GETAWAY CAR

Several years before, the Daughters of Bilitis, a lesbian organization, had been founded in San Francisco, and they had chapters throughout the country. Some women and I started the Philadelphia chapter. We started putting out a newsletter. We tried to distribute it very widely, and not very many places accepted it. Even the bookstore at Penn. We weren't asking them to sell the newsletter. All they had to do is give us a space to put the newsletter out, and they said no. It occurred to me that there were other ways to approach it. So at lunchtime, I would go to the bookstore and fold the DOB newsletter and put it inside books on the shelf, particularly in the outrageous books they used to publish about the sickness of homosexuality. That was perfect. People who bought the book got the newsletter free of charge. I don't know how much good that did, but it gave me a great deal of satisfaction.

One night, the police raided Rusty's, the main lesbian bar in Philadelphia. That wasn't unusual, but that Saturday they actually took about a dozen women to jail. They stayed in jail overnight. That was the procedure, but it went on their record, so obviously they were unhappy. They came to our chapter of the DOB, and they said, "Do something about it."

We went to Barbara Gittings [Editor's note: Barbara Gittings (1932–2007) was a prominent LGBT activist] and asked Barbara for guidance, and she put us in touch with the American Civil Liberties Union. We then contacted the police and asked for a face-to-face interview. I didn't go to the interview because I wasn't a citizen, so I couldn't show my face, but I did drive the people there, so I used to say that I drove the getaway car. Barbara got somebody from the ACLU to come to the interview to act as a legal adviser. The police denied that they were out-of-bounds for what they did. Some of the women had refused to give their IDs. The term that they used was "resisting arrest."

A few weeks later, on a Wednesday night, we all went to Rusty's. Barbara didn't like to go to bars because she didn't smoke and it was too noisy, but it was a hot summer night, so she went for beer. We had hardly sat down when the bouncer came in and pulled the jukebox and turned on the lights. We knew that there was going to be a raid. By now, I had applied for my citizenship and I was going to have my interview in a couple of weeks. It was foolish of me to have taken that chance. On the other hand, I said, they never raid bars on Wednesday nights because there's not enough people, but they did.

When they came to our table, they asked for IDs and everybody pulled their driver's license, and Barbara pulled her membership card in the American Civil Liberties Union. It was a miracle. They took a look at that and they didn't say a word. They left.

Ada protesting the 1992 film *Basic Instinct* for its portrayals of gay and bisexual relationships

That was a good lesson. I mean, it is important that we let the authorities know that we know our rights.

REMINDER DAYS

In the mid-'60s, the Mattachine Society in New York and Washington together with Barbara Gittings and the photojournalist Kay Lahusen (p. 98) organized demonstrations in front of Independence Hall in Philadelphia on the Fourth of July. They were called Reminder Day demonstrations, and they went on for five years from '65 to '69. By 1968, I had become a citizen, so I was able to march. I marched and I went around trying to listen for comments from the spectators. I was surprised how many of the comments were positive.

We had connected our demands to the Constitution. It wasn't a question anymore of tolerating us. We were full citizens and we required, we demanded our rights.

In the 1970s, the movement started building national organizations staffed by professionals, and we started going into the legislatures. I was part of a group called the Homophile Action League, and that was one of the things that HAL did, which was a first in Philadelphia. We got politicians to come talk to us. Milton Shapp, a wonderful governor of Pennsylvania, was one of the first to come and talk to us and was open to our demands. The mood of the country had become much calmer. The way in which we approached the fight was different. We started fighting through established channels, which is not a bad thing.

In 2015, in Philadelphia, we had an exhibit at Constitutional Center that was the fiftieth anniversary of those pickets. It was very well attended—you can't imagine. It's almost like it took fifty years to go from the front of Independence Hall across the mall to the Constitution Center. Two blocks. It took fifty years, but we made it.

OUTWORDS interviewed Ada in April 2018 in Philadelphia. Although sad that Ada was forced to leave her homeland to find freedom, we're glad she found it in Philly, and grateful for the spark and spirit she brought to America's gay rights revolution. And we love the image of Ada driving a getaway car. Go, Ada!

KYLAR BROADUS

TRANSGENDER LEGAL PIONEER

WASHINGTON, DC

Kylar William Broadus was born on August 28, 1963, in Fayette, Missouri, and designated female at birth.

While still presenting as female, Kylar made his first foray into the world of politics, winning election as student body president at Central Methodist University during his senior year. Kylar then earned his JD at the University of Missouri School of Law.

In the late 1990s, after informing his employer of his plan to transition from female to male, Kylar's work environment became increasingly unwelcoming and unsupportive. After being forced to resign, and having realized it was (and still is) completely legal in Missouri for companies to discriminate based on gender, Kylar undertook a long, committed journey to develop federal, state, and local protections for people regardless of their gender identity or gender expression. His many scholarly articles on transgender advocacy in family and employment law fundamentally shaped academic and legal discussions of gender. In 2010, Kylar founded the Trans People of Color Coalition (TPOCC) to fill a gap in the private and nonprofit sectors. In 2012, Kylar became the first openly transgender person to testify before the US Senate in support of the Employment Non-discrimination Act (ENDA).

In 2011, the National LGBTQ Task Force honored Kylar with its Susan J. Hyde Activism Award for Longevity in the Movement, and the Freedom Center for Social Justice presented Kylar with its Pioneer Award.

I was born in Fayette, Missouri, on August 28th, 1963, which was the historic march on Washington, on that very same day.

Everybody talks about the Emancipation Proclamation and when slavery ended, but sadly my parents suffered lots of hate, were subject to Jim Crow laws, and suffered all the atrocities that were the new framing of slavery. When I grew up, signs were still separate for restrooms. I still remember going to the drugstore for entertainment and then going to the bathroom, and then this woman putting her hand in my face, being a little kid, saying you can't go there and me reading the signs. They were labeled Negro and White, and then Colored and White.

My parents focused on us. They wanted to make our lives better than their lives. They

Five-year-old Kylar with his father and "BFF for life," William, in 1968

taught us how to navigate this world as black Americans. They taught me, yes, when an officer pulls you over, what you have to do and how clean you have to be as a black person, because police harass black people just for being black. They taught us you're always going to be targeted because of the race of your skin, and you're always going to have to jump twice as high because of the race of your skin.

My first job came at five years old. I went with my father to his night job, and I'll never forget, I was so happy to be promoted from emptying the trash cans to cleaning the water fountain. My dad's coworkers would say, "Oh, you brought your son with you today," and he'd say, "Yep," and he'd just keep it moving. Never bat an eye.

In the second grade, I began to act out. Trans children act out and have anger, and that's how they find out that trans children are trans early on, because there's a certain

way we act out. My father became great cover for me, because my mother would lay out outfits, and then he let me change them to more masculine outfits.

I prayed to God every day to fix me, because that's what I knew and I grew up in the Bible Belt of this country, which is Missouri, and so that was the religion. But nothing ever changed.

Finally, one day when I was twelve or thirteen, I found this *National Enquirer* with an article about Billy Tipton. [Editor's note: Billy Tipton was an American jazz musician. Although he lived his adult life as a man, it was discovered after his death in 1989 that he was assigned female at birth.] I hid this *National Enquirer* in our house like it was a *Playboy* magazine, so I could come home and look at it. And I stopped praying to God every day, because at least I then had a role model in Billy Tipton.

Billy died in poverty before his time because he didn't want to seek medical intervention to blow his cover. And still, just learning about him gave me a grounding to know that I wasn't crazy. There are people out there like me, that I can relate to, and I can figure out hopefully how to move forward.

NOTHING OUT HERE FOR TRANS PEOPLE

After law school, I got a job with a financial services company and wanted to move up the ranks. But their rigidity towards women, which I was classified as, was very sexist, and I didn't fit that whole sexist mark. I was wearing suits all day every day and looked like I do now, with a short haircut. Then I told them I wanted to change my name to what people called me, which was KB. They said that that wasn't proper for a woman. I said, "You have other employees that use their initials, so why can't I use mine?" That's where it began.

My boss started calling me every hour on the hour in the evenings, creating ridiculous projects that were due the next morning. I'd stay up all night and get them done. Then he'd be shocked, because they'd be done, but they just kept pushing and pushing and pushing. It was like, "It's clear you don't want me here," and so we parted ways.

That's when I knew I needed to go into advocacy because there were no laws to protect me. I went from making significant income to no income, and then to having my career destroyed. I said, "Wow, there's nothing out here for trans people. I've got to get on this, because I don't want anybody to go through what I've gone through."

INTERSECTIONS

In 2010, after waiting for other and younger people to form some sort of intersection of people of color and trans people, I formed the Trans People of Color Coalition. I just kept seeing the lack of intersectionality. As I traveled and did my trans work, I would hear from every pocket, whether it was rural or whether it was metropolitan: "I don't feel anybody's doing any work for me. I feel isolated." And I heard that from every trans person of color. So we formed.

It's great to have allies, but it's also great for the impacted group to be the speakers for that movement. I don't just mean trans people of color, but trans people in general. We sometimes think that because I'm oppressed in one way, then I understand every form of oppression. But how can I understand your struggle as a gay white man, when I'm not? And what makes you think you can understand my struggle as a trans black man, if you're not?

We have to have an openness to understanding that. If we're not open to that, then we need to be having a discussion about why not. If we're mindful, we can learn lots from each other.

The *Time* magazine cover gets us visibility [Editor's note: In May 2014, *Time* magazine ran a cover article under the headline "The Transgender Tipping Point: America's next civil rights frontier"], but we still have to change hearts and minds and get those rights. A magazine cover is not a piece of legislation. It's not a court case. We need social change, not just visibility. Black Americans have been visible forever. It takes more than that.

OUTWORDS caught up with Kylar at the 2016 Lavender Law conference in Washington, DC. Although bone-tired, Kylar gave a compelling account of his transformation into the man he was born to be—a man who has fundamentally altered the legal standing for transgender people in America.

JACK MYERS

GAY BAR OWNER

JACKSON, MISSISSIPPI

> Jack was born in Pelahatchie, Mississippi, in 1944. His father owned a logging and lumber business and later a small-engine repair shop. His mother came from a family of sharecroppers and poultry farmers. Jack trained as a radiologic technologist before deciding that what he really wanted to do was create places where gay people like himself could congregate. Shortly after his twenty-first birthday, Jack and a business partner opened Mae's Cabaret, the first of several LGBTQ watering holes that Jack would own over a fifty-year stretch.
>
> In 2016, Jack closed the last of his bars. That same year, the *Washington Post* dubbed him "the patron saint of Mississippi's gay scene."

When I was an x-ray student at UMC, which is now University of Mississippi Medical Center, in 1964 or '65, three civil rights leaders came down from New York to Philadelphia, Mississippi, and subsequently were murdered by the sheriff's department up there and were buried in a pond dam. I think they found their car burned up, and it took them several weeks to find the bodies. They shipped the bodies to the UMC, and I was there working that night, and the senior student and I had to do complete body x-rays on them.

The x-rays revealed some shots and some broken bones and different fractures. Some to the head, some bullets in some of them, broken arms and stuff.

These guys gave their life for something they believed in. They were trying to get the black and white community to come together, and they just went to the wrong town. It was sad to see those three young guys, their lives ended so violently—because I saw what happened to them, the results of what happened to them.

MAMA AND PAPA JACK

One of the hardest things I ever had to do in my life was to tell my parents that I was opening a gay bar. At that time, I had not come out to them. They were visiting me and were getting ready to leave, and I just kept trying to get up the courage. "You've got to tell them, you've got to tell them."

I finally got up the courage when we got on the front porch. I just told them that I was opening a bar. They said, "Oh, really?" "Yeah, but it's gonna be a gay bar." Daddy made the comment, "Well, I'm not going." And Mama said, "Well, I'm going. If you don't want to go, you can stay at home. I'm going." So then after that, they started working the door at my clubs.

The whole time I had nightclubs, my parents ran the door. Everybody called them Mama and Papa Jack. When my dad got sick, they moved in with me. My dad died in 2006, and my mom passed away in 2015.

GO, JACKSON

I thought about hanging a shingle one time. "Spiritual Adviser, Marriage Counseling." Because people seem to open up when they've had a few drinks, get stuff off their mind, talk about it. Talk to somebody that's not gonna tell everybody what their business is. Confide in me.

I used to get letters all the time, thanking me for giving people a safe place to go when they didn't have any place else to go. "Thank you for protecting us, and looking out for us, providing a safe place." A lot of them were gay people that feared for their jobs. They could come to the bar, to come out and be themselves for a while. It means the world to me now that they felt safe coming to the bars that I had.

On weekends, we always had an off-duty policeman in uniform at the door. Occasionally, in those days, you'd have a pickup truck of guys come by and scream different stuff, "fags" and all this stuff, but as far as stopping and trying to start any problems with people, or trying to do something in the bar, that never happened, because when they saw a policeman there in uniform, you know they're not gonna fool around that much.

One time when I had the saloon on Capitol Street, we had some guys that tried to cause some problems. They got out of their car, and we chased them off down the street with a baseball bat.

The next day, I was down there working, and one of the guys came by and he said, "I wanted to stop and apologize to you." I said, "What are you talking about?" And he said, "For y'all standing up last night, when we yelled stuff about you being gay and all this stuff. You guys really stood up for yourself." And he said, "I admire you all for that."

It made me feel better. I know it took a lot for him to come back and say that, you know, but he did.

The other day, I saw two guys walking down the street holding hands. Go, Jackson. So I guess, by now, people here realize they're gonna have to put up with us.

OUTWORDS interviewed Jack at his rambling old home in Jackson's Fondren neighborhood. Out behind Jack's house is a 1949 Cadillac, pining for a paint job. The best things in life—like Jack's brand of authentic Southern hospitality—never go out of style.

JEWEL THAIS-WILLIAMS

DISCO CLUB PIONEER

LOS ANGELES, CALIFORNIA

Jewel Thais-Williams was born on May 9, 1939, in Gary, Indiana, and moved with her family to San Diego when she was four years old. After attending UCLA, she held a wide variety of jobs, from grocery clerk to women's prison guard, and eventually opened a clothing store with her sister. In 1973, Jewel purchased a bar that had previously shunned black patrons and transformed it into Jewel's Catch One, one of America's first black discos, and a place where everyone, regardless of race, gender, or sexual orientation, was welcome to come and have a good time.

In the late 1990s, recognizing the black community's lack of medical options, Jewel earned a master's degree in Oriental medicine. She then opened the Village Health Foundation next to The Catch, using proceeds from the business side to ensure that no one would be turned away for lack of funds.

Jewel served on the board of AIDS Project Los Angeles and cofounded the Minority AIDS Project. In addition to the Village Health Foundation, Jewel and her wife, Rue, own and operate Rue's House, providing services to women and children living with HIV/AIDS. In 2012, Los Angeles Mayor Antonio Villaraigosa presented Jewel with the Dream of Los Angeles Award for her contributions to the LA queer community and the entire City of Angels.

When the recession hit in 1970, '71, women stopped buying their clothes as much. I said, "I need something that's recession-proof." I thought about owning a bar. I said, "I can do that probably."

Every day I would get the *LA Times* and check out the clubs or restaurants or bars. One night in 1973, I saw an ad for a place called Diana's Club. I said, "That must be the little club that's down on the corner of Cren-shaw and Pico." I drove over. I didn't even go home that night. I just stayed around waiting until morning.

The bar opened at seven o'clock in the morning, but they told me that the owner wouldn't be in until about ten o'clock. I came back at ten o'clock. The owner was the widow of the man that had had the club for twenty years or so. Her name was Mary. I asked how much she wanted for it. She said, "$18,000." I said, "Okay." We signed on it.

The next step was to raise enough money to pay for it. The club was $18,000, and I gave her $1,000 down. I had thirty days to raise another $17,000, and no really good ideas about where that was going to come from. I went to everybody and every institution that I thought would. There was a lot of no's in between.

The day I walked in and presented Mary with the check for the balance of the money, I just started wondering about the next thing. I've never been one to jump up and down for joy, because if you jump up, you might come down on a nail or something. Just keep your feet on the ground.

JEWEL'S CATCH ONE

I didn't change the bar's name at first. It was Diana's Club. People would call me Diana. It was okay with me. I had no problem with that. After maybe four or five or more years of working and not taking a vacation, one day my sister came in and presented me with a ticket for a cruise. It was a Caribbean cruise. She said, "You're going on vacation. Plane leaves tomorrow, going to Miami. Yes, I used your money to buy it, but you're going to go on a vacation."

When I got back, my sister had taken the neon Diana's sign down and put up Jewel's. That's how Jewel's was born. Then a friend of mine and I came up with the name Catch One. 'Catch one' was a saying that guys used. They were going out catching. Talking to my friend, I said, "What

about Catch One?" He said, "Yeah, that's cool."

By now, the sexual revolution was taking place. When I got my first business cards with "Jewel's Catch One" on them, I put "or more" at the bottom of it.

In the early days, I still had the white clientele, older white retired clientele, the ones that didn't want the black folks to drink with them. It morphed into what I call my three masks or my three faces that I would have to put on. I'd have the older white folk during the daytime, and then the African-American blue-collar workers and that. They weren't that gay-friendly, either. They would come in and have their beers and whatever, and go on home. Then around ten or eleven o'clock, I call them my children, that's when my children arrived.

In the beginning, we had live acts. Etta James and Esther Phillips, occasionally local people, sometimes we would get folks from the Atlanta Underground, the popular local singers from there to come. One of the first people that I had was Sylvester. At that time, he played with a live band. Then in 1975, disco hit. I said, "Hooray!" because I didn't have to pay a band and all that. I could pay one disc jockey.

In the '90's, Madonna was the attraction, and Sharon Stone. You might run into any of those kind of folks here. That's when the big influx of white folks started coming. Those that were in the know, like Madonna, knew that this was a banging place. The music was the best. I have to say so myself. We could stay open until four or five o'clock in the morning, six o'clock if we wanted to. They could go to other places and still come here and do the after-hours thing.

Naturally, the black kids jumped into me about having white people here. I used to say, which wasn't quite true, but I'd say it anyway, "It's whoever is paying. If I have one thousand baboons at the door, then it's baboon night. That's just the way I roll. I got bills to pay."

COMING OUT

I came out to my mom and dad when I was fifty. When my girlfriend, Rue, and I were gonna have our commitment ceremony, I went to my parents and I said, "I know you have to know, but I need to tell you, because I need to speak this out loud to take the power out of the stigma of my being who I am with you. I don't want you to wonder, is she or not? I am, and Rue and I are going to get married, and I would like for you both to come."

My dad said his religion wouldn't allow him to come. A day or two before the ceremony, my mom calls and said that she's not going to attend. She didn't want to be bothered with that junk, she said. I said, "Okay. Sorry you feel that way, but bless you anyway."

The day of the wedding, my mom arrived with one of my sisters. I guess she and my sister just couldn't stand not knowing, so they were there. My mom had the best old time at the reception and meeting people and seeing, because it was big and it was glamorous. It was flawless. I guess she wanted that for her other daughters too, and she didn't get it. She was cool.

OUTWORDS interviewed Jewel inside the rambling 1925 building that used to house Catch One. Today it's a nightclub called Union—a fitting name for the space where Jewel Thais-Williams drew together diverse elements of the LA scene for love, friendship, and fun.

RAY HILL

REFORMED OUTLAW, RADIO HOST, ACTIVIST

HOUSTON, TEXAS

Ray Hill was born in Houston, Texas, in 1940. He came out as gay during high school and was equally bold in his choice of "profession": burglary. In 1970, Ray received a 160-year prison sentence, but won parole after five years for good behavior. From that point forward, Ray became a mouthy, tireless advocate for gay rights and civil rights.

Just days out of prison, Ray created a radio show about gay issues for a local, progressive radio station, KPFT FM. By 1980, he was manager of the station. He later dreamed up a groundbreaking radio program called *The Prison Show*, providing a platform for inmates, family members, and corrections employees to talk out their issues. In the meantime, Ray cofounded the Houston Lesbian and Gay Pride Week. In 1979, he served as the chair of the executive and coordinating committees for the first national March on Washington for Gay and Lesbian Rights. In the decades that followed, Ray founded numerous organizations to fight for First Amendment rights, LGBTQ equality, and the rights of the incarcerated.

Ray won four federal suits against the city of Houston for police abuses, including the landmark 1987 Supreme Court case *Houston v. Hill*. Ray also helped John Lawrence usher his case against sodomy laws through the US federal court system. In 2004, the Supreme Court ruled in John's favor in *Lawrence v. Texas*, ending the criminalization of gay male sex in America.

In 1999, Ray received a lifetime achievement award from the Houston chapter of the ACLU.

I started studying homosexuality when I was in high school, and the way you have to do that when you're in high school is you have to go to the college library because the high school library didn't have any of that shit. I slipped into the closed shelves and learned about who homosexuals were from Edmund Bergler and the most voracious, anti-gay writers of the era. Edmund went into great details on what queers did when they were being queer. And it was like a training manual. I needed access to that material at the time and needed to know how to make these things fit. And Edmund Bergler, one of the

Ray at the historic 1979 March on Washington for Lesbian & Gay Rights. Ray helped plan the march and later served as on-stage director.

most homophobic writers of all times, gave me all of that in aces. So I didn't know the word "gay," but I did know the word "homosexual," and it was just time to be honest. This was 1958.

And so I went into the kitchen and my mother, Frankie, was in there, and I said, "Frankie, I'm a homosexual." And she took a puff of her cigarette and a hit off her coffee and she said, "Well, that's a relief." "What do you mean, 'that's a relief'?" She said that she and my father, Raymond, had noticed that I tended to dress up more frequently than the other boys in the neighborhood. And they thought that I was pretending to be wealthier than we were. They were afraid I might grow up to be a Republican. But if I was gay, they can handle that.

WILDE N STEIN

In 1975, a week after I got out of prison, I started doing a gay radio show on KPFT called *Wilde N Stein*, named after Oscar Wilde and Gertrude Stein. What I had in

mind was to build community with radio. So while my friends were going to meetings with fifteen or twenty people every two weeks or once a month, I'm reaching thousands every week over the airwaves. They're all in their closets. They're all scared. I'm not doing much about their self-oppressive guilt and shame, but I am role-modeling not being in their closets, the guy that talks about being gay, and I open the phones. You want to call and straighten my ass out, come on down. I can't lose an argument. I got the buttons and the switches. So I'm always going to get the last word, sucker. So I play the radio for all that it's worth, and that starts building toward a community.

Wilde N Stein was on the air for about five years. And then KPFT needed a manager. The previous manager had quit. She left a note and said, "This is the worst damn job I've ever had in my life. I'm outta here."

So we cast lots and I lost, and they decided to make me manager. Then someone says, "Stop. This cannot happen." "Why?" "Well, the FCC has a rule that managers of licensed broadcast facilities have to be persons of good moral character." And I said, "What exactly does that mean?" "Well, we don't know, but certainly no ex-convicts and no perverts." Eventually, the FCC's legal team told the FCC that *Black's Law Dictionary* does not have a specific definition for "good moral character," therefore we suggest you abandon the rule. And I became the first openly gay ex-convict to manage an FCC facility in the United States, laying the way for all the rest of the fools that have gotten those jobs since.

"HOUSTON AIN'T A DEMONSTRATING TOWN"

In 1977, Dade County, Florida, passed a nondiscrimination ordinance protecting employment for gay men and lesbians. Passing an ordinance to protect employment rights of gay people was a big deal in the '70s. In response, Anita Bryant formed an organization called Save Our Children to call a referendum on that ordinance. That became a national story, and so everybody in the country knew who Anita Bryant was and that she was against queers. [For more on Anita Bryant, see pp. 237, 254–55.]

Anita Bryant becomes the devil incarnate to gay people. She is a threat to our burgeoning struggle. We're a long way from being equal in those days, but she is a threat to the promise of all of that. And then all of a sudden, an old lesbian columnist in the *Houston Post* writes a column that says, "Guess who's coming to dinner?" And it's Anita Bryant. She's coming to Houston and she's going to be singing the "Battle Hymn of the Republic," her biggest song, for the State Bar Association at the Hyatt Regency Hotel. And I am the only advocate of onto-the-street-and-raising-hell action in Houston. Everybody else is quasi-Republican. "Let's go to the cocktail party so we can convince ourselves how good we are." I said, "If I could get them on the streets, it would change Houston from a passivist town to an activist town." This was my opportunity. I can't screw this up. I gotta get this right.

I go meet with Pappy Bond. Pappy Bond at that time was a captain of the Houston Police Department. He said, "I heard you all were going to have this demonstration, and how many people you expect at that demonstration?" I said, "About five hundred." He went to laughing. He said, "Houston ain't a demonstrating town. I've been through with Civil Rights and women's rights and abortion and anti-war, and fifty to sixty people are about all anybody can draw in Houston." And I said, "Pappy, you better count on a few more."

We had twelve thousand people. Twelve thousand. Houston had never seen a demonstration that large, and they were angry. Their hopes and their dreams and aspirations were being threatened by this woman. And so by the time they got to the Hyatt Regency Hotel, they were venting all that anger. We're talking about gay people who were afraid and ashamed and guilt-ridden. We're talking about people who didn't want to be seen in public as gay people, but all of a sudden they weren't alone.

Ray Hill passed away on November 24, 2018, at the age of 78. His funeral was held on the steps of Houston City Hall.

DON QUAINTANCE

RURAL PRIDE ORGANIZER

CENTERVILLE, MICHIGAN

Don Quaintance was born in 1941 on a farm in Cherokee, Iowa. In 1967, after serving in the Navy, he moved to Minneapolis and began his life as a gay man. For three decades, he never fully came out. Then, in 1999, Minnesota state senator Michelle Bachmann began a strident antigay campaign throughout the state. As a veteran, Don felt he had a right to make his voice heard. He started marching and writing editorials. When his picture appeared in a Twin Cities newspaper, Don was out for good.

In 2000, seeing that East Central Minnesota had no gay organizations, Don and four friends founded the East Central Minnesota Men's Circle. Five years later, they came up with the idea of inviting Minnesota's entire rural LGBTQ community to a picnic. That event became Pride in the Park, the second rural Pride event in the United States.

I was the oldest of eight kids. We moved around quite a bit, always living in rural parts of Iowa, southern Minnesota, and northern Minnesota.

Growing up as a gay young boy, I wasn't picked on, as I know many people were. But I just knew I was different. I tried to get along with everybody. Maybe we moved so much, people never got to know me. I did always feel ashamed of who I was. I felt defective. I had no role models, nobody to look up to for advice. I just felt like I was alone.

I didn't know anybody that was gay until I left school and came to the city for business college and met my first gay men, gay people. I was so surprised to find how many gay people there were. I thought I was, not the only one, but one of a few.

A MEN'S CIRCLE

Around 1999, I said to some gay friends, how do you meet people in the rural area? One person suggested that we could run an ad in the paper, and maybe we can start a men's circle up here. And I'm thinking, a men's circle? What's that?

Anyway, we ran a bunch of ads in all the local newspapers. We had a meeting, and about twenty-five people showed up. I was totally surprised that in a rural community, that many came. So that was in April 2000. That's where the Men's Circle started.

Some of the men would come thinking that it was a group of men getting together for sexual things. We right away said no. We're just a group of friends. We get together once a month in a safe place, usually a restaurant, meeting room, or something, to talk about issues that affect us in the rural area, or just affect us period. Sometimes we have speakers.

Five years after we started the Men's Circle, we decided, well, we've been together five years. Let's run an ad and invite the whole GLBT community and just see what happens. So that actually was the start of our Picnic in the Park in Pine City. I think this is now the seventeenth or eighteenth year of the Men's Circle, and the fourteenth year of Pride in the Park.

It's now called East Central Minnesota Pride in the Park. In 2005, one hundred people came. Then the following year, two hundred, three hundred. So now we have about five hundred people that might come, which is quite a few for a rural community. There are gay people, there are allies, friends, families. We have a barbecue where we serve food. We have entertainment. We have vendors from a lot of different places.

It's probably the same thing at Pride in San Francisco or New York, except being a smaller community, you're raised to know all these people, especially when they're coming back every year. You get to know their names, and if not their names, their faces at least. It's like a big family with four or five hundred other people.

A GOOD ROLE MODEL

Recently, I was at a wedding of one of my nephews, and I got a thank-you note from him just last week. He thanked me for coming and was glad to see me and whatever.

Then, the very last sentence, he says he was very proud of me for being a good role model for him. I have tears in my eyes because I thought, well really?

Also since that time, since the last couple of months, two nephews have come forward asking me about their kids. Both of the kids are saying they're bi, so they're asking me about what can they do, what should they do. Who should they see? That kind of thing. I guess they trust me, and they look in my direction.

Suddenly you understand that you are making an impact. Maybe you did some good, you know. Especially in your own family. That was your desire I guess, to help somebody out there, and now it's back in your own family.

In March 2018, OUTWORDS navigated a rapidly intensifying snowstorm to interview Don at his home in Centerville, Minnesota. In contrast to the weather outside, Don's home was warm and inviting, decorated with flowers, native American art, and family photos.

INTEGRITY

ALEXEI ROMANOFF

UKRAINIAN IMMIGRANT, ACTIVIST

LOS ANGELES, CALIFORNIA

Alexei Romanoff was born in the Ukraine in 1936, fled with his family to the United States during World War II, and came of age as a gay man in New York's Greenwich Village during the 1950s.

By 1966, Alexei was co-owner and manager of a Los Angeles gay bar called New Faces. On New Year's Eve, New Faces, the nearby Black Cat, and two other gay bars were raided by the police. Six weeks later, Alexei helped organize a protest at the Black Cat. Taking place more than two years before the Stonewall riots of June 1969, many people regard this event as the true genesis of the modern gay rights movement.

A lifelong activist, Alexei worked to establish gay-friendly medical clinics, fought against California's anti-gay Briggs Initiative, fought for AIDS research funding, helped convince Alcoholics Anonymous to list LGBT meetings, and cofounded the Avatar Club of Los Angeles to promote safer sex education for the leather community. In 2017, Alexei served as Grand Marshal of the Los Angeles Resist March, which took the place of that year's traditional Pride march.

When I was sixteen or seventeen, in New York City, it was really hard to rent a place for two men. Two women could rent together, but they would not want to rent to two men, particularly in the Village, of all places. I had this partner and we saw an advertisement for an apartment with a view of the river. It didn't say East River. It didn't say Hudson River. Just "view of the river."

We went and looked at it. The view of the river was, if you went out to the fire escape and hung over about two feet, you could see about two inches of the river way down there.

But we liked the place. We talked to each other. We talked to the landlord and said we'd like to take it.

The landlord said, "What's the relationship between you two?" I stopped for a minute and I stuttered and I said, "He's my partner and my lover." I looked back at my boyfriend and he was looking at me with his mouth hanging open and eyes wide as though to say, "What the hell have you just done?"

The landlord then said to me, "Can you guys afford the place?" I said, "Yes, we have your first month's rent here. We both work

PRIDE (Personal Rights in Defense and Education) led hundreds in protest of the riots that occurred when police raided the Black Cat and other bars in the Silver Lake neighborhood of Los Angeles and brutally beat patrons and the bartender. February 11, 1967.

part-time. We're going to the university. I sit out on the street on weekends and sell my artwork, and I study." He said, "Okay, give me the first month's rent. Here's the keys."

To this day, I have never lied. To this day, if someone asks me, I tell the truth.

FACE DOWN ON THE SIDEWALK

I arrived in Los Angeles on February 15, 1958. Eventually, I was working in a bar called the High Spot. It was on Hyperion Boulevard down in Silver Lake. Evidently, my reputation got out as being friendly, because I've always been a talker and a person who likes to meet new people. In 1964, this woman, her name was Lee Roy, came over to the High Spot and she said, "I'm trying to open a bar here on Sunset Boulevard. We've already got the place rented. I would like you to come and help me set it up."

I thought it was a really good thing. Lee ended up giving me part-ownership of the bar for helping to set it up. That's how I got involved in New Faces.

On New Year's Eve 1966, the police raided another bar up the street called the Black Cat. After they played "Auld Lang Syne" and everybody was hugging and kissing, that's when the raid started. These people ran out of the Black Cat and ran down the block to New Faces. The police followed them. Of course, they were plainclothes. They weren't uniformed officers. Evidently, they saw somebody who ran away from the Black Cat in a white dress.

The people from the Black Cat ran into New Faces, and the police followed them in. Because it was New Year's Eve, Lee Roy was dressed in a white gown. The cops said, "Who is the owner of this place?" The bartender said, "Lee Roy," which sounded like a man's name, and pointed at Lee. The cops went over and grabbed her and started beating her because they thought she was a cross-dresser. They broke her collarbone. Then the bartender came over, and they grabbed him and they pulled him across the bar. He had a ruptured spleen. Both Lee and the bartender ended on the sidewalk outside, face down. When they found that Lee wasn't a cross-dresser, they didn't press any charges on her. Both she and the bartender ended up in the hospital.

FROM BUNKER HILL TO THE BLACK CAT

After the events of New Year's Eve 1966, a demonstration took place at the Black Cat, in February 1967. The Black Cat had the most damage from what had happened on New Year's Eve. We made a lot of signs. We made flyers at a printing store because nobody had printers. If someone dropped a flyer, we would run and pick it up so that the police couldn't bust us for littering. We kept moving so the police couldn't bust us for loitering. It was five to six hundred gay men and women, lesbians, and those who support us. We marched up and down and chanted.

We were afraid the news media would show. We were afraid because if our pictures were in the paper, we would lose our jobs. We would lose our homes. None of the mainstream media showed up, but the free press showed up. They covered it with the pictures, all the pictures we have today. Years later, I met with Chief Bill Bratton of the Los Angeles Police Department. We were looking at the pictures from the demonstration. I said to him, "Do you see anybody smiling?" He looked at them and he said, "No." I said, "They weren't. They were scared as hell."

About two years, we had the Black Cat designated a historical landmark. An Asian man led that charge. His name was Wes Joe. He's still around today. I was asked why I wanted this place declared a historical landmark and a plaque put outside. I said, "Just like you have Bunker Hill, you have Gettysburg, you have Selma, Alabama. Some young gay man who's maybe eighteen, when I'm no longer here and able to tell him what had happened, he has a place to go to that's a physical place with a plaque outside. That's why we need that. We need to remember where we came from."

Today, Alexei lives with his husband, David, in Los Angeles. With his twinkling blue eyes, it's easy to imagine Alexei as a Ukrainian immigrant charming the pants off New York queers in the 1950s. But Alexei's fighting spirit is never far away—it's what has kept him going all these years.

JUNE LAGMAY

LOS ANGELES CITY CLERK

LOS ANGELES, CALIFORNIA

June Lagmay was born in Yokohama, Japan, and grew up in Historic Filipinotown in Los Angeles. In high school, she fell in love with Rita Romero. The two have been inseparable ever since.

After college, June became involved with Dignity Los Angeles, the first gay and lesbian Catholic group, which at the time was still meeting in secret. She helped manage the campaign of Don Amador, the first openly gay man to run for City Council, and she later served as the first co-chair of Asian/Pacific Lesbians and Gays.

In 1988, after working for two Los Angeles council members, June became a legislative assistant in the LA city clerk's office. This led to a long career under five Los Angeles mayors, culminating in 2009 when Mayor Antonio Villaraigosa appointed June as Los Angeles city clerk, the first Asian American and first openly LGBTQ person to hold this post. During these years, June helped start an LGBTQ organization for City Hall employees. After thirty-two years with the city, June retired. In 2014, she was honored by API (Asian and Pacific Islanders) Equality–LA for decades of human rights activism, and by the Los Angeles City Council as part of its LGBT Heritage Month celebration.

My mom and dad met in Japan, post–World War II. My dad is what in Filipino we call a mestizo, half white, half Filipino. He was born in Brooklyn, New York. He was an American soldier in the war, who then found employment in Japan as a civilian. My mom was a soldier too, but for the Japanese army, and then she also found civilian employment. They met. He courted her. I was born in Japan, and then we all came over in a tramp steamer, arrived in San Francisco.

My mom was not a submissive type. She grew up in a tough time. She's from Yokohama, which is a port town, so they're used to foreigners. They stand their own ground, and they carry their own weight. As I grew up, it started to bother me when people would say racist stuff about Asians. Asians are the good minority, right? People would say, "Oh, you never get in trouble. You always play the piano, keep your head down. You walk behind people." That just started getting on my nerves more and more.

RITA BANDITA

In high school, I was such a good Asian girl. I played the piano. I was best in my class. I got all A's. I was teacher's pet.

Rita, they used to call her Rita Bandita. She was naughty. She snuck cigarettes. She was moody. She played the guitar.

I think our oppositeness just attracted so much. I never met anybody as deep and internal as she was. I got on her nerves because I was so good and because I was so predictable. We were mutually attracted and repelled at the same time.

Eventually we became very good friends, always at each other's houses, long nights on the telephone. A couple years later, in senior year, it became physical, and it was intense.

SPACE FOR EVERYBODY

In the 1970s, my dear friend Paul Chen became one of the first co-chairs of Asian/Pacific Lesbians and Gays. The people that I

June and Rita Bandita

met in APLG were the most loving, powerful, strong people that I'd ever met.

Within APLG, you could do what you wanted. There was space for everybody. You could be Japanese, Chinese, Korean, Southeast Asian, Indian, male or female, transgender. If you wanted to be a separatist lesbian, you could. If you wanted to hang out with the guys, you could. If you wanted to wear jeans, you could. If you wanted to wear a dress and makeup, you could.

There were some members who were FOB, fresh off the boat, who hardly spoke any English. Some were so deeply closeted that it was painful for them to even be alive. Others were open and out and much more advanced in their activism. The only thing that we understood is that we had been oppressed and that we all liked rice. How that oppression took effect and how we dealt with it, there were as many ways of dealing with it as there were types of people. It was just a wonderful experiment.

PUSHING BOUNDARIES

Early in my career, I was assistant to the candidate Don Amador, who was one of the first gay candidates to run for city office. Don and Harvey Milk were very close. They had this plan that Harvey would win a gay seat in San Francisco and Don would win a gay seat in Los Angeles, and then they would sort of "cement" the two cities.

When Don didn't win, I was a council field aide for a few years, then I worked for an assemblywoman. Eventually I got a job in the city clerk's office, and when Richard Riordan was elected mayor, I joined his staff. When he was turned out, the new mayor, James Hahn, picked me up. I worked for him for his whole first term. Then he was beaten by Antonio Villaraigosa, who picked me up, and I worked for Antonio for eight years.

All this time, I felt like I wanted to push boundaries. I didn't want to be a typical meek Asian. I wanted to do the job that I was given my way. My way.

I remember when I was in a low-level position in the city clerk's office, there were hearings and discussions before the City Council on gay issues. I asked my superiors, "Can I have permission to go and testify?" They said, "Are you sure you want to do that, June? It's one thing to have a personal life. If you do this, everybody will know and you can't ever take it back." I said, "I don't see the harm in any of that. That's fine with me."

When the City Council was deciding whether to grant domestic partner benefits, I went to Zev Yaroslavsky. Zev was chair of the council's budget committee, and they had the decision whether or not to do it. I remember approaching him and saying, "Councilman, you should know, I'm your assistant on the budget committee, and I'm a gay woman, and we really need this, because if my partner gets sick, there's no way that she can be taken care of. It may not be the fiscally wise thing to do, but it is the right thing to do."

By the time I became city clerk of the city of Los Angeles, I was very open about being lesbian. I always remembered, "If I stay closeted, I disrespect my partner. It doesn't matter what happens to me, but I must not do that."

At June's OUTWORDS interview, she and Rita proudly showed us a tiny photo from their high school days, literally stuck to its glass frame (p. 37). But they are proudest of their legal marriage in October 2008 and the 2018 "golden anniversary" of their life together.

PHYLLIS RANDOLPH FRYE

JUDGE, TRANSGENDER ACTIVIST

HOUSTON, TEXAS

At her birth in 1946, Phyllis Randolph Frye was named Phillip. Growing up in Texas, Phillip became an Eagle Scout and commander of his high school ROTC program. He graduated from Texas A&M with degrees in civil and mechanical engineering. By that point, Phillip was married and had a son.

Coming to terms with the fact that he was (in the vernacular of the day) transsexual, Phillip came out to his family and the military, who promptly rejected him. Unable to get a job, Phillip found an unlikely ally in his second wife, Trish, who encouraged him to transition. When Phil, the born-again Army lieutenant, wrote a letter to his neighbors introducing himself as Phyllis, they responded with eggs, slashed tires, and spray-painted obscenities on her driveway. To protect herself and others, Phyllis decided to become a lawyer.

After law school, Phyllis couldn't get a job. But in 1986, a closeted military service member was slapped with a DWI after leaving a gay bar. Phyllis took his case, kept it out of the newspapers, and used the fees to launch her transgender law practice. Five years later, she created the International Conference on Transgender Law and Employment Policy, bringing together lawyers and activists to draft policy goals and lobby Congress. On November 17, 2010, Houston mayor Annise Parker appointed Phyllis to the municipal bench, making her the country's first openly transgender judge. Three years later, the Transgender Foundation of America honored Phyllis with its Lifetime Achievement Award. In 2015, leading transgender attorney Shannon Minter (p. 159) called Phyllis "the grandmother of our movement."

When I graduated in high school, I had a four-year military scholarship to the Texas A&M College of Engineering. I was a big deal with respect to the military. They were investing a lot into me. I was on a career path. While I was still in college, in 1968, I got married.

It wasn't until my wife and I were overseas in Germany, with my baby son, that I came out to her about my desire to cross-dress. I figured that I had to come out to her, because I had been cross-dressing secretly during our marriage for a couple of years. I was hoping that it was something that she would accept and that I would be able to indulge to some degree. Well, she didn't.

The military found out, and they started trying to run me out. I was so despondent, I cut my wrist. They wanted to give me a general discharge. I said, "No, I'm going to fight for an honorable." I threatened to embarrass them by coming out to the press because I was one of their superstars. I finally got my honorable discharge.

By September of '76, I was working as an engineer in Houston, when it became known that I cross-dressed. I was fired, and no one would hire me. I couldn't get a job. By now, I was divorced and remarried. My wife and I went from a combined income of about $32,000 to $10,000. We had a mortgage payment, car payments. I still paid child support for my son. It was really, really tough. I would get so depressed. I was so angry.

My wife knew about my cross-dressing. She finally said, "These people aren't going to hire you because of who they think you are. You might as well go ahead and be who you are."

GET OVER IT, JUDGE FRYE

I was appointed seven years ago as a municipal court judge in the city of Houston by then-mayor Annise Parker, who was the first out lesbian mayor in a major city in the United States. I am the first out-of-the-closet, transgendered judge in the nation. Can I

be active politically? Yeah. In this last legislature in Austin, when they were trying to run through a bathroom bill, private citizen Phyllis Frye was there. I was lobbying. Every time somebody said, "Judge Frye this," I'd say, "No, I'm not Judge here. I'm Phyllis Frye here. Anything I'm saying in this interview is from me as a private citizen, not in my role as judge."

When I first became a judge, I went to a trans event, and suddenly I was the keynote speaker. I'd just been appointed a couple of weeks before. Everybody was just so excited. Big smiles, Judge Frye, Judge Frye, Judge Frye. Well, I wasn't handling it yet. I said, "No, no, no, I'm still Phyllis. I'm still Phyllis. You can call me Phyllis."

Well, one young FTM trans man, his name is Lou Weaver, very active nationally with Lambda Legal, he grabbed me by the arm and carried me over to a quiet space in the corner. He put his finger in my chest and he says, "These people need to be able to call you Judge Frye, so get over it." So I got over it.

GIVING PEOPLE BACK THEIR LIVES

I told my wife what I want on my gravestone is "She opened doors." What else can you ask for as an epitaph? That's what I feel that I've done.

I take transgender people through the courts all the time. I first started in the '80s. The judges didn't know much about us. They wouldn't even change the name unless you'd had full below-the-waist surgery. Well, how in the world are you going to get a job if you're Ralph, presenting as Tammy, for three or four or however many years until you can put your money together to jump through all the hoops to have your surgery? I began to convince the judges that it was important to change the name at the very beginning.

Then, in the early '90s, more and more people said, "That's great, but it still says M or F on my driver's license or my passport." For a transgender person, a change of name, without also changing the gender marker, was an incomplete change of name. I invented that concept of gender marker. I started taking people through the court without any surgery of any kind, at the beginning of their transition, to get their name and their gender marker changed. They could go to the Department of Public Safety, who does our driver's licenses, and get a new driver's license with their new face, that had their new name, and if they were male-to-female it said F, and if they were female-to-male it says M. That was a big deal. A lot of other people around the country have copied that.

Another thing, it used to be you could not get your name changed if you had a felony conviction. The state didn't want people who commit felonies to try to get under the radar by changing their name, so they can do more bad stuff.

Twenty years ago, I had a trans woman come to me. She was almost forty years old. She'd been living full-time as a woman since she was a teenager. She was a florist. She had been to several attorneys, trying to get her

Phyllis speaking at the second national transgender lobbying day in Washington DC in 1996

name changed. They all said, "You have a felony." I asked her, "What was the felony?" She says, "Possession of marijuana when I was seventeen." I said, "This is stupid. That's not even a felony now."

I explained all this to the judge. The judge says, "Makes sense to me." The judge signed the name change order. We walk out. As soon as we go through the door, I hear a thud. My client had passed out. She hit the floor. A bunch of people ran over. We helped her to a bench in the hallway. She woke up. She saw me. She started crying. She says, "You gave me back my life."

I get to do that. I do it every single month. I'm giving people back their lives. It's a lot of fun to give people back their lives.

OUTWORDS interviewed Judge Frye at her Houston office in May 2017. When it came time for portraits, we thought it would be funny to use a gavel as a prop. Phyllis wasn't having it. The lifesaving power of the law is serious business to her.

Phyllis addressing the audience on the eve of the 1993 March on Washington for Lesbian, Gay, and Bi Equal Rights and Liberation

ABILLY S. JONES-HENNIN

BISEXUAL ACTIVIST AND ORGANIZER

WASHINGTON, DC

ABilly Jones-Hennin was born in 1942 in Saint John's, Antigua, and adopted at age three by civil rights activists with nine other adopted kids. After growing up in South Carolina and Virginia, ABilly served in the US Marine Corps and graduated from Virginia State University in 1968. After marriage, three kids, and a divorce, ABilly came out as bisexual.

In 1978, ABilly helped launch the National Coalition of Black Gays (NCBG) in Columbia, Maryland, the first national advocacy organization for African-American gay men and lesbians. A year later, ABilly helped mobilize the first March on Washington for Lesbian and Gay Rights—and that same historic weekend, he helped convene the National Third World (People of Color) LGBTQ Conference at Howard University, which gave rise to Howard University's Lambda Student Alliance, the first LGBTQ organization at an HBCU (historically black college or university).

Over the subsequent decades, ABilly has taken on countless leadership roles within the black and LGBTQ movements, including minority affairs director of the National AIDS Network, founding member and co-chair of the National Coalition of Black Lesbians and Gays, board member of the National Gay and Lesbian Task Force (today known as The Task Force), and board member of BiNet USA.

After high school, I went to Virginia Union University and flunked out after a year. I wasn't quite mature enough for college, but I had a lot of fun that first year. Then I attempted to join the Marine Corps. Their slogan at that time was "A few good men." I was like, "Oh, that's for me."

I was only seventeen, so I had to have my parent's signature. Initially, they were like, "Absolutely not." Then my father said, "Well, maybe it would be good for him. It'll help him settle down." My mom cried and my dad signed the paper, and off I went into the Marine Corps. I was on active duty for four years and inactive duty for three more. I did find a few good men.

The Marine Corps got me through college, and I enjoyed it. I learned a lot of discipline and leadership. Of course, you had to be discreet about relating to other men. At that time, there was like an underground, closed community of military personnel

Abilly in 1964

WORD OF MOUTH

In the '70s, organizing events, conferences, and meetings for LGBT organizations, the way we did it is we send out snail mail, which is unheard of almost today. We made phone calls and we put flyers up in various places. It was by word of mouth. If you had a meeting, you announced when the next meeting would be, and people would write it down and remember. That's how we organized. That's how we organized the first March on Washington in 1979, which I was one of the national logistics coordinators for. We did not have cell phones. There was no texting. There was no social media. Yet people got the message and came together.

My days of marching are over, but I definitely am politically involved, and I plan to be as long as I live. There's so many issues to be addressed, you pick your issues. You know the expression "Think Global, Act Local." It's so, so important. You gotta do what you can. Send money when you can. Write a letter when you can. If you can't march, at least attend a rally and cheer on the sidelines.

who got together and fraternized with each other and had sex with each other. You had to trust who was there, but at any moment if someone got busted, they could then turn on other people who were in there. You could use a false name, but if you were in the same unit with other folks, it could be risky. All it would take would be for one person to turn you in, and you could be in trouble.

I was turned in at one point. I was grilled, and grilled, and grilled. I think what rescued me is that my lover at that time was the chaplain, a captain in the Corps. I think that saved me. But that was a scary moment.

THE JOURNEY

It's hard to be totally out always. There are always situations that most of us decide, "Is this a safe environment for me to say that I'm bisexual?" I don't walk into the room and say, "Hi. My name is ABilly and I'm bisexual." You weigh the odds of doing it. You have to work through the fear of knowing that you will probably be put down. You have to decide how much education you wish to do or how much energy you have.

At this point in my life, I most strongly identify as a bisexual activist. I feel more empowered to put myself out as a bisexual without having to apologize for it, without feeling ashamed or embarrassed about it, without being closeted about it. The biggest commitment that I have right now to myself is that I will not lie or deny that I'm bisexual. If I'm invited some place to speak, and I identify myself as bisexual, invariably some youth will come to me and say, "Thank you. I identify as bisexual too." Both youth and even older persons. I'm often thanked, but quietly. That person may not be quite strong enough to come out, but they are grateful that somebody did.

ABilly lives in Washington, DC, with his partner of forty years, Cris. Between them, the two men have five children, nine grandchildren, and six great-grandkids. They spend their winters in Quintana Roo, Mexico.

GRETHE CAMMERMEYER

NURSE, ARMY COLONEL, DADT ACTIVIST

WHIDBEY ISLAND, WASHINGTON

Colonel Margarethe Cammermeyer, commonly known as Grethe, was born in 1942 in Oslo, Norway. At age nine, she and her family immigrated to the United States. At eighteen, she became a US citizen. A year later, she entered the Army Student Nurse Program and, in 1963, earned her nursing degree from the University of Maryland. While serving in Germany, she married a fellow soldier. Together, they went to Vietnam, where Grethe served as head nurse of a neurosurgical intensive care unit, garnering a Bronze Star for Meritorious Achievement. Returning home, she raised four sons while working in VA hospitals and earning her master's degree and PhD in nursing from the University of Washington.

In 1988, divorced and having attained the rank of colonel, Grethe transferred to the Washington National Guard, assuming the role of chief nurse. That same year, in her self-described "aha" moment, she met and fell in love with Diane Divelbess, an artist from California. A year later, during a security clearance interview, Grethe disclosed that she was a lesbian, leading to her involuntary discharge two years later. Grethe filed a federal lawsuit against the Department of Defense, and in 1994, district judge Thomas Zilly ruled her discharge unconstitutional.

After her retirement from the military in 1997, Grethe devoted herself full-time to overturning the military's "Don't Ask, Don't Tell" (DADT) policy. On December 22, 2010, Grethe led the Pledge of Allegiance at President Obama's signing ceremony to finally repeal the much-despised statute.

I was born in 1942 in Oslo, Norway, during the Nazi occupation. My father was a neuropathologist and my mother a nurse, and they were involved with the Nazi resistance. In fact, we lived across the street from Nazi headquarters, and so very early on I became involved in the resistance. When I was an infant, my mother would put me in a baby carriage, and underneath my mattress, she would store guns for the resistance forces. Then she would walk through town, and turn into an alley, where some people would jump out, and take the guns from underneath my mattress. I attribute the fact that I can sleep anytime, anyplace to having been raised on guns.

As I got older, I recognized that my parents' involvement in the resistance was necessary to prevent evil, even though they lost friends and many had to flee. I read books about Norwegian women in particular, who were influential in the resistance forces. And I wondered if I would have been as brave. Would I have stood up? Would I have taken the challenge, regardless of the risks?

Much later, during my years in the military, there were times I had to challenge what I was ordered to do, that I did not think was ethically correct. Even though it may have been correct in terms of policy, it was not ethically correct for me as a nurse.

In one example, I was a young lieutenant in Germany. I had seventy-six patients, including a number that had had heart attacks and were at risk of dying at any particular point. I was ordered to leave the ward to go down to sign in with the chief nurse. It was a direct order. I felt that I could not leave my patients, and told them so. They ordered me again, and I refused again.

It was intimidating, because after all, I was in the military. I was supposed to obey lawful orders. I didn't consider that a lawful order, because my patients came first.

Eventually, someone came and covered for me on the ward, so that I could leave to sign in. At that point, they apologized because they had not realized what the clinical situation was that made me decide that I couldn't come down.

Every time I withstood the challenge, I felt a certain satisfaction that I did the right thing. I was willing to take the consequences

Grethe receiving the Bronze Star, Vietnam, 1968

for that. I think the more a person does that, the more you realize that the world does not fall apart if you say no. You come to believe that doing the right thing ends up with the right consequences.

DISCHARGE

Six months after I disclosed that I was a lesbian to the investigator, seeking a top-secret clearance, I was told that they were going to discharge me. I was stunned because I had been in the military for twenty-five years. I had served with distinction in Vietnam and throughout my military career. The president of the board said, "Margarethe, we consider you a great American, but because of the regulation, I have to recommend that your military designation be withdrawn." It was a policy at the time that the military had instituted, saying if you were gay you had a mental illness, that it would be bad for the unit, that sort of thing.

I was stunned. I believed that by coming out, that I would just be allowed to continue to work. I believed that President George Bush would see that this was an error and that I could continue to serve. When that didn't happen and I was discharged, I lost my blind belief in the military. And yet I knew that what I was standing for was the right thing to do. It cost me my career and gave me my integrity.

FIGHTING BACK

The Lambda Legal Defense and Education Fund agreed to take my case. They took it on and for two years worked with me and fought the government on my discharge, and subsequently, we won. I was reinstated in the military. By now, "Don't Ask, Don't Tell" was in place. My attorney said, "Wouldn't it be a shame to have you muted, because you've won your case?" That's when I had to remember that it wasn't for me that I was doing this. I was trying to help change the policy so others wouldn't have to go through what I had gone through.

When you start that journey, it really is lonely, because you don't know the direction that it's going to take. Even though I had been told by my attorney that there was going to be a lot of notoriety around my case, I didn't know what that meant. She did, but I didn't.

Once "Don't Ask, Don't Tell" was overturned, there was the euphoria of the event. I was in Washington, DC, for the signing ceremonies. I was asked by the White House to lead the Pledge of Allegiance. It was a big deal for everyone there, a huge deal. We cried because now the Pledge of Allegiance applied

to all of us, and the flag not only was representing America, but it was representing us.

Once the euphoria subsided, I thought, "What do I do now with all this energy and all of this drive for creating a greater good?" That became a real personal crisis for me. I had done over 125 lectures at different universities. Suddenly, I felt like a has-been. I had to come to terms with that.

The exciting thing now is that there are gay generals in the military that are out and involved. They're doing what I used to be doing, and I am delighted for them. Occasionally, there is a tinge of, "Well, gee, I wish I was there." My wife, Diane, reassures me that I'm okay. It's time for the next generation to take over. My personal victory helped improve life for so many people.

Today, Grethe and Diane live on Whidbey Island, Washington, with their two rescue dogs, Bella and Stryder. They are very close to Grethe's sons and their children. In person, Grethe is tall, strong, and very direct—the kind of person one would want as an ally in any campaign for justice.

DOC DUHON

ENERGY EXECUTIVE, LONGTIME AIDS SURVIVOR

PALM SPRINGS, CALIFORNIA

Doc Duhon was born in 1954 in Reno, Nevada. In high school, Doc began experimenting with drugs and alcohol. He dropped out of college, got married, and had a daughter named Arielle. At thirty-four, having come out of the closet, he finally got sober. He participated in many AIDS protests, including a 1988 die-in at the California state capitol building in Sacramento. In 1991, a broken condom changed his HIV status and the course of his life.

In subsequent years, Doc became a leading energy efficiency expert for the utility PG&E, serving as the first chair of the California Commissioning Collaborative, a group dedicated to maximizing the potential of high-efficiency buildings. In 2006, HIV health issues forced Doc to retire.

My father was a traditional Cajun man. Rowdy when he drank, quiet the rest of the time. He came into my bedroom when I was twelve years old. It was about ten o'clock at night. We lived in a very small place, all four of the children shared one bedroom. My older sister was away, my younger siblings were asleep.

My dad looked at the floor, never looked at me, and he said, "Your mother and I would really appreciate it if you are not one of those awful homosexuals." Got up and left the room.

I dived into a closet. A deep one.

When I finally came out, my father had a very difficult time. He finally came to some element of acceptance. The reason I know my father turned a corner was, much later,

I walked into the living room at my parents' home. My father had a propensity for yelling at the TV. He was screaming at Newt Gingrich for making a homophobic statement. I thought, "Okay, we've done it. We've made it over the edge."

MAKING UP FOR LOST TIME

My first couple of months after I seroconverted, I had a really tough time. I was working for PG&E, Pacific Gas and Electric, a company that through the 1980s had lost so many people to the epidemic that they had become hugely supportive of their gay and lesbian employees. I finally went to my boss and said, "I'm HIV-positive. I don't know what to do." The company put me directly

Doc participates in a 1988 "die-in" on the steps of the California state capitol to protest governmental inaction on HIV/AIDS.

into therapy; they got me in line with the best medical practitioners they had available. They were magic. It really helped.

By the late 1990s, I'm starting to show a little wear and tear from the anti-HIV drugs, but I got my life back, I'm going to live, I'm responsive to the meds, my career is finally going somewhere. I'm involved in energy efficiency and climate change, I'm making presentations to the governor's office, I'm going to Washington, DC, and talking to the EPA.

I worked so hard that I got sick and lost weight again. Towards the end, I can remember sitting at my desk in tears, because I could no longer keep up with the demand, and I

didn't know what to do. Finally one day, my boss came into my office and basically said, "You need to leave." I said, "What do you mean, I need to leave? It's December 19th, it's the end of the year." I had thirty employees and a $65 million budget. "I got work that's got to be done. My reputation is on the line here!"

My boss looked right at me and he said, "You've been my friend for a really long time. You look like you are dying, and you are not going to die at your desk."

I got very upset. I went home. I called my AA sponsor and said, "My life was my job, and I made a difference in the world," and all this stuff. She said, "Honey, I have something to tell you. It's not going to be easy to hear." I said, "What is it?" She said, "You used to be important, and now you are not. Get over it."

NOT HIDING ANYMORE

My take on being gay has always been, I'm not straight, living in a house with a wife, 2.2 kids, a Volvo, and a white picket fence. I don't want to be gay, living in a house with a husband and 2.2 Lhasa apsos and a Volvo and a white picket fence. I just don't want to do that. I'm a big fag, and I need to embrace that. I can be kinky, I can be poly, I can have open relationships.

My family today is very conventional for me, but it doesn't look very conventional for the rest of the world. My partner, James, and I have been together since 1991. I have somebody in my life who is my dominant. I submit to him. He sets the rules in many areas of my life. My dominant has another submissive who lives with me. I call him my brother; his name is Scott. I have two submissives of my own, one who serves me and calls me Master, and another who I mentor like a son, who calls me Daddy. My biological family, the ones that choose to still be part of my life, know the people in my kink family, and vice versa.

I've been through too much in my life to not be who I am in the world. It's not worth it for me to hide any portion of myself anymore. As long as I'm being responsible, being loving, taking care of things as things go, I don't need to make excuses so that people won't be upset, and I don't need to explain away my life.

There are two ways to deal with people who react badly to who I am. One of them is, "Fuck you. I'll do what I want," and the other one is, "Everyone is entitled to their opinion. Your opinion of me is none of my business. Go with God."

I try to practice the latter.

Today, Doc lives in Palm Springs, California, where he's deeply involved in the leather and polyamory communities. Doc volunteers with the LGBT Community Center of the Desert, as well as Let's Kick ASS (a long-term HIV survivor support network).

CHUCK WILLIAMS

FOUNDER, THE WILLIAMS INSTITUTE

LOS ANGELES, CALIFORNIA

Chuck Williams was born in Los Angeles to parents who moved to California to get away from their uptight religious families in Texas. Chuck grew up enjoying the beach, surfing, and riding around on his pet donkey. After studying business at UCLA, Chuck got married, entered the Air Force, and was sent to Scotland. He and his wife soon had a son.

Returning to the United States, Chuck's marriage fell apart. Soon after, Chuck met a man named Stu on a waterskiing trip. They've been together now for more than fifty years. Chuck meanwhile entered the burgeoning computer business at RCA. After RCA was acquired by the Sperry Corporation, Chuck moved east with Stu to head Sperry's US and international operations. When Sperry was acquired by Burroughs in 1986, Chuck stepped down, returned to California, worked as a consultant and professor for a time, and ultimately turned to what may be considered his true life mission: establishing the Williams Institute at UCLA Law School.

Chuck donated $2.5 million in 2001 to found the Williams Institute. At the time, it was the largest donation ever given to a college or university in support of a gay and lesbian academic program. The institute's mission was and is to conduct rigorous, independent research on sexual orientation and gender identity law and public policy. Over the years, Williams Institute experts have authored dozens of public policy studies and law review articles, filed amicus briefs in key court cases, provided expert testimony at legislative hearings, and trained more than three thousand judges in sexual orientation law.

I started out at UCLA working as a student to get a degree as an x-ray physicist. When I was a sophomore, a professor had written formulas all over the chalkboard. It was a very high-end course. He spun around and he said, "What is this?" and I said, "I have no idea," and he said, "You are not a scientist," and I said, "I think you may be right."

That's when I changed degrees and began a degree in business and a master's degree in economic theory, and then I eventually worked on my doctorate in the same field.

I entered the Air Force and was an officer, headquartered in Scotland. It started my international thing. I have been an internationalist ever since. I've been in seventy-five countries, and I'm still going to more.

Just before I entered the Air Force, I got married. My son was born in Scotland.

I came back from the Air Force to Long Beach and lived in Long Beach for a while, and I was working on my PhD at UCLA. I was excited about hanging out with professors. We'd talk about stuff and it all made me feel very good and very intrigued, and I'd come home and my wife was upset because we weren't going to the country club for dinner. I didn't like the country club.

Then there was a question of, what kind of life are we going to live. I wanted to get my doctorate and be a professor. You're not going to get very wealthy that way. We fell apart over that. There's no doubt, toward the end, there was some indication on my own part that I wanted to be with guys, but it was a combination.

RESEARCH THAT MATTERS

At a certain point, I was beginning to accumulate money, and you gotta take care of it if you die [*chuckling*], even if you don't while you're alive. So I was working on my will and trust. I said I'd like to do something with some money that's left after people are taken care of.

I have never been one that worked on charity operations that a lot of people do. I'm not belittling it at all. It's a good feeling to go out and find somebody on the street, pick them up, take them in for dinner, and give them a bed to sleep in. My position is, I want to find out how they got there and why.

A company photo of Chuck during his RCA years

Therefore, I said, if I'm going to do something for society, well, who? Well, the society I'm interested in is mine, which is the gay and lesbian society. Okay, then, what do you want to do? My thing was, I'd like to try to end discrimination, which is prevalent throughout everything—legal, judicial, regulatory, society itself. I want to try to help reduce that or solve it. So I said, we need somebody that's going to really study the issue and see what they can come up with. It had to be practical in nature, and that's why I decided to put it in a law school because, regardless of what you think of lawyers, they're practical.

For example, there are judges judging cases related to gay and lesbian issues who never had a course on gay law. So we have to train judges. You look at the legislators: they're passing laws every day and some of them don't have an understanding of what's going on, so we've got to teach them. They're not just there to beat up on gays and lesbians, so we got to teach them how not to do that.

We went to fifteen universities with the request for proposal. I narrowed it down to three universities: Harvard, Stanford, and UCLA. The dean at the UCLA Law School was excited about it, and they put together an excellent proposal. Then I didn't want somebody waking up and saying, "What are we doing with this queer stuff?" So I had lunch with the chancellor of the university, and he finished and stood up and said, "This is an issue whose time has come."

Then I met with the president of the university system, and he agreed, and then I said I want to meet with the Board of Regents, and they agreed. So I said, "It's done. We'll do it," and that's why we set up the Williams Institute at UCLA.

Chuck attends graduation at the UCLA School of Management, where he taught for several years.

Initially, I made an investment of two and a half million. We had to have an endowment, because people say, "How long are you going to be in existence? You just opened the door." If you have some little endowment, at least then your strategy is to build a bigger endowment. I said, we want to have a 20 million endowment when we're ten years old, and we did. We now have about a 30 million endowment. The institute has really accomplished a massive amount. Our byline is "Research that matters," and I think that's valid.

WINNING A WAR

The classic example of what we do at the Williams Institute was a case called *Lawrence v. Texas*. That was a case in which two guys went to bed together in the privacy of their apartment and were arrested and were convicted of a felony for having sex. They were convicted all the way up through the circuit courts, and it went to the US Supreme Court.

We got involved in *Lawrence v. Texas* when it started. We knew it was going to go to the Supreme Court because of the way it went through the circuits. We got together twenty-eight law firms to help us pro bono, and we had a staff of four people in Texas. We studied what gays or lesbians were doing in every county in Texas. There are doctors, lawyers, merchants, chiefs; they sell newspapers, anything they do. The majority of those professions require the rights of the state. Example, if you're going to be a hairdresser, you have to have a license from the state to be a hairdresser. You couldn't get such a thing if you were convicted of any felony. *Lawrence v. Texas* was a felony case, for having sex in their home.

We went and we presented all our research to the Supreme Court in an amicus brief. We also had a guy working for us who had been a clerk for Justice Kennedy. That was a great tie-in.

Long story short, they ruled in our favor. They said that law is not valid, and not only is it not valid but the prior ruling, which was *Bowers*, was invalid when they ruled it at the Supreme Court. So here's the Supreme Court ruling not only that this is no good, but everything we did about it previously is no good. I said that's where we won a war. Really did.

We were quoted in the Supreme Court ruling [*choking up*]. It was very exciting. The institute was very, very changed in how big we were, how strong we were, and how much money we could raise, as a result of the *Lawrence* case.

THINKING ABOUT MARRIAGE

At the beginning of the marriage equality effort, I thought Evan Wolfson [see p. 116] was nuts. He and I were both being honored by some organization. He and I both spoke because we both were being honored. He spoke with this conviction that we should have marriage next week, and I thought, "Is he nuts?" I said, off the record, "You got to walk before you run, and you're trying to win a four-hundred-meter race, and it's just not going to happen."

I felt that you've got to do what would be the simplest, easiest thing first. How about some little rights? Give people some little rights and make that phase one, and then keep going to the final phases. That's pretty much what I thought.

Then, in California, we had a case of two ladies, lesbians, who lived in an apartment house. One of them came home with the groceries and was attacked by a dog and killed. They had no rights at all, zero. The surviving partner couldn't sue for wrongful death.

At the institute, we never are activists. That's not our role. But we went to the state legislature in California. I went myself to the state legislature. We stayed until they passed a bill, which was three days. In three days, they passed a bill to give partners the right to sue for wrongful death.

At that point, my thinking got firmer in that, yeah, we should think about marriage.

OUTWORDS interviewed Chuck in April 2017 at the home that he and Stu built in Malibu, California. Below us, the sun-struck Pacific Ocean stretched to the horizon and beyond.

JAN EDWARDS

SCHOOL TEACHER AND COUNSELOR

SONOMA, CALIFORNIA

Jan Edwards was born in 1938 in Cleveland. From early on, she was a take-charge person, captaining street ball games and later serving as class and student council president. Because her mother was an invalid, Jan also took over the running of her family household, becoming a sort of second mother to her younger sister, Faye. She enjoyed being a spokesperson for others, a role she still values today.

Jan graduated from the College of Wooster in Ohio, then embarked on a forty-two-year career as a teacher and school counselor in middle schools, high schools, and colleges. Along the way, she married an Air Force officer and pilot and had two children. As Jan realized she was a pacifist and a lesbian, her marriage ended. Jan later had a twenty-eight-year relationship with a woman; but at seventy-five, she left that relationship and struck out once again on her own. In what she describes as a strange twist of fate, Jan was subsequently diagnosed with a vocal tremor that makes it difficult for her to sing (a lifelong passion) and, at times, even to speak. "Note to self," Jan says, "don't wait to speak."

When I married my husband, Jim, I think I thought I was following the natural path. In the late '50s, if you went to college, you usually met someone, you married someone, you had children, you became a wife and mother. That was the expectation.

Having said that, there were certainly times where I had second thoughts. I thought they were second thoughts about Jim. In retrospect, they were probably second thoughts about getting married. The university where I was teaching had spoken to me about the possibility of staying on and getting more classes, and later perhaps getting my PhD

there. That had a lot of appeal to me. But I felt like I was in too deep at that point. I had given my word that I would get married to Jim. I never realistically considered that his plans would dictate my plans. I was so naive.

Jim joined the military and trained to become a fighter pilot. He got stationed at Travis Air Force Base in Fairfield, California. During the late '60s, when Jim and almost every other man in our circle was in Vietnam, all of the wives were left at home. Some had small children, and we had activities out at the Air Force base for officers' wives specifically. We had luncheons galore. We had wine, parties. Most of us just assumed that we were all doing our civic duty.

Then, when Jim was in Vietnam, I got seduced by a woman, another officer's wife.

This woman informed me that this was quite common, that many of the wives got together while their husbands were gone, that this was nothing other than normal military absence behavior. Even though I was with her on several occasions, I remained puzzled. Engaged, but puzzled, and never quite comfortable with the whole thing. I was cheating. I was cheating on my husband.

Right before Christmas of 1967, Jim, the perfect Air Force officer who never did anything wrong, went AWOL and flew home to Fairfield. I knew, day 2 of his being home, I was pregnant. That recommitted me to the idea of, this is my marriage. This is my family. We have a two-year-old daughter, another child on the way, and this is our happy family.

1968 was a cataclysmic year in our country. When I realized I was pregnant and that Jim was still in Vietnam and that the war showed no signs whatsoever of cooling down—on the contrary, there was a significant buildup, the Tet Offensive—I was scared stiff. I thought, what is going to become of the three of us, soon to be four of us? How are we going to possibly manage? This child I'm carrying is never going to know his or her father. The little girl, my daughter, what will she remember of her father? Myself, who will he be, if he comes back? If he comes back, what will he be like? My son was born in September 1968. Over the course of the next five or

six years, Jim and I grew very, very separate. Ultimately, in 1975, we divorced.

THE FINAL CHRISTMAS

Over the years, it crossed my mind that my son might be gay, and it certainly crossed the mind of many of my friends, both male and female, particularly my gay male friends. They would often say, "Jan, Jay is gay. Has he come out to you yet?" It was a different time period, and he was still in high school at that time. I said, "Well, no. He has never addressed it at all."

Later, when Jay was in his twenties, he came to me one day and he said, "Mom, I need to tell you something." Mind you, I had not come out to him yet, either, although my partner and I were living together and sleeping in the same bed, and I'm sure he

Jan with Jim in 1963

knew that we were a couple. He said, "I am a homosexual," which was sweet, and I said, "You are?" He said yes, and I said, "And I am too."

Over a period of time, it became very obvious that my partner was not comfortable with the amount of time that I wanted to spend with my children. When they were visiting us, there were very stringent conditions placed upon when they could arrive, when they must depart, what meals they could have with us, how late they stayed up, or whether they were noisy or whether they could flush the toilet in the middle of the night. All the while, she tried to convince me that they were adults. That they didn't need their parents butting in their lives, and if they wanted to see me more, they would make more of an effort to see me. I opted to let that continue for way, way, way too long.

The final Christmas that I spent with my partner, my son and his husband and my daughter were invited to our house for approximately a two-hour period that would encompass brunch from, as I recall, eleven a.m. to one p.m. I vowed at that point there would never ever be a Christmas like that again. I knew I had to go.

I have never felt more desperate in my life. It felt like my life depended on it. I can't imagine being more frightened or needing to do something extreme than if somebody had entered my home with a weapon and was about to shoot me. It was on that level. It was so extreme. At the age of seventy-five, after being in a relationship for twenty-eight years, I waited until my partner was going to be away from the house for a couple of hours. I loaded some clothes in black garbage bags and snuck down the stairwell of a fire escape and shoved things in my car, scared, really frightened, and left.

I frankly don't see myself being partnered again. What I still would like is a close pal, a pal. I just can't come up with a better word. A woman, probably gay, who is just available. A woman who calls when I get home from a trip and says, "Tell me all about it," or, "Let me bring over a sandwich. I want to hear about your adventures." Some close person that would just check in and for whom I would do the same.

It's not sad for me. It's okay. It's quite okay.

Today, Jan lives in Sonoma, California, where she serves as a hospice volunteer and in her church's lay care ministry. Jan's happiest times are spent with her children, Leah and Jay, Jay's husband, Mason, and her granddog, Henri.

JEAN TRETTER

GAY HISTORIAN

MINNEAPOLIS, MINNESOTA

Jean Tretter was born in 1946 in Little Falls, Minnesota, into a German Lutheran family that had immigrated to the United States a century before. To avoid persecution, Jean's parents hid their German roots and passed as Norwegian Americans, even speaking Norwegian at home. As a result, Jean grew up thinking he was Norwegian.

Jean served as a decorated linguist in the Navy during the Vietnam War. He left the Navy in 1972 and, inspired by the Stonewall riots three years earlier, came out as a gay man. [For more on the Stonewall riots and their cross-country ripple effect, see pp. 68, 99, 104, 193, 196, 201–202, 209, and 225–227.] That year, he helped organize the first Stonewall commemoration in Minneapolis–Saint Paul. The event became the annual Twin Cities Pride Festival, one of America's largest LGBTQ celebrations.

In the 1970s, Jean also began collecting gay and lesbian books and other materials ranging from documents and photographs to artifacts like buttons and campaign posters. Later, he produced and hosted a gay and lesbian music radio show and co-chaired Minnesota's Gay Games committee. Since the 1980s, Jean has dedicated himself full-time to the preservation of LGBTQ history. In 2000, he donated his entire collection to the University of Minnesota Libraries, where it receives rightful recognition and respect as the Jean-Nickolaus Tretter Collection in GLBT Studies.

One of my only real claims to fame is I grew up in the same hometown as Charles A. Lindbergh, which is Little Falls, Minnesota. My family came to Minnesota before Minnesota was even a territory. My great-grandfather was a stonemason in Germany and helped to build the Morrison County Courthouse.

Northern Minnesota was a great place to grow up. I was particularly interested in nature, collecting bugs and insects and all that kind of stuff. The variety of wildlife up there was tremendous. We had wolves and bears and porcupines and raccoons and white-tailed deer, and fish, all types of fish. We went fishing often.

As you know, Minnesota's nickname is the "Land of 10,000 Lakes." We have lots of ponds and lakes and glacial depressions with water all over. In the middle of winter, I loved to go out in the middle of some of these little ponds with the fresh snow on top of them. I realized that nobody had ever maybe stepped in this place, in this pond, or this lake. That was real exciting and adventurous for me to be able to step somewhere where no other explorer, no other person had ever been. That was important to me.

BE GOOD AND KIND

I did some things in the Navy of which I'm actually quite proud.

The Navy was very uptight about people being gay at that time. We're talking '60s and '70s now. They weren't necessarily kicking people out, because this was the Vietnam War and they needed bodies; they needed cannon fodder. That was important.

When I was at security school in Pensacola, Florida, there was a young Jewish guy from Texas. They had found out that he was gay, so they were going to kick him out. We were being primed for getting our security

clearances. The FBI had interviewed our family and friends. He couldn't have a security clearance.

The reason I say I was kind of proud of myself is because of all the people at Pensacola, Florida, I did not abandon him as a friend. I stuck with him. Part of it was the fascination of him. He was Jewish, and he taught me a lot about the Jewish religion. He'd take me with him on Fridays to the Jewish ceremonies and all this kind of stuff. I was learning all kinds of things from him.

I didn't admit to being a homosexual, but I defended my friend. I said, "These are people. We can't be prejudiced; we shouldn't be prejudiced. We've got to be kind and good to them." I think it helped me come to terms with my sexuality, in the fact that I could look back at myself and say, "I had enough courage to stand up and defend homosexuals, even though I didn't have enough courage to come out of my closet at that time."

SAVING MATCHBOOKS

I got out of the Navy in 1972. That was at the same time that Jack Baker had run as an openly gay man and had won the position of president of the student body at the University of Minnesota. Chicago asked Jack Baker to come out and be grand marshal at their Pride event, because, after all, he had gotten to be one of the big important gays in the United States at the time.

After Jack had gone to Chicago, my gay friends and I sat around, and we said, "We can't be letting our people go to Chicago and celebrate Pride in Chicago. We need to cele-

In 1982, Jean (front row, far right) served as co-chair of the Minnesota Gay Games team.

brate it here." That was when we got together and decided that the next year, 1972, would be when we had our first gay Pride here in Minneapolis–Saint Paul.

I started to notice that whenever we held an event, the stuff would disappear. In those days, one of the main ways to communicate was to stand outside a bar on Saturday nights and say, "We're going to have such and such an event"—whether it was a dance at the university or whatever it was—and we'd hand out fliers. The fliers either got thrown away, got crumpled up. Some people kept them but if that person left, died, or anything like that, his relatives or whatever would throw them all away.

I realized I had to start picking stuff up and preserving it myself because that was the only way it was going to get saved. I couldn't count on anybody else. Whether it was matchbooks or whatever, you saved it all somehow because that was the only way you could keep it from being destroyed.

When I first tried to study gay and lesbian history at the University of Minnesota, they weren't interested. I even picked, as my primary adviser, a professor in the Anthropology Department who I knew was gay because I kept seeing him down at the gay bars on weekends. He was like, "You should really pick something else." Nobody believed in gay history or gay culture, lesbian history or lesbian culture, because we were just a sexual anomaly. We weren't real. And therefore, we weren't worth studying.

We need to have some way of proving to the disbelievers that if you are gay and you live and you do anything, that you produce history. If you create anything, you're creating gay and lesbian art. If you build anything or cause a social custom to happen, you are creating gay and lesbian history, you're creating gay and lesbian thought, you're creating gay and lesbian music.

It was a very hard lesson to learn. People still don't believe us sometimes.

An extremely humble man, Jean Tretter expressed deep appreciation that OUTWORDS was willing to travel all the way to snowy Saint Paul, Minnesota, to interview him. He is a titan in the field of LGBTQ history, and it is our honor to thank Jean here for his service.

LIBERATION

JUAN-MANUEL ALONSO

CUBAN-AMERICAN FASHION DESIGNER, LONGTIME AIDS SURVIVOR

PALM SPRINGS, CALIFORNIA

> Juan-Manuel Alonso was born in Havana, Cuba, in 1952. After Fidel Castro took power in 1959, Juan-Manuel's family emigrated to America. Juan-Manuel studied at City College of New York and the Fashion Institute of Technology, was the head of design studios for Nino Cerruti, Sahara Club, and WilliWear, and had his own fashion label. In 1997, battling AIDS, Juan retired from the fashion industry and turned to painting, which, in his own words, kept him from feeling like he was waiting to die. In all of his paintings, Juan-Manuel tries to convey messages of beauty, hope, and solidarity to the people around him.

I was born in Cuba in 1952.

My memories of Cuba were the beach, and horsemanship, and jumping with horses in competition. They kept me very busy. I got into a lot of trouble because I've always been very—not mischievous, but if you tell me no, that's what I will do.

I left Cuba in the '60s with my family. We went to New York. In high school, I used to hang out with a group of kids who were also Cuban. The girls protected me. I didn't realize why. Whenever we went to the city, to a party, or anywhere that we took the subway, one of the kids would always pick me out. The girls had to get in the way to say, "Why are you doing this? He hasn't done anything." It was this anger that this kid had, and he used to call me "faggot." Maybe he felt something in himself that he had to take it out on me. That happened to a point when

I got a stick, and I beat him up. Then that stopped.

Later, in New York, I got married, I got divorced, my parents never asked a question. I started living with a man. They came to visit. My father said, "Oh, there's only one king-sized bed?" I said, "Yeah, and the couch, and you know." That was the only question.

After my dad died, and my mom became very ill before she passed away, she said she had something to tell me about my ex-wife. She said, "I don't want to die with this, but I didn't mention anything because I didn't want you to have an argument with her about it." She told me that when we got divorced, my ex-wife called my parents. She asked for my father to be on the other extension, and she told them, "You raised a faggot."

My father's answer was, "Whatever my son is, he's our son, and we love him."

Juan-Manuel at his 1989 wedding in San Francisco to his partner (since deceased), long before marriage equality was passed in California and across the US

FACING DEATH

I was diagnosed as HIV-positive in 1982. I kept working as long as I could to hide it, but it got to the point where my platelets were coming down because the HIV was eating them. The only person that knew was my assistant, and she would back me up whenever somebody asked why I wasn't there. It was either, "He's at the market," or "He went to see fabrics," or something. "He went to see the merchandise in the store" was a good one too.

I was being treated with WinRho. [Editor's note: WinRho is used to treat primary immune thrombocytopenia, a blood disorder frequently experienced by HIV-positive individuals.] It got so expensive. The last year that I worked, when I did my taxes, it was $55,000 of my salary that went to infusions. I was very fortunate at the fact that I was able to afford something like that. Every time before going on a trip for work, I would have to get an infusion two days before. Because of the cabin pressure on the plane, if it's New York–Tokyo, which is twelve and a half hours, I could have bled out. The injections helped. They brought my platelets up, sometimes even to the point that I was able to come home again without receiving another infusion, until one of the trips. I was in India and had to stay a little longer because my collection wasn't finished. My assistant came into my room in the morning. I saw her face. I said, "What's the matter?" She said, "Oh my God. You're full of blood." I was bleeding through my pores.

She called immediately the doctor, and he came. He freaked out. He goes, "You have appendicitis." I said, "No, I don't. You're not going to touch me. Just cauterize my nose if you're able to." I told my assistant, "I'm flying to New York." I came back to New York, and they gave me an infusion.

The next time I went to the doctor I mentioned it, and the doctor said, "Do you want me to do the papers for your disability?" I said, "I think so. I think it's time." I wasn't feeling too well, and I was losing weight. I was experiencing all the things that happened to everyone who is HIV-positive back then, when there was no medications or anything. It was deterioration. It was fast. I became disabled and sat there. I had no idea what I was going to do.

I am not a person that will sit and not think of what to do to make this better. I said, "Oh my God. I like painting, so I'll start painting."

I moved to Palm Springs, and it was like I had to readjust to the slower life and I had to readjust to everything, but then it gave me time to learn to be by myself, to enjoy being by myself, to create. I'm not by myself. I have so many artist friends or wife-of-artist friends, that it's amazing how much acceptance, how much togetherness, how much of a family we

have been able to build, I have been able to build. I realized that I had to just do what I like, and that will keep me alive. Some people say, "Your paintings look like child's work." I think, "Do they realize that it took Picasso his entire life to learn to paint like a child?"

My name is Juan-Manuel Alonso. I'm an artist. I'm alive, and I care.

In addition to the hours he spends painting, Juan-Manuel mentors high school art students, teaches painting at a senior center, and volunteers at the Desert AIDS Project.

MISS MAJOR GRIFFIN-GRACY

TRANSGENDER ADVOCATE

OAKLAND, CALIFORNIA

Miss Major Griffin-Gracy was born in the 1940s in Chicago, Illinois. When she came out to her parents as transgender, they tried a psychologist, exorcism, and prayer before finally kicking her out. The pattern continued when Miss Major was expelled from two colleges for wearing dresses. Moving to New York, Miss Major performed in various drag revues, relying on sex work and petty crime to cover her bills. A rough-trade gay club called the Stonewall Inn was one of the few places where she felt welcome. On the night of June 28, 1969, when the Stonewall was raided for the umpteenth time by the police, Miss Major and a group of fellow transgender women were on the front lines of the crowd that finally fought back. The revolution had begun.

For well over forty-five years, Miss Major has advocated for the rights, equality, and safety she stood up for at Stonewall. From 2006 to 2015, she was a key member and executive director of the Transgender, Gender Variant, and Intersex Justice Project (TGIJP), an advocacy group for transgender people in prison and after. Miss Major wrote letters, met with prisoners, and helped newly released individuals go to school and find jobs. A documentary about her life entitled *Major!* was released in 2015, garnering multiple best documentary awards and screening at festivals from Sweden to India to Brazil.

I was a preemie baby. I was due to be born in December and wound up being born in October at Saint Luke's Hospital in Chicago, Illinois. They had a hard time keeping me alive. They had to create special milks and things for me to sustain myself off of, and they had to give my mother shots so that her milk would help me to grow and not die. That was a pretty rough start. I've been a strug-

gling bitch from the moment I took breath. Fighting to hang in there and survive and be here and make myself known.

Around fifteen, sixteen years old, I started scooting around the house in mother's stuff every now and then with my sister, and telling my sister, "Don't tell Mother." Of course, Mother noticed one day that her shoe backs were mushed, because my feet were bigger

Miss Major at the Gilded Grape, a legendary 1970s trans nightlife venue just west of Times Square in New York City

than hers. My mother yelled at my sister and smacked her hand on the table, and my sister told my mother everything.

After that beating, I realized: don't tell your sister shit, and don't say nothing to your mother about this. Just keep on the down-low, as they call it now. From then it was trying to figure out how best to do it. I met some friends who also were little drag queens and got to hang out with them after school. Got painted and dressed up at their houses sometimes. They made me look like the worst imaginable. They told me, "Girl, you can only wear flats because you're so tall. We have this Lane Bryant dress for you," which made me

look like a wall instead of a person. The little flowers and daisies that they used to make bad girls wear. Then these horrible brown wigs that they would cut the bangs short, so the bangs would jut out of your forehead.

Then I met an older woman who used to do drugs named Kitty. Kitty put me in blonde hair and gave me heels, the little opera pumps, white, which is still my favorite color. Dressed me up, painted me. It was a yellow dress. I felt like Natalie Wood.

I decided from that point forward, I'm only wearing blonde hair. I didn't give a shit what people had to say about it. "You think you're white." I don't think a damn thing other than you should mind your fucking business.

THEY NEVER INVESTIGATED ANYTHING

After Christine Jorgensen came out it was like, okay, she's in New York. I need to go to New York.

New York was wonderful at that time in the '60s. Everybody was searching for who they were as a group. It wasn't an individual thing. It was blacks wanted their rights and other folks wanted the Vietnam War to end. Women wanted equal pay for equal jobs. Everybody in some form or another was fighting for their group.

At that time, Forty-Second Street was in its heyday. Just that one block from Forty-Second and Broadway to Forty-Second and Eighth Avenue, walk that block and every-thing you can imagine that's in New York is somewhere in that block. Hooking back

there at that time was a blessing. All you've got to do is let people know what you're looking for, and it'll find its way to you. The johns all knew who we were. We didn't have to explain anything. They liked picking up transitioning women and then sucking their dick. They would slow down and talk to us and ride with us a little bit and then drive onto the bridge or the tunnel. It was fun. You felt safe.

There were whites and Hispanics, but there was always more black girls than other girls. The black girls came out earlier than everybody else. The family catches them and throws them out. Of course, we looked out for the white girls and the Latin girls because they were our sisters.

Somewhere around '67 to '68 it got kind of dangerous. There was some guy killing the girls and stuff there. The police didn't care. I lost a really good, good, good friend there. She was killed in her apartment, drowned in her tub. We tried to tell the police, "Investigate her boyfriends." They took the list. They never investigated anything.

After that we started keeping track of johns that the girls were going with. We would pay one of the girls so she wouldn't have to hook. She could just pay attention to the cars that we got in, write down the license number and a little description of the car and the driver so that if anything happened we knew what was going on.

As time progressed, boys started coming over from New Jersey, four or five in a car, high off of beer and stuff and throwing full beer cans at the girls as they would drive down the street. We figured out a way to stop that car. They would get out. We would physically fight them. The police would come and have a boy who had a black eye from one of the girls. They would tell the boy, "Go back to Jersey. Don't let me catch you over here again."

My concern was keeping my community alive and keeping us going and keeping us safe. We're not safe. We're just out there heart on our sleeve, head in our hand, doing what we need to do to be okay.

PASSING

As a trans person, you become obsessed with passing and being unrecognizable to the world as to who you actually are. It's an obsession because it's your driving, moving, motivating force for everything that you do. Everything aims, points, pushes, coddles over, covers up, reshapes, and rebuilds it to make that a viable thing so that it's never penetrated so that no one ever sees through it. Getting caught up into that, it's kind of like painting a floor. You start over here by the door and you paint yourself up until you've painted yourself in a corner. You can't get out of the corner for three days because it takes that long for the floor to dry. If you step on the floor, you'll stick to the floor. You're stuck there.

Passing became so important simply because you get tired of being beaten up and chased and harassed and berated for who you are every day. When you step out your front door, you never know if you're going to get back to it. If you do, it's like, "Whew, I made it back home. Thank God." We shouldn't have to live like that. It should be, "I made it back home. Let me fix something for dinner."

OUTWORDS caught up with Miss Major in Oakland, California, in the summer of 2016. Today, Miss Major lives in Little Rock, Arkansas. In December 2018, she announced plans to build a home called Oasis for her trans and gender non-conforming community.

DONNA SACHET

DRAG QUEEN, COMMUNITY ACTIVIST

SAN FRANCISCO, CALIFORNIA

Donna Sachet was born Kirk Reeves in 1954 in South Carolina. Kirk's young life was marked by a violent, alcoholic father and a mother afraid to fight back. After graduating from Vanderbilt University in Tennessee, Kirk headed to New York to work in retail fashion. He spent the 1980s there, watching AIDS grow into a full-throttled epidemic. In 1990, Kirk was offered a job in San Francisco, just months after the city was devastated by the Loma Prieta earthquake. Kirk was ready for upheaval. He headed west.

A few years later, Kirk found himself performing in drag at a talent show. The crowd went wild—and Donna Sachet was born.

Over the past two decades, Donna has entertained at venues as diverse as San Francisco's Great American Music Hall, the foot of the Washington Monument, the New York Marriott Marquis Hotel on Broadway, and the International Mr. Leather competition in Chicago. More importantly, Donna has helped raise millions of dollars for various causes. She has won dozens of awards, including the 2005 San Francisco Police Officers Pride Alliance Award, the 2011 Bank of America's Local Heroes Award, and the 2015 Horizons Foundation's Leadership Award. For twenty-five years, her annual Songs of the Season musical cabaret show has raised money for the AIDS Emergency Fund. In 2009, Donna became the first drag performer to sing the national anthem at a Major League Baseball game. She did it at AT&T Park, in her adopted hometown of San Francisco.

My upbringing was pretty typically Southern. My father was the breadwinner, and he ruled the house with an iron fist. There was never any question of disobeying him because there was corporal punishment. He was a heavy drinker, and my mother was just cooperative with all of that and let whatever happened, happen.

I played with dolls since I was really a small child. I wasn't able to own dolls, so I'd make pipe cleaner dolls and make clothes for them out of paper and pieces of fabric I found. It was very minimal, but I just loved the creative process of it. I watched black and white movies, and I thought, this is like Audrey Hepburn, big hats or something.

One day, my father found me in the backyard playing with a girl from next door.

We played with dolls together sometimes, creating outfits. My dad was just outraged. He ran home and he grabbed everything up. We built a bonfire in the backyard, and he made me throw in all the dolls. They weren't store-bought; I'd made them. They were characters in my life.

He said, "Do you have anything else?" I never disobeyed them. I just lived in terror. So I brought this box of scraps that I was going to make things out of. That all went in the bonfire. And then he took my hand and put it in the ashes to reinforce the lesson: "This is wrong. There's something wrong with you."

NOW, VOYAGER
Growing up, I loved those movies with Bette Davis and Joan Crawford and strong female characters. Or the Bette Davis movie *Now, Voyager*. She's transformed from this ugly duckling to this chic woman on a cruise ship. I mean, that was a dream for many of us. I could relate to these women's power and their clothes and their mannerisms. Some of it was the very stuff I was being teased for in school. "Why are you walking down the hall like that?" "What are you strutting for?"

At that time, I was like, why can't I hold my hips straight? Why am I walking funny? But then you watch those movies and those women didn't just come down the staircase, they owned the staircase. I wanted to do that too, but I was a guy and I was never going to be in the movies. It was so frustrating to see that gap between what I wanted and what I saw there.

I don't think I was dealing with the gay

Donna performs at her annual holiday "Songs of the Season" cabaret, a fundraiser for the AIDS Emergency Fund.

part of myself yet, as much as I was dealing with the gender-specific roles that we play. I think that continues today. I don't think I've fully defined it yet. Why do I want to do the things I want to do? Because it feels good to me. So many people put drag on. I feel like I let drag out, that there's this character in here that I sat on for so long and that so many people around me forced down, and now I'm able to fully express that character.

"LOOK AT THAT SASHAY!"
In 1990, I moved to San Francisco. New Yorkers said, "Didn't you just see that earthquake that happened there? Are you crazy?" I was so ready for change.

About a year after arriving in San Francisco, I joined the Gay Men's Chorus, which was a big thing for me because in New York I never joined anything that was openly gay.

The chorus was eye-opening for me. Some of the members were rich, some poor, some students, some successful, some were older, some were younger. I began to have gay friends for the first time.

The Gay Men's Chorus used to take retreats once or twice a year at a camp up in the woods, to rehearse music and kind of get to know each other. Before one of the retreats, they announced they were going to have a talent show contest on Saturday night. I thought, "Oh, I'm just so tempted to do this." That person living inside me for all those years wanted to come out.

I practiced a Donna Summer number, lip-syncing of course. I didn't have a dress, but I had this Asian-style robe, with the dragon on the back. I didn't have high heels. I used ballet slippers. I did buy a wig. I practiced my song for many weeks and got it all down. At the contest, I introduced myself as Donna Winter, because she was Donna Summer. She's black, so I was Donna Winter.

I don't know how I got the courage to do that.

As I left the stage, everyone exploded in applause. I heard this guy in the aisle say, "Look at that sashay!" Everything kind of fell in place. Not "Look at that stupid walk!" or "What's wrong with you?" but "Look at that sashay!" with admiration. The character inside of me had finally been released. I changed my name to Donna Sachet right on the spot.

In July 2016, Donna invited OUTWORDS to record her story at her stylish home just above San Francisco's legendary Castro neighborhood. After talking openly about her wretched childhood and the freedom she finally found in the City by the Bay, Donna sounded a wise warning against divisiveness and complacency within the LGBTQ community: "United we stand; divided, they get us one by one."

BLACKBERRI

SINGER-SONGWRITER, HIV ACTIVIST

SAN FRANCISCO, CALIFORNIA

Blackberri was born in 1945 in Buffalo, New York, and named Charles Timothy Ashmore.

At nine, Charles picked up the harmonica. Soon he was playing just about any song that came out of the radio. He served in the Navy, then won a music scholarship to the University of Arizona; but after arriving and being told the university "didn't teach his kind of music," he returned the scholarship and made his way to San Francisco, where his music career finally took off. By that point, Charles had taken the name Blackberri, after an Arizona friend told him he was "black and sweet."

In 1975, Blackberri shared the stage with Steven Grossman at KQED's *Two Songmakers* concert, marking the first time two openly gay musicians had performed on public television in San Francisco. In 1979, Blackberri's song "When Will the Ignorance End?" was chosen as the theme for the first National Third World Lesbian and Gay Conference (organized in part by OUTWORDS interviewee ABilly Jones-Hennin, p. 43). Two years later, Blackberri released his first solo LP, and in 1989 his song "Beautiful Black Man" became the centerpiece of Isaac Julien's movie *Looking for Langston*. Blackberri's music was also featured in several Marlon Riggs films, including *Tongues Untied* and *Black Is . . . Black Ain't*. In between these projects, Blackberri traveled and performed extensively overseas.

Beyond his musicianship, Blackberri has devoted extensive time and energy to HIV work. He is also an ordained Lucumi priest.

I always tell musicians, especially African-American musicians, they need to leave the United States. Because once you leave the country and you're in another environment or another country, you see that people see you very differently there than people in the United States see you. You get a whole different sense of yourself.

In the US, even though I was playing music, sometimes the audiences were sizable and sometimes they weren't. And there was always this thing somewhere in my head that I'm probably not good enough; that's why people don't appreciate me. Overseas, I wasn't begging people for work. People were coming to me and wanting me to work with them. Instead of telling me how much they're gonna give me, they would ask me how much

I wanted. Which puts you in a very different ballpark.

So I realized that traveling was definitely the way to go, and I was fortunate. I met lots of interesting people. People would turn me on to other people.

When I moved to the Bay Area and I was living in the Haight, I found out a gay singer-songwriter named Steven Grossman was living in the Haight also, so I made an effort to reach out and meet him and I did, and we became friends. We liked each other's music. I played for him, he played for me, and we swapped a lot of stories.

Later, this Canadian radio guy named Steven O'Neill saw me at a coffeehouse, and he said, "How would you like to do a show with Steven Grossman? I have a connection

with KQED, the public television station, and I'm gonna put a proposal to them to do this show."

So we did this show called *Two Songmakers*. It was the very first time that gay music was ever on public television in San Francisco. Very first time.

BEAUTIFUL BLACK MAN

My song "Beautiful Black Man" came from an encounter that I had in Milwaukee, Wisconsin. I went to do a series of shows there. I go out one evening, I go to this bar, and this really beautiful black guy walks into the bar, and I go, "Wow, he's really fucking hot." So I go over to him and we talk, and eventually I invite him to come home with me. We're leaving the club and he said, "I don't see what you see in me."

One of the lines in the song is about being discriminated against in bars. It says,

> *Beautiful black man, did they ask for ID?*
> *Did they want two pictures, or did they*
>   *want three?*
> *I know it's hard but sometimes we must*
> *Just walk away, shake our heads, and*
>   *discuss*
> *You're such a beautiful black man, but*
>   *somehow, you've been made to feel*
> *that your beauty's not real*
> *You're such a beautiful black man, but you*
>   *walk with your head bending low*
> *Don't do that anymore.*

And that's where I use what this guy said, "I don't see what you see in me."

*Beautiful black man, I'm glad you look
  my way
Let's go home together, what more can I say?
You say you don't see what I see in you
I see the beauty I wish that you knew.*

Black people have always been considered ugly. So there's a lot of internalized stuff around how we look, how we are, our hair, our lips. That internalized self-hatred has driven the AIDS epidemic. People didn't feel they were important enough to take care of themselves.

When AIDS first happened, it was outside of my circle. And then it came into my circle and it touched people that I knew closely, and it was really crazy. There was so much hurt and pain from the loss in the community. And there was a way to prevent it.

When we found out there was a way to prevent it, that's when I made the decision that I didn't want to see anybody go through what I've already seen. If there's any way that I can save people from that experience, that's what I want to do. So then I just put my music aside and I went into HIV work. I started working at San Francisco General on the AIDS ward. I worked with the Shanti Project. I became a death and dying counselor. It was good work. It was hard work.

And then I decided watching people die is a little bit too heavy for me. Why don't I get them before they get to that place? So then I went into prevention, and I started doing the education of how to not get this disease.

My goal was to help these brothers see that they were worth something and that they were important and they were worth saving. That somebody did love them, even if they didn't love themselves.

At the end of every OUTWORDS interview, we ask our subjects "What's your hope for the future?" When we posed this question to Blackberri, he instantly replied, "I don't do hope. I do prayer."

DIANA RIVERS

PIONEER OF WOMEN-ONLY SPACES

MADISON COUNTY, ARKANSAS

Born in New York City in 1931, Diana Rivers grew up Diana Smith in an artistic and liter-ary family. While studying sculpture in Maine, Diana met her future husband. The couple had three sons and lived for a time in an artists' community in Stony Point, New York. After her divorce in 1970, Diana took the last name of Rivers, in honor of her newfound freedom. She traveled extensively through the American West, then made her way to Ar-kansas with the dream of establishing a women-only community. Her vision was realized in the Ozark Land Holding Association—280 acres on a steep, forested hill, where women built homes for themselves and one another, a community house, and a peace garden. Over the years, many women have come and gone; but Diana lives there to this day.

Diana has published several works of fiction exploring women's struggles, loves, conflicts, and triumphs. She helped organize the Women Vision conference in Kansas City, the Women's Conference and Festival at the University of Arkansas in 1990, and the Goddess Festival, held each March to coincide with the spring equinox.

I got married at eighteen. I think I wanted to get married because I had come from such a fractured family situation that I wanted to jump out of that into something definite. The marriage produced three children, and lasted twenty years, so that was a pretty good jump.

I pictured that my husband and I would get old together. We were both sculptors, and we shared a lot of things. We loved travel. We traveled a bunch with the kids. We went out West and we went on camping trips. At some point, we went on a canoe trip with the three kids up in the Adirondacks.

The community where we lived was pretty radical. We were involved in a lot of demon-strations against the Vietnam War, some of them very illegal or quasi-illegal. For me, there was a sense of desperation. It felt like it didn't matter what we did. It didn't matter if we lay down on the road in front of the trucks. They were going to do their war no matter what.

Eventually, my husband fell in love with somebody else. That's not what broke up the marriage, as far as I'm concerned. What broke up the marriage is he couldn't be nice to two women in his life. I was getting the wrong end of it and finally thought, "This is abusive. I can't do this anymore," and then left.

DYKE MOUNTAIN

I'm enough of a separatist to think it was very important for women to have their own space. How would we ever know what we would do if we don't have the space to do it and to try it out?

I began looking around for some women who were interested in looking for land. It was basically, I want to live in the country, but I don't want to be isolated in the country. We eventually collected a bunch of twenty women and had a meeting when we made the shaping decisions. At that point, I started looking for land. We found this mountain. There's a creek down at the bottom by the swimming hole. There are very wild spaces, big pastures, and woods. It became the Ozark Land Holding Association.

The people in this county, they're my neighbors. Some of them I know; some of them I don't. I tend to be shy around them. Sometimes they clearly disapprove. There's no question. Somebody will look at me and pretty much turn their back. Other times, they're very friendly. They all know my name, and they know who I am.

There was a moment when a bunch of us were down at the main house, and we got a phone call. It was UPS. They had a package for us and were trying to figure out how to get here. In the background, we heard somebody say, "Oh, you know where that is. That's up there on Dyke Mountain."

DAUGHTERS OF THE GREAT STAR

My book series is called the Hadra series. The way this story started is, I was in town. It was a summer day. I was sick. I needed shelter. I needed just to stop. I knew where the keys to my friend Mary's house were, so I went in her house. She was away. I was trying to just lie down and go to sleep, and this little story came into my head about this woman going to the ocean to drown herself. She had a name, Sair.

I'm thinking, "What? Who? What is this about?" All I wanted to do was go to sleep and get better. "I feel lousy. I'm not interested in this." But it kept replaying like a little tape. I got up and wrote it down. Then, I saw the women who came to save Sair—very wild-looking women, called the Hadra. They've been following Sair, and they've been watching her, and they see her do this. She's not pleased when the Hadra fish her out of the ocean, but she eventually ends up living with them and going through a lot of adventures with them. She has a new life.

The first draft of this book got written at night, in a week and a half. Nothing like this has ever happened to me since. As I was writing it, it was like, "Who are the Hadra? Where did they come from? How did all this happen?" I backed up 200 years and wrote what is now the beginning of the series, *Daughters of the Great Star*, where I could explain to myself and everyone else where the Hadra came from and how it all began.

MICHAEL HICKERSON

BARTENDER, CARNIVAL PERFORMER, SOCIAL WORKER
SLIDELL, LOUISIANA

Michael Hickerson was born in New Orleans in 1955. As a kid, he was "the gayest kid in the neighborhood." When bullies showed up, he defended himself, sometimes with humor and sometimes with his fists. The bullies learned he might be gay, but he wasn't a pushover.

After a stint at Southern University in New Orleans, Michael began tending bar at various mostly white New Orleans gay clubs, whose owners used Michael's blackness, good looks, and charm to attract customers. Working in the bars paved the way for Michael to participate in New Orleans's famous gay carnival balls—to be in the spotlight—which he loved.

During this time, Michael contracted HIV. Knowing that if and when he got sick, he would no longer be able to work in bars, Michael re-enrolled at Southern, earned his bachelor's and master's degrees in social work, and embarked on a long career of helping people with HIV/AIDS and others in need. Ultimately, Michael founded In This Together (ITT), a nonprofit community-based organization providing comprehensive supportive services to individuals and families. Along the way, Michael served as vice-chair of the Louisiana State Board of Social Workers, as an adjunct professor at Southern University's School of Social Work, and on the board of the Hurricane Katrina recovery agency Lower Nine.

I was born to Sadie and Charlie Hickerson. We lived in an area of New Orleans called Central City. Central City is an African-American community. Very, very poor community, but a very loving and happy community. It was a wonderful place to grow up in.

When I was twelve, my parents mustered up enough money to purchase a home, took us from the ghetto, and moved us uptown to a street called Octavia Street. We moved into an area that we really knew absolutely nothing about. The community was totally white. My mom told us it was a better place for us.

So, we moved there, and then the strangest thing happened. All of these "For Sale" signs started popping up all around the neighborhood, especially the block where we lived. Well, we were kids. I really did not understand that until much later in my life, that this was a racial thing. That people were moving out, or were trying to sell their homes because we had moved in.

When I was about twenty-one years old, that isolation that we experienced when I was twelve years old, when we moved to the white neighborhood, I experienced it again.

I ran across some magazines that a neighbor put in his trash. In all the magazines was this word "gay." Through those magazines, I found some addresses and I ventured out. I found bars and stuff. Some of them still exist now.

I dressed up, I got pretty, and I finally got enough nerve to walk into the bars. When I walked in, I began to experience that same thing again. That isolation, those signs coming up, "For Sale." The same thing. It was a period of time when gay bars and the gay community were predominately white. There were not very many African Americans in that community, and I began to experience the same thing. Being last to be served at the bar. You're sitting up at the bar and all the white guys are getting their drinks before you.

In those magazines, I saw all of this fun, I saw all of this excitement, I saw all these people laughing and talking. And you're thinking, "I want to be a part of that," never realizing that "Hmm, there're no black people in these pictures."

Back then, and I think now as well, bartenders controlled the space. They controlled who could come in and who could not come in. Black people had to have three or four cards to get in the bar, while our white counterparts didn't need anything to get in. All they needed to do was be white to get in.

I never stopped going. I endured it. I would sit there, by myself. I eventually got to meet the bartenders, and they got to know me. I became a regular there. Then they started introducing me to other clientele that was there. So I used that. I used them knowing me to get my friends in. "They're with me, they're with me, they're with me." But during that period of time, we had a little protest. We had a little protest about the bars carding African Americans. Some of our white counterparts joined the protests. They joined the protests. And it wasn't that big, but it was effective, it was effective.

NOW PART OF SOMETHING

When I was in 12th grade, in 1973, I worked the concessions stands at the New Orleans Municipal Auditorium. Municipal Auditorium, it's right outside the French Quarter in the Treme neighborhood. It was a venue where all the concerts, all the Mardi Gras Balls, and all of this kind of society stuff was held.

I saw these men having this Mardi Gras Ball—but I didn't know they were men. They were these women in beautiful dresses and feathers, having this thing where they promenaded around the floor, and they bowed, and it was just so elegant. I had never seen anything like that in my life. I was just fascinated. I heard the name. It was the Krewe of Apollo. I was 16, 17 years old, and I thought, "Ooh, I want to do that." I did realize that there were no blacks, and I respected it. I was a young kid that knew absolutely nothing, and I took it for what it was.

Fast forward to my times in the bars. The name Apollo popped up again. I met

Michael at the 20th anniversary ball of the Krewe of Amon Ra.

some people who were a part of the Krewe of Apollo, and I got invited to some of these balls and stuff. Then I heard about a krewe called the Krewe of Celestial Nights, and the Krewe of Celestial Nights had two black guys in it, and I thought, "Wow. Ah-hah! This is my opportunity! Yes, this is my opportunity." So, I did some talking and researching and realized that a lot of the members hung out at this bar, and I went to that bar, and I tried to schmooze up to them. And I was successful! Yes! I joined the Krewe, yes. I was able to join the Krewe.

To be a part of a group, to be a part of something, when you once were an outsider, when you once were a loner, when you once felt isolated. Now, you're a part of something.

In the early '90s, I joined the Krewe of Amon Ra. They had never had a black in their organization, and some of the members did not want it. As a result, I think a third of the organization quit.

Later, at our ball that year, I received the President's Award for being one of the hardest workers in the organization. I was shocked. It was very nice to be honored for the work that I contributed to the organization. But I also think that was their way of saying, "We're sorry for what happened." I think it was a way of saying that.

YOU DUST YOURSELF OFF, AND YOU FIGHT ON

When HIV hit our community, it was something that all of us did not understand. We saw this happening, and then that happened, and then a person died. We did not understand any of this stuff.

I have so many friends, so many friends who I have lost to HIV. So many. So many. Yes, so many . . . [*crying*]

So, what do you do? You try to live, and you try to help people live a better quality of life. You try to help them understand that you can live, and there are ways to do it.

Because I was well known in the community, I was invited to join the board of a startup organization that was providing housing for persons with HIV. From there, I got an opportunity to work as their volunteer coordinator. But after about a year, I realized I wanted to do the social work piece of it. So I went back to school. I got my bachelor's degree. And I got hungry, so I continued, and I received a master's degree. And then I was ready. I did social work. I did case management for a few years with an agency.

Then, you learn things, and you learn disparities. You learn that services aren't being provided equally. And I saw that some parts of our community were getting this, and others weren't. So, I started a nonprofit organization that provides HIV services and that would focus on the African-American community receiving those services. That's the organization that I run now. The name of the organization is In This Together.

Today, we don't provide HIV services any longer; we provide behavioral health services to our community. We're a small organization. We have like nineteen employees that work out in the community. It's pretty successful, and when I say "successful," it's be-

cause of the feedback that you hear from the people that you serve. As long as the feedback is positive, we're going to continue going the way we are.

It's important to hear this stuff from a black perspective. To understand that we, in our small little ways, contributed to where we are today. It's an experience, it's an adventure, it's a journey. Sometimes crippling, but you get up, you dust yourself off, and you fight on.

OUTWORDS interviewed Michael in July 2017 at the offices of ITT, during an intense thunderstorm. Inside the building, Michael was warm, funny, and loquacious, but at a couple of points, his memories of the AIDS epidemic and the many friends he lost rendered him speechless with grief.

MIA YAMAMOTO

CRIMINAL DEFENSE ATTORNEY, TRANSGENDER ACTIVIST

LOS ANGELES, CALIFORNIA

Mia Frances Yamamoto's parents were among 127,000 American civilians of Japanese ancestry sent to concentration camps by the US government after the bombing of Pearl Harbor in December 1941. This is how Mia came to be born in 1943 at the Poston Internment Camp in Arizona and how, from an early age, she became a crusader against injustice in the legal system.

Upon graduation from UCLA in 1966, bewildered by her gender issues, Mia enlisted in the US Army, served in Vietnam, then enrolled at UCLA School of Law, where she founded the Asian/Pacific Islander Law Students Association and organized with black, Chicanx, and gay law students around social justice causes. With time, Mia began more actively confronting her gender dysphoria; but it was only at age sixty, in a classic case of "better late than never," that she finally came out publicly as transgender. Since then, she has been an ardent advocate and spokesperson for the trans community in the legal profession and beyond.

As a lawyer, Mia's awards and honors include being appointed to the Judicial Council Task Forces on Jury Improvement and Fairness and Access in the Courts, the Rainbow Key Award from the city of West Hollywood, multiple designations as Criminal Defense Attorney of the Year, and recipient of the Harvey Milk Legacy Award.

My first job out of law school was as a legal aid lawyer. I worked there for three years until I realized that this work bored me to death. Then a friend of mine had an interview at the public defender's office and said, "I can't go. Won't you go down there and take my interview?" I went down to the public defender's office, filled out the application, and got the job.

During my ten years as a public defender, it was absolutely the greatest job I've ever had and the proudest job I've ever had. When you're fighting for somebody's life or their future, all of a sudden everything becomes way more vivid and way more immediate.

When I was in law school, I had already started to cross-dress. I would actually go out on the streets. I would mingle with the other drag queens, female impersonators. Once I got a job, I was able to start my therapy. Then

Mia (right) in 1971, graduating from UCLA law school

I'd see these same people at group therapy, and I was able to get to know them. Their stories were so remarkably similar to mine. The same childhoods, the same feelings. A lot of them, their parents had sent them to therapy, or their wives and their children sent them. I remember the Hollywood group in particular had more attrition than my units in Vietnam. More people were lost to suicide, to homicide, to reckless behavior than any unit I was ever with in Vietnam.

It was dangerous, depressing. It's probably a little bit like the AIDS epidemic during the '80s, when people started dying left and right. There were a lot of unhappy people out there, and a lot of people who were unhappy with them. I felt like there was just no place for me in the world. The only place I ever knew of transgender people was out on the streets, drag queens and street queens, or on the stage, female impersonators. I couldn't relate to any of those lifestyles. I thought, "If that's the only thing that's open to me, I think I'd rather be dead."

At the same time, I felt like to take my own life would have been the worst thing I could do. I was going to be hurting so many people. For years, I basically felt held back by my clients. It wasn't even my family anymore. It was my clients. I kept thinking, "I can't let these people down. I've got death penalty cases. I've got people whose lives are riding on my decisions and my presentation, so I can't do it."

LIBERATING THE COURTS

I turned sixty. I turned 6-0. Somebody threw me a surprise birthday party, and all of these people are talking about how wonderful I am. I'm thinking, "I'm just a total asshole." I'm thinking, "I'm a complete phony. I'm a coward." I was so depressed. I never thought I'd live this long. My dad died at fifty-four, so I never figured I'd last as long.

So, I remember saying at that point, "I don't care what happens. I don't care what it takes. I don't care what I lose. I'm going to transition." At that point, I started coming out to all of my best friends, my family. Whatever shame or guilt I experienced would be nothing compared to the shame and the guilt I feel by not transitioning.

Coming out is a very litmus-test time for your friendships, for your family, for all the connections that you have. It tests all of them. And every one of these people has a different reaction. One of my brothers completely rejected me when I told him. Our conversation ended up with him saying, "I'm not your brother. I want you to keep away from my family and my kids and grandkids. I'm never going to talk to you again." So I said, "Okay. If I'm never going to speak to you again, I want to thank you, because you were the rebel of the family. You were the one that taught me I didn't have to be what everybody wanted me to be. Thank you very much. Goodbye."

When I told my office partner John, he couldn't believe it. He said, "How can you do this now? You're in the twilight of your life. Why would you throw everything away this late in your life?" And I said, "Because it's the truth. I've got to deal with the truth, and that means everybody else is going to have to deal with it too."

Next, I started coming out to my clients, the next most important people after my family. I came out to each one of them individually. I told them, "I'm going to be changing my gender. I'm going to be presenting myself as a woman from here on in. If you want to leave, I will completely understand, because I came to you as Michael. I'll find you somebody good. I will make sure that you're taken care of." I was amazed. I didn't get a single person who jumped ship on me.

The night before I went into court for the first time as Mia, I needed some kind of a motivation to get me going. I thought, "Tomorrow I'm going to liberate the criminal courts building, and after I do that I'm going to liberate the jail. After that, I'm going to liberate the prosecutor's office. I'm going to go to all of these places where nobody has ever seen a transgender woman before in their life, and I'm going to make it normal." When I came into court, the prosecutor on my case looks at me and says, "So, what are we calling you now?" I said, "That's the perfect question. I call myself Mia."

I have to admit, I was moved to tears by how little I expected of my peers and from the court. The women were like, "Welcome to the club." The guys were like, "I got your back, homey." The prosecutors especially are people I beat up on pretty much every day. We're fighting like crazy all the time. Yet they were incredibly embracing when I finally came to court. Who could ever expect that? I'm grateful beyond my ability to express it, because all these people were amazing, and they still are.

A few months after her OUTWORDS interview in April 2017, we invited Mia to say a few words at an OUTWORDS fundraiser. Mia got up and basically set the room on fire with her speech about the importance of recording LGBTQ history and defeating the forces that would like to relegate queer people to the margins of society—literal or figurative 'camps' like the one her parents were sent to during World War II.

BREAKING
GROUND

CLIFF ARNESEN

BISEXUAL VETERANS ACTIVIST

BOSTON, MASSACHUSETTS

Cliff Arnesen was born in Jersey City, New Jersey, on Thanksgiving Day 1948. At age three, Cliff was sent to an orphanage after his father drunkenly threw him against a wall. His troubled childhood continued until he joined the military at age seventeen, where he was dishonorably discharged for homosexuality—but not before the Army forced him to masturbate with another soldier to prove that he wasn't faking his condition.

Returning to civilian life, Cliff attended Bunker Hill Community College in Boston, becoming the first in his family to graduate college. He became president of the New England Gay and Lesbian Veterans in 1988, and in 1989, he testified on behalf of bisexual service members before the Eighth Congressional Speaker's Conference on the Concerns of Vietnam Veterans, making him the first and only openly bisexual veteran to testify before members of Congress.

In 2018, Cliff successfully won a lawsuit against the US military for service-connected PTSD/military sexual assault and trauma during his tenure in the Army. He and his girlfriend, Claudia, whom he calls "the love of my life," have been together for over twenty-five years.

When I was sixteen, I wanted to do something with my life. I asked my mother one day, I said, "I'd like you to sign a waiver. I want to join the Army." She said, "Son, you know there's a war going on now in Vietnam."

It took a little prodding, but she finally agreed. I quit school in the tenth grade. My mother signed a waiver. I joined the United States Army.

At that time, the war in Vietnam was escalating. They were really pushing people to go. Eight weeks of basic training, boom, you were off on a plane to Vietnam.

While I was still in basic training, I got word that my mother's life was in danger. I went AWOL. My mother was living with another alcoholic. She said, "He punched me." I didn't return back to my unit. I overstayed, just to keep an eye on my mom. I went to Greenwich Village to hide out from the military police. I was gone a total of three weeks.

Finally I turned myself in. They arrested me. They drove me back to Fort Dix. My company commander put me under house arrest to await a court-martial, which normally would've been just an Article 15, which is like a slap on the wrist. But during my interrogation, I told my company commander that I was bisexual. He said, "I'm going to teach you a lesson."

I was sentenced to one year of hard labor in the military prison. I was in the general population. Then a group of soldiers came to me one night, and they said, "This is your last night on earth." I said, "What are you talking about?" They said, "We're going to kill you tonight."

So the military removed me from the general population and put me in segregated confinement for my own protection. I remained there for three and a half months. In 1967, after two years, the Army gave me an undesirable discharge based on homosexuality, which precluded me from obtaining all medical or educational benefits from the military.

Five months after my discharge, my mother died of breast cancer. At that, I lost the last thing that I truly loved in my life.

A REPRIEVE

After being expelled from the military, I began to drink a lot and take drugs just to drown out the pain, the sorrow. I moved to

Albany, New York, where I met a guy named Donnie, who was my first love. We got an apartment for about a year or so. Our relationship ended because of my drinking. After that, I was almost homeless.

I was really empty in life. I was just kind of drifting along. In 1973, I moved to Boston and went to a gay bar. I met some people. I found a gentleman who worked as a sexton at a church. He provided me a place to live until I could get on my feet, get a job. I continued to drink. I was always drinking.

I drank up until 1983. I ended up in the VA hospital dehydrated, and needles in my arms, and just a total wreck. Twenty-some years of drinking. I had always thought, "I never want to be like my father," but I ended up like that, just like my father. I was drinking a quart of vodka a day. The doctor said, "If you keep on drinking like this," he said, "you're going to die. It's that simple."

I left the hospital. I joined AA. I was working as a house painter and a carpenter. Somebody told me, "Why don't you go to school? Take a course at Bunker Hill Community College." I said, "I can't." They talked me into taking a course. I took one course, and I got an A. I was about to leave the school, and one of the teachers stopped me in the hall and said, "Where are you going, Cliff?" I said, "Well, I got my A. I'm going back to my job." She said, "Take another course."

I took another course, and I got another A. I said, "Maybe I can do this." It took me four years. I had two jobs. I finally graduated from Bunker Hill Community College in 1987 with high honors, with a 3.9 average.

Cliff testifying before a congressional committee on veterans affairs in 1990

I n 1987, I went to my first meeting of the New England Gay and Lesbian Veterans. Mr. Bob Derry was the cofounder. I told him, "I'm a bisexual veteran." Eventually I was elected president of that group.

In 1989, we had a meeting with Dr. Paul Camacho, a Vietnam veteran who had arranged conferences in Washington, DC, with minority veterans groups. We told him we wanted gay veterans to testify before Congress. But he said, "I don't know how we're going to do this. It's never been done before." Finally it was decided we would put gay veterans on as part of a medical platform, to advocate for veterans with HIV/AIDS and who suffered from PTSD and other illnesses.

The first testimony came on May 3, 1989. I had the honor of testifying as an openly bisexual veteran, with a gay veteran who had HIV. We testified before Congress on AIDS and PTSD. I testified again in 1990.

I never thought that a poor kid from Brooklyn would end up in the marble halls of Congress.

On countless occasions, Cliff has thanked the OUTWORDS team for interviewing him, and for our efforts to preserve bisexual history as part of LGBTQ history. To him, we say, "Thank you for your service."

DONNA BURKETT

MARRIAGE EQUALITY PIONEER

MILWAUKEE, WISCONSIN

Donna Burkett was born in 1946 in Chicago, Illinois. Her grandfather owned Black King, Milwaukee's first black sit-down restaurant and, by all accounts, the best barbecue joint in town.

Donna graduated high school, joined the Army, and returned to Milwaukee in 1970, whereupon she met Manonia Evans and fell in love. In 1971, Donna and Manonia applied for a marriage license at the Milwaukee county clerk's office. Unsurprisingly, the county clerk turned the lovebirds away, so they filed a federal lawsuit. Although their lawsuit was ultimately unsuccessful, the argument they used—equal protection under the Constitution—was cited by US District Judge Barbara Crabb more than forty years later, in 2014, when she overturned Wisconsin's ban on same-sex marriage.

On Christmas Day 1971, Donna and Manonia were married in a private ceremony. The local press picked up the story, and the ensuing controversy took a toll on the young couple. Not long after, Donna and Manonia split up.

I grew up with my mother and my sister. My mom was not married. We had no dad in the house.

I didn't have any problems with my mother growing up. When I was about fourteen or fifteen, my mom told me I should start trying to not be so rough and tomboyish. I should start trying to do other things instead of running and playing and fighting and all of that. But I didn't have those problems that some people do have about coming out and keeping it a secret from your family.

I used to take my mom out sometimes. We'd go out to the gay bars together. She just loved the light. I'd turn around, and she was up there on the dance floor dancing by herself.

MANONIA

I don't remember where I met Manonia. All I remember is I asked her to meet me at this bar. When I came in the bar, I didn't see her so I walked back by the pool table. Then she came up and she said, "You ain't even going to speak to me?" I looked. I said, "I didn't even recognize you." She looked all different. She had put on a little makeup and stuff.

I liked the idea of getting married. We went down to the courthouse to apply for our license. We filled out the card they gave us, turned it in. Then the lady at the counter went, "Oh my God." Then she walked off and she went and got somebody else, and then they came over. They said, "Is this information correct?" "Yeah, it's right. You don't think I know my name?" Then they went in some back room, and then they came back out and they said, "You can't get married."

When we got out in the hallway, that's when all these reporters came. That's how it took off. That's how the press got involved. The people at the courthouse must have called their buddies or something. I don't know what they did, but that's how it took off. They caught us right in the hallway, and when we got outside they caught us.

We had a private ceremony. Father Joseph Feldhausen, he married us. He was an Episcopal priest. We had to go through I forget how many months of counseling. We had a ceremony, and then we had a reception. Still wasn't a lot of our friends there. They didn't want to come because they thought the newspapers were going to be there. They said they didn't want their picture and their name and their jobs in the paper.

Manonia got kicked out of school. I got some kind of little job. We had a rough time. We moved in with a couple of guy friends until we could get back on our feet. Back then, Milwaukee was a horrible place to be, and be gay. It really was.

When marriage equality finally passed, the Milwaukee LGBT Center gave me an award, the Vanguard Award. The newspaper came out to do an interview. They told me that they were going to be giving me an award.

It was a really nice function. It was at Potawatomi Casino. The room was really elegant, a big chandelier.

People kept asking me, did I ever think that it was going to take this long. I told them, "I never said, 'Let's go do this so we'll be important later on.'" I never thought anything of it. Once our case was over, it was dead.

You know with the Wright brothers and the airplane, okay? Somebody will pick it up and they'll keep going and keep improving on it, until it's there. So I shouldn't have gotten an award. Everybody that is gay should get an award because what I did would have been forgotten had not somebody else kept it going.

JAMISON GREEN

AUTHOR, TRANSGENDER HEALTH ADVOCATE

UNION CITY, CALIFORNIA

Jamison Green was born in Oakland, California, on November 8, 1948, and designated female at birth. In his early forties, he was able finally and fully to transition to his male identity. From that point forward, he threw himself fully into transgender activism. He developed a local San Francisco support group for transgender men into a global organization and, in 1994, wrote the San Francisco Human Rights Commission's report on discrimination against transgender people. In 2007, he founded a transgender training and policy consulting group for business, education, and government. He also published his prize-winning book, *Becoming a Visible Man*, which has become a classic text, informing and inspiring transgender and cisgender people worldwide. [Editor's note: The term cisgender describes types of gender identity perceptions in which an individual's experiences of their own gender agree with the sex they were assigned at birth.]

In 2009, Jamison became the first transgender person to receive the Distinguished Service Award from the Association of Gay and Lesbian Psychiatrists. From 2014 to 2016, he served as president of the World Professional Association for Transgender Health (WPATH), just the second transgender person to hold this position.

The first time I realized that it was possible to transition was when I saw a man named Steve Dain on television. This was in 1976. He was a teacher of girls' PE in an Emeryville high school. He transitioned over the summer one year and came back in the fall and, "Hi, I'm a guy now." The administration just flipped out. The school board fired him, and he fought it. He was the first really visible trans man in this country.

Steve was very good looking, very articulate, very relaxed, poised. Everything about him was perfect. I'm watching him on television on a talk show thinking, "Oh my God, it really is possible." That scared me. It's like, "Now I really have to choose."

A year later, a friend of mine transitioned. He said to me, "Oh, you should do this. You would really love it." One thing he said was, "Now, I get the respect that I deserve." I was like, "Well, wait a minute. Women deserve respect. People who are different deserve respect. People who are androgynous deserve respect. I'm not going to go there for that reason. If I go there, it won't be for that reason." I pulled back at that point. It literally took me almost ten years to start moving forward again.

I thought very seriously about this. You can't make a change like this without a huge ripple effect. I thought, "I would lose my family. I would lose my friends. I would lose my job. I would lose everything." At the same time, I thought, "I would be happy in my body. I would be present. I would be visible. I would be able to be seen for who I am. I would be more solid in the world, more grounded and solid."

That's pretty much what happened. I did lose some friends, including a few who really

Jamison in 2000, addressing an audience of 750,000 people at San Francisco Pride—the first trans man ever to speak from the Pride main stage

surprised me, because I thought they were people who really loved me and cared about me. I had a lot of trouble with my mother. My mother didn't want me to tell any of the other relatives about my transition. She regressed into calling me the name that they had given me at birth, which I had not gone by for over twenty-five years. Much later, I think my daughter was about five or six. My mom was referring to me with feminine pronouns and this other name. My daughter said, "Grandma, don't call him that. His name is Jamie, Jamie, Jamie, Jamie, Jamie, Jamie, Jamie, Jamie."

It wasn't until maybe the last year or so before my mother died that she was really able to accept who I was, and understand that I was male and that the rest of the world perceived me as male, and that I was doing fine.

A BRIDGE-BUILDER

In 1997, I went to a conference of the Harry Benjamin International Gender Dysphoria Association, the people who were dealing with practices and policies that affected trans people's lives. And I was blown away by the fear that the professionals had about trans people. Most of them were very, very tense. They had the same shame that trans people have. They felt there was a lot of responsibility in deciding whether or not someone could have surgery. They were very nervous they might be perceived as being influenced by their patients. There was just a lot of trepidation everywhere. Those attitudes made trans people very angry.

Jamison in Provincetown, MA, in 2002, performing in the cabaret at Fantasia Fair, the world's longest-running transgender conference

I thought, "Trans people need more support, and professionals need to be less fearful."

One of the things I said very clearly to the professionals was, "If you don't want to be perceived as gatekeepers, don't be gatekeepers." People literally went, "How can we do that?" I said, "Stop trying to put brakes on people, and start trying to help them. Your role is not to distance yourself from your client or judge your client. Your role is to say, 'How can I help you be more comfortable in your gender, whether that means transitioning, not transitioning, transitioning to an in-between state, whatever makes you comfortable that may be different than the stereo-

types that you've been operating under?'" It's all about really seeing people.

Eventually, I was invited to join the organization. Then the board actually debated for nearly four years about whether or not I could be allowed to vote. There were people on the board who felt that I had too much power in the community and that I was dangerous. Yes, I did intend to change things, I am maybe provocative now and then, but I'm not unreasonable, and I'm not dangerous. I understand their perspective, and I understand the community's perspective. I'm a bridge-builder.

Today, the organization is called WPATH, the World Professional Association for

Transgender Health. Lots of people in the community hate this organization, but without this organization people in prison would not have access to transition-related care. People in many clinics across the country getting public health would not have that access. People who were being sued for custody of their kids because they're trans would not be able to win their cases.

The first Standards of Care for transsexualism, if you will, were developed in 1979. In 2011, Version 7 of the Standards was published, and that document is a radical change from past documents. The Standards used to talk about what the community had to do in order to qualify for treatment. Now they talk about what professionals have to do to provide good service to the community. That was one of the reasons that I joined this organization, was to change that.

NO REASON FOR FEAR

What some people still don't understand is that trans people are not trying to deceive people. We are not trying to be something we are not. We are actually trying to be our authentic and actual true selves, no matter what that looks like on the outside to anyone. We may look like very, very tall women with square jaws or whatever. That doesn't mean we're not comfortable in our skin. Trans men are often shorter than average. So what? Why should we make people feel bad about the way they look? There are things that they can't help. But when trans people do what they can to make themselves feel more at home in their body, to make them-

selves feel more productive in society, then society says, "Oh no, I'm not at home with your body. I don't want you to be productive in my society."

Why is it that we can't look at the issues that trans people are actually struggling with and not judge them for being different, for not looking right, for having a gender variance that doesn't feel comfortable for the observer? Let it go. Let it go. There is no reason for you to be frightened of me.

KAY LAHUSEN

PHOTOJOURNALIST

KENNETT SQUARE, PENNSYLVANIA

Kay Lahusen was born in Cincinnati, Ohio, in 1930. After college, she moved to Boston to work in the reference library of the *Christian Science Monitor*. There she discovered *The Ladder*, published by the Daughters of Bilitis (DOB), America's earliest lesbian civil rights group. Through the DOB, Kay met Barbara Gittings, and over the course of forty-six years together, Kay and Barbara became two of the most influential activists in the early LGBTQ movement.

Through the 1960s and '70s, Kay photographed countless activists, demonstrations, and marches of the LGBTQ movement, establishing herself as America's first openly gay photojournalist. She also helped found the Gay Activists Alliance and in 1972 co-wrote one of the earliest anthologies of gay activism, *The Gay Crusaders* (subtitled *In-depth Interviews with 15 Homosexuals—Men and Women Who Are Shaping America's Newest Sexual Revolution*). As a team, Kay and Barbara were active in the American Library Association's Gay Task Force and were instrumental in persuading the American Psychiatric Association to remove homosexuality from its list of psychiatric disorders in 1973.

In 2007, Barbara passed away. Kay subsequently donated their joint collection of photos, writings, and papers to the New York Public Library.

I was interested in photography as a kid, before I ever had a notion I was gay. I just loved to take pictures with little cameras. My dog, the little boy next door, the fish pond next door, all of that stuff. I never had an expensive camera. When you're dealing with a group of people, you just can't expect them all to hold still while you fiddle with your camera, and you have to just shoot on the run. So, I always had inexpensive cameras. All I brought to photography was my own love of

photography and love of my subject matter.

When it came to photographing marches, they were just something I wanted to do, whether I was photographing or not. We picketed both in Washington and Philadelphia. I'm seldom in the picket line because I'm always behind the camera. I would jump in the line, picket a while, get back out, get behind the camera.

I never thought of these pictures as being terribly significant, but I hoped they might

Kay in a picket line in 1969

might encourage people to come and harass them, throw rocks, who knows. But the event went without any trouble at all. So then they decided, let's picket the White House, invite the press, send a letter in to the president with our demands, our wishes, and walk around for a couple of hours in the sunshine.

Some people wore sunglasses, and others just thought it was too much to come out in that setting, but that was the first substantial picket.

In those days, you walked around, went to the grocery store like an ordinary person and all of that, and nobody thought you were gay. There was no problem in everyday living. But when you got in a picket line and carried a sign like our signs, people automatically thought you were gay. Not invariably. I know one woman looked at our picket lines and she said, "They're all actors." She thought nobody could possibly want to do this.

A group of us felt that the Gay Liberation Front wasn't gonna get anywhere. [Editor's note: Founded in 1969 shortly after the Stonewall riots, the Gay Liberation Front (GLF) is commonly credited with organizing the first Pride march to build on the momentum created by Stonewall.] They were so chaotic in their meetings. Everybody yelling and screaming and calling each other names. Twelve of us went our separate way and formed the Gay Activists Alliance. We drew up a constitution, worked by Robert's Rules of Order, and had membership. We were militant without being nasty or disruptive, although we did disrupt a day of business at *Harper's*.

be someday, and apparently they are. Some are in the Smithsonian, and New York Public Library has five hundred of my pictures. It's very gratifying to still have these pictures.

PICKET LINES

The picket lines were born in Washington in 1965. At first Frank Kameny thought maybe it was a foolish idea. [Editor's note: Frank Kameny (1925–2011) was one of America's most prominent early gay rights activists.] Then Frank thought better of it and said yes, we should try that. And so that's the way the picket lines were born.

The first time they went out and picketed, I think they were ten people, and it was thought that they shouldn't have publicity because it

In 1970, *Harper's Magazine* published an antigay article. You can't believe it, but in those days, they really did. We invaded their headquarters. We were there early in the morning when the secretary was just opening up, and we all went in, and we were very nice, very pleasant, and we served coffee and donuts. When the phone rang, we took over the phones, and we'd answer, "We're having a sit-in at *Harper's Magazine* because they published an antigay article." We went and talked to the editor. I remember one of our spokesmen saying, "You knew that article would be harmful to homosexuals! You knew that!"

News travels fast in New York. The New York radio stations were saying, "A bunch of homosexuals has taken over *Harper's Magazine*, and they're doing a sit-in there." It was a fun event. We were very polite. Nobody was harmed, although the editors never responded or discussed the sit-in in print.

THE KISSING BOOTH

My partner, Barbara, was a great bibliophile. She was collecting books with mentions of homosexuality. Eventually, Barbara was able to join ALA [the American Library Association]. Believe it or not, she didn't have to be a librarian to join it. She formed a group of gay librarians, went to ALA meetings and the ALA convention, and handed out a flyer she'd made up with a bibliography of gay-positive literature that could go into libraries. You had to just think of everything you could possibly think of in those days to promote yourself.

Eventually the gay librarians' group was given an eight-foot-by-eight-foot booth in the exhibit hall at ALA. The title of the booth was "Gay, Proud, and Healthy: The Homosexual Community Speaks." We thought, "What are we going to do to draw attention to our gay booth? We'll have a kissing booth!" Barbara and a writer named Alma Routsong stood under a sign saying, "Gay kisses for women." Then we had a couple of guys under a sign, "Gay kisses for men."

No men came into the booth. But some other ALA members wanted to help us out. So they came to the booth and they hugged Barbara and Alma, and they sort of had a love-in, a very random, crazy, hug-a-homosexual time. It's fun if you have a certain amount of moxie to get out there and do these inventive things.

Because Kay doesn't use email, it took a while to schedule her OUTWORDS interview. We actually had to communicate via old-school letters carried cross-country by the USPS. But the effort was more than worth it. Kay understands journalism, history, and how small, determined steps can add up to a revolution.

DEAN HAMER

SCIENTIST, FILMMAKER

OAHU, HAWAI'I

Dean Hamer was born in 1951 in Montclair, New Jersey. He graduated from Trinity College in Connecticut and earned a PhD from Harvard Medical School. After determining that medical research was more compelling to him than treating individual patients, Dean spent thirty-five years as an independent researcher at the National Institutes of Health (NIH).

In the 1990s, Dean began studying the relationship between human behavior and genetics. In 1993, his research group's first paper, published in *Science*, presented the first-ever findings linking homosexuality to a particular region of the X chromosome—the so-called gay gene. Dean's book on the topic, *The Science of Desire*, became a *New York Times* Notable Book of the Year. His second book, *The God Gene*, explored the relationship between faith and genetics. In later years, Dean developed a potential form of HIV prevention, which is currently entering preclinical testing. His research has been cited by medical scholars nearly twenty thousand times.

In the early 2000s, Dean met filmmaker Joe Wilson. Together they produced the Emmy Award–winning documentary *Out in the Silence* (2009). After moving to Hawai'i in 2011, Dean and Joe produced *Kumu Hina*, a documentary about gender diversity among Pacific Islander peoples. Their most recent film, *Leitis in Waiting* (2018), explores gender diversity in Tonga, the last remaining monarchy in the Pacific.

I've always been curious about how things work. I'm always wondering, why does A lead to B? Or what is causing C? When I graduated from college, I'd already spent two summers in a laboratory. I knew that I loved research, but everyone told me, "You should go to medical school. You'll make a much better living. You can do research on the side." Then I got accepted at Harvard Medical School, and everyone again told me, "You can't turn down Harvard Medical School. You gotta go there."

I didn't love medical school. I found a lot of it was rote learning. I wasn't all that keen about dealing with patients. I was like, "Oh my God, they're complaining about their illness again." After a year of medical school, I just said, "I'm going to go on leave of ab-

Dean in his laboratory at the National Institutes of Health, 1981

sence and do research full time." I remained on leave of absence from Harvard Medical School for the next twenty-five years.

I started my scientific career at a really auspicious point, because it was just at that time when we were progressing from a general idea of what genetics were, to a very specific ability to actually isolate genes and to look at them and to manipulate them.

I started thinking and thinking. I was thinking, "I could study alcoholism, or I could study depression." Finally, at some point, I think actually my partner at that time said, "Why don't you study sexual orientation?" I was like, "Oh my God, that's really a good idea." I went rushing to the library and realized no one had studied anything about sexual orientation at a molecular level ever. It was a completely wide open field. We set out

to find out whether there is a genetic basis for sexual orientation, and if so, how it works.

As I was doing the research, it was never much of a concern to me what the reaction would be, because I had spent my whole life with other scientists. The criterion there is good science or bad science, important science or not important science. I felt that if we were able to crack this at all, it would be of course good science, because we're doing it the right way. And it would be important, because that's the fundamental question. Sexuality is the driving force of biology. Sexuality is how we pass on our genes. It's everything.

Our original research was actually pretty simple. We looked at a bunch of families of gay men and asked about their gay relatives and noticed there was a pattern that most of the gay relatives were on the mother's side of the family. That was really interesting. The next step was to look for actual DNA sequences on the X chromosome that were associated with sexual orientation. To do that, we got a bunch of gay brothers, forty-four pairs of gay brothers. We found that there was one specific region called Xq28 that the gay brothers shared far more often than would be expected by chance. Their straight brothers usually didn't have that region. That told us there's some gene in that part of the chromosome that is somehow tipping the scales and making these guys more likely to be gay. That became the somewhat misnomed gay gene.

When that research came out, it caused a huge sensation. It was on the front page of every paper, not just in the United States but all around the world. I was on every news show. I got on the *Oprah* show. I did Ted Koppel. It was a huge big fight, and I stepped right into the middle of it. There were some people, especially gay people, who thought this is great because if we can prove that being gay is not a choice, that will take away a lot of the prejudice. There were a lot of the antigay people, especially the religious people, who were infuriated by the research because it is their firm belief that people choose to be gay, and it is a bad choice and that's what makes it a sin. Therefore this research couldn't possibly be right. Then there were also people, gay people, who were very concerned that the research would be misused and that gay fetuses would be aborted and that the military would be doing secret testing. They were very concerned about that as well. It was a very, very split and controversial reaction at the time.

I know it's an old adage, that the truth will set you free. What I know for sure is that the untruth and wrong thought will never allow you to be free. I believe that.

Watching Dean paddle out with Joe to catch a few waves on Oahu's North Shore, you might think time has mellowed him. It hasn't. Dean today is as fiercely determined as ever when it comes to searching for truth and defending every individual's right to enjoy the ancient Hawaiian values of pono ("doing the right thing") and aloha ("living life with love").

DICK LEITSCH

PIONEERING PROTESTER

NEW YORK, NEW YORK

Dick Leitsch was born in 1935 in Louisville, Kentucky. In high school, he came out to his Catholic parents, who surprisingly took the news in stride. Dick stuck around Louisville a few more years, raising hell in whatever gay bars he could find; but he needed a bigger stage for his boundless energy. In 1959, he moved to New York, where he supported himself for nearly six decades as a journalist, waiter, bartender, painter, and holiday decorator.

In New York, Dick met and fell in love with Craig Rodwell, a former ballet student. Craig invited Dick to the meetings of a nascent gay rights organization called the Mattachine Society, and by 1964 Dick was the group's president. Two years later, in a rascally mood, Dick, Craig, and a couple of buddies came up with the idea of "sip-ins" (fashioned after the sit-ins of the civil rights era) to focus attention on bars that refused to serve gays and lesbians. The brilliant stunt ultimately helped establish queer people's right to peacefully congregate in bars—or wherever they chose.

Listening to the radio on the night of June 28, 1969, Dick heard something about trouble at the Stonewall Inn. Hopping a cab, he arrived in time to witness the flashpoint of the gay rights revolution. Dick's account of the Stonewall riots was later published in *The Advocate*.

In New York, when I moved there, there were strictly gay places. Straight people didn't go to them. Nobody danced, nobody touched, nobody did anything. That was all against the law. Dancing was allowed, but you had to stay in a line and everybody danced in line. One of the employees would stand there and yell, "No touching! No touching!" You couldn't touch anybody, because the police would bust the place if they heard about that.

I came to New York with a lover, and we had a little apartment at Seventy-Second and Fifth Avenue. We were together for a couple of years, then we broke up. So I was just wandering around being single. One night, it was very cold that night, I walked to the Village and met this guy, Craig Rodwell. So we went off and had sex. He liked me and he called me back, and we started hanging out. He told me about these meetings of the Mattachine Soci-

Dick as president of the Mattachine Society

ety, and he wanted me to come with him and I said, "Well, I don't know much about that." I was never interested in that. He said, "Oh, it's very important and nah, nah, nah," and I said, "All right, if you want."

At the meetings, they all talked about making a better world for homosexuals and all that kind of stuff. It seemed to me they never had any ideas about how to go about doing it. I just stayed around because Craig was fun.

After a while I got tired of Craig, but there was this guy named Julian Hodges, a very smart politician sort of guy. He wanted to make Mattachine bigger and actually do political activities and change laws. Everybody else seemed to mostly talk about being polite and not causing trouble, and he actually wanted to change the world. I liked his idea, and we became very close.

Julian was running for president of Mattachine, and he was going to lose. So he said, "You run. You'll win." I said, "I can't do that. I don't know anything about being president. I'm just a nice little queen here, that's all." He

said, "You're just going to be the talking head, and I'll tell you what to say." I said, "Fine, I can do that." So basically Julian became president. I just used my name, and he actually did all the work.

Then Julian lost his job and left New York. Now he's gone. Everybody says, "You're the head of the Mattachine." I said, "Yeah, right." So I was head of Mattachine.

People would call up: they want someone to be on television, they want somebody to write an article, they want somebody to this, somebody to do that. "Dick, somebody's got to and I'd love to do it, but I can't because my mother can't know I'm gay." Or "I'll lose my job. I'm a teacher, I'm a priest, I'm a whatever. I can't do that. You got to do it. Dick, you got to do it." So I signed my name, I went on television, I was in the newspaper, my picture was here, there, and everywhere. Time after time. That's how I became the most famous homosexual in the whole world.

In those days, all the people in Mattachine were trying to be nice gay people, nice organized people, churchgoing people. "We don't do drag queens, we don't do leather, we don't have sleazy sex." I said, "No, no, no. There's thousands of ways to be gay. Be any kind of gay you want to be. If you want to have babies and puppies and live in the suburbs, you do that. If you want to do drag, do that. If you want to wear leather and go on motorcycles, we can all be happy doing it. Everybody has to be able to do what they want to do. Just don't hurt anybody else. Just don't mess up everything. Do it your own way, for yourself, if it makes you happy."

THE "SIP-IN" THAT STARTED A REVOLUTION

Back in the early, mid-1960s, the police kept closing bars. As fast as you open a bar, if gays came in, the police would close the bar, and we had no place to go and no place to hang out.

One day I was talking to some friends and I said, "Everybody comes in and says we have no place to drink and eat. It's like black people in the South." They say, "Oh, yeah, yeah, yeah." So we decided we would do something about that.

I talked to a lawyer. I said, "Why are they making laws against gay people drinking and eating when we have the right to do everything we want to do? The law says that everybody has to be free, so why can't we do that?"

Restaurant and bar owners were afraid of being closed by the police, because if you had the gay people in it, the cops would come and close it. So they put signs up saying, "If you're gay, don't come here." Various signs saying that all over town. There was one in the East Village that said, "If you're gay, please go away." I said, "That's the place. We'll go there." We decided to go in at noon, and we told the media. But when we got there, the place wasn't open. A guy from the *New York Post* was there. He said, "We told them what you were going to do, and they closed up. They

Dick famously being refused service at Julius's bar in 1966—the "sip-in" that helped launch a revolution

don't want to deal with it." I said, "Oh shit. What are we going to do?"

So we decided to try this little Mafia place around the corner. We walked in, sat down. The media came and sat at the next table. The waiter came over, and we gave him a little piece of paper. It said, "We are three homosexuals. We're orderly, we don't intend on being disorderly. We just want service." The waiter said, "Huh, wait a minute." So the manager comes out, and he's this big Mafia guy with $500 shoes. He says, "What's going on here?" I said we were homosexuals, and we wanted to be served. He said, "They ain't doing anything. Give them drinks on the house." Oh God! We were trying to have a demonstration!

Finally we remembered this other place called Julius's that was famous for cheese-burgers, and so we went in there. We had heard that Julius's refused to serve gays. So we went in, we sat down and said, "We're homo-sexuals." And the waiter said, "I can't serve you," and there was a photographer. He got a picture of him, and that's how we got that famous picture of them.

[Editor's note: The actions of Dick Leitsch, Craig Rodwell, Randy Wicker, and John Timmons at Julius's bar in April 1966 are regarded as one of the earliest acts of LGBTQ civil disobedience in America. The "sip-in" gained coverage from the *New York Times*, which referred to Dick and his friends as "de-viates," and *The Village Voice*, prompting the head of the state liquor authority to publicly deny that his organization threatened the liquor licenses of bars that served gays. Two years later, a case brought by the Mattachine Society against three New Jersey bars made it all the way to the New Jersey Supreme Court, where the justices ruled that "well-behaved homosexuals" could not be denied service.]

OUTWORDS recorded Dick's story in August 2016 on our first East Coast interview trip. In early 2018, Dick was diagnosed with terminal cancer. After making arrangements to donate his files and photos to the New York Public Library, he celebrated his eighty-third birth-day by attending the Broadway revival of The Boys in the Band. *Commenting on the steady stream of visitors after his cancer diagnosis, Dick said, "Had I known how much fun this would be, I'd have done it a lot sooner."*

MARY MORTEN

COMMUNITY ACTIVIST, FILMMAKER
CHICAGO, ILLINOIS

Mary Morten was born on Chicago's South Side. In 1984, fired up by Geraldine Ferraro's historic campaign for vice president of the United States, Mary started volunteering with the Chicago chapter of NOW. Soon she was spearheading the formation of a lesbian rights committee and a women of color committee, and at twenty-nine, she became Chicago NOW's first black woman president.

In June 1997, Mayor Richard M. Daley appointed Mary as his liaison to Chicago's gay community. Mary served in this role until 2000, when she was named director of the violence prevention office for the Chicago Department of Public Health. Along the way, Mary also cofounded the Illinois Safe Schools Alliance, an organization promoting inclusion and safety for LGBT youth, and developed an LGBTQ anti-racism program called "The Color Triangle: A Different Look at Race in Our Community."

Mary has also used radio and film as a force for change. In the early '90s, she co-created the documentary *The Nia Project: Images of African American Lesbians*. She also produced *Leaving the Shadows Behind*, a short documentary on activism in the African-American LGBT community. In 2011, Morten directed her first full-length documentary, *Woke Up Black*, chronicling the lives, dreams, and struggles of five young African Americans in Chicago. In 1996, Mary was inducted into the Chicago Gay and Lesbian Hall of Fame.

I walked into the Chicago office of NOW during the Mondale/Ferraro campaign. I said, "Oh gosh, I think I'm home." I was longing for a place where I could have deep conversations about issues that I cared about, and I was not really around folks on a regular basis where I could do that. I walked in and knew, "I want to get involved."

As often is the case, and was the case even then, and especially then, I was the only black woman in the room. I remember saying to the associate director, who became the executive director and a very close friend, I said, "Why aren't there any other black women or women of color here?" She said, "That's a really good question," and we had this long talk about it. I felt like she wasn't just giving me lip service, and that was refreshing because early on, when that question got asked, people would often say, "Well, we built it, why aren't they coming?"

As I got more involved with the organization and eventually became president of Chicago NOW, first black woman to be president in twenty-five years, first out lesbian, I had to really look at these issues of NOW being either not for women of color and not being for anyone who might be a lesbian.

I think that's always what's challenging about having multiple identities. I'm not black here and a lesbian there. All that comes with me. I felt that Chicago NOW was a welcoming space, but externally that was not understood. So we started a lesbian rights committee, and we started a women of color committee. I really couldn't do one without the other, and so we established those committees while I was president of the board.

FIRST AND ONLY

In my life, I have been "the first" or "the only" woman, or lesbian, or African-American woman, or African-American lesbian in almost every position I've had. Sometimes I didn't know I was going to be the first or the only or whatever. I would find out later.

As I got older and found myself in these situations where I was the only or the first, it was enormously challenging, at times overwhelming. Certainly when I was president of NOW I felt that way. I became the first African-American president of the board for Chicago Foundation for Women, which was one of the largest women's funds in the world. I absolutely felt and feel the weight of being out there and being a role model.

I know that it's important for people to see other people that look like them in certain positions and in certain organizations, so they can say, "This is a place where I can come and where I can feel safe." I understood that early on. I didn't shy away from it. It comes with the territory. But it is hard. It's hard. It will wear you out because of the expectations from your community and also folks from other communities, in terms of what they expect you to do and how outfront you will be on particular issues and how vocal you will be.

Everything from how I dress to, certainly when I was younger, how I wore my hair, all that is put through this filter of, you are a black woman living in a white world. You have to be better than everybody else, and you always have to be prepared, you always have to be ready. Let me just say, my theater background came in handy because I'm a huge proponent of "fake it till you make it." You got to step up and you have to exhibit a certain amount of self-confidence even if you don't feel that way, because if not, they will just eat you alive.

DISRUPTERS

LAMAR VAN DYKE

TATTOO SHOP OWNER, ARTIST

SEATTLE, WASHINGTON

> Lamar Van Dyke was born Heather Elizabeth Nelson in Canada in 1947 and grew up in Buffalo, New York. At nineteen, she had a daughter whom she gave up for adoption. Over the next four years, she got married and divorced three times. At that point, as far as Lamar was concerned, she was done with men.
>
> After traipsing around the United States and Mexico with a bunch of rowdy lesbian separatists, Lamar opened a tattoo shop in Seattle in 1980. Ink and leather became the focus of her life, and her shop became a key epicenter of Seattle queer life. She also became a "queen-pin" in the local S&M scene.
>
> In 1994, Lamar's daughter contacted her out of the blue. They connected and are still in each other's lives today.

When I came out, it was in the '70s and feminism was on fire. We were on fire with feminism. We were going to change everything for women. Everything was going to be different. We were running around with hammers and power tools and fixing our own cars and doing all of that and setting up programs for women to move forward.

After a few years of that, it became pretty clear to a certain group of us that we just needed to go and do something. That was us removing ourselves. We purchased a farm. We were going to move to the country and live the good life and make our own tofu and grow our own vegetables, and we were going to take care of ourselves. That lasted for one Ontario winter, where the snow was up over the windows of the house. When spring came, I took off.

I started with one woman, and I went off with her in her van. We had a great time, and I said, "I love this lifestyle, but I need my own van. I cannot live in a Volkswagen van with another person anymore." I bought a step van, and off we went. Then we found other women with vans, and we became the Van Dykes. We traveled all around North America and Mexico. We shaved our heads, we ate vegetables and drank water, and I weighed like 130 pounds. We were going, going, gone.

Everybody had a Van Dyke name. Ann changed her name to Brook Van Dyke because she babbled all the time. Chris changed

Lamar (laughing at bottom edge of frame) and friends down some beers to celebrate rebuilding the foundation of a 100-foot-long barn on their farm in Cavan, Ontario.

her name to Thorn Van Dyke because she was very thorny. I took the name Lamar because, as a kid, I used to run around saying, "I'm Hedy Lamarr, the movie star. I'm Hedy Lamarr, the movie star."

We didn't speak to men unless they were a waiter or a car mechanic or somebody that we needed. Then we would speak to them, but if we didn't need them, we wouldn't speak to them.

After the Van Dyke thing imploded, I legally changed my name to Van Dyke because I loved the idea of having a reservation in a restaurant and having them say, "Van Dyke party of six," and having six dykes stand up to go to the table.

THE RAILROAD TRACKS

As separatists, our view on women's sexuality was that men have been attempting to control women's sexuality since the beginning of time. That's what monogamy was all about because men certainly are not monogamous. We decided that that was bullshit and that we could have sex however we wanted with whoever we wanted, whenever we wanted.

When I came to Seattle, I was looking for women who were like-minded, and I found them. There were women in Seattle who were doing sadomasochism, or SM, but they weren't talking about it. It was a secret. I was talking about it. I had jewelry on my leather jacket, like a little whip and stuff, and so people were identifying me and coming to me and telling me, and I felt, "There's actually a lot of SM dykes here. They're just not connected." I started connecting them. So the whole dyke SM thing in Seattle erupted all around me. Pretty soon, there was a huge vibrant community of motorcycle-riding, leather-jacket-wearing, carrying-on dykes that were having a blast.

We'd be hanging around in my shop and I would get out the Polaroid camera, and we'd start just dressing up. Then I decide, "Okay, it's *National Enquirer* time," so we put electrical tape on our nipples and we put on blindfolds, and we have people posing and everything, and then more women come in and the whole thing grows, and then I'm

just going, going. Let's do this or let's do that. Let's go downtown and tie you to the railroad tracks. We would do it. That was heaven for me. It was a very safe environment, and people were having lots of fun and living out their fantasies, and having things happen that they'd never thought would happen before.

SM really created a situation where I totally trusted myself. It made the rest of my life a little calmer, a little easier. It helped me sort it out in a way.

Although Lamar today speaks with men, works with men, and graciously allowed a man to interview her for OUTWORDS, she still feels like a wild pirate of a woman. Life for Lamar will always be about change and adventure—otherwise, why bother?

EVAN WOLFSON

MARRIAGE EQUALITY PIONEER

NEW YORK, NEW YORK

> Evan Wolfson was born in 1957 in Brooklyn, New York, and grew up in Pittsburgh. His dad was a pediatrician; his mom was a housewife and later a social worker. From day one, Evan was intensely aware of American inequality, appalled at the injustices foisted upon minorities, and determined to make the world a better place before he kissed it goodbye.
>
> After high school, Evan headed off to Yale College, served with the Peace Corps in Africa, and then entered Harvard Law School. In his 1983 law school thesis, he took up the issue of marriage equality, essentially drawing the road map for the next thirty-two years of his life.
>
> In 2001, after stints as an assistant district attorney and with the organization Lambda Legal, Evan formed the organization Freedom to Marry on the strength of a $2.5 million grant from the Evelyn and Walter Haas Jr. Fund. Over the next fourteen years, Evan engineered a four-pronged "multi" campaign—multi-year, multi-state, multi-partner, and multi-methodology—that boosted public support for same-sex marriage from 27 percent in 1993 to 63 percent in 2015 and that ultimately resulted in the 2015 US Supreme Court decision that made marriage equality the law of the land. In 2004, *Time* magazine named Evan one of the one hundred most influential people in the world.
>
> In 2011, after joking or whining for years that the marriage movement would benefit everyone except himself, Evan tied the knot with Cheng He, a molecular biologist originally from Beijing. The couple's wedding ties were emblazoned with the Chinese symbol signifying "double happiness."

By my third year in law school, in 1983, I had come out in progressive degrees to friends and roommates and family and the world. That year, we had to write a third-year paper in addition to our regular coursework as part of the graduation requirements.

In thinking about what I wanted to write, I knew I wanted to write about something advancing gay rights.

As a twenty-one- or twenty-two-year-old, I realized that who you are is profoundly shaped by the choices your society gives you. Not only the choices in terms of law and

In 2000, Evan represented gay Scoutmaster James Dale before the US Supreme Court in a case that ultimately upheld the Boy Scouts' right to exclude homosexuals.

opportunity, but even the language that your society gives you. And then I asked myself, "Why is there this stigma against people like me?" And I concluded, "It's because of who we love." And then I asked myself, "What is the primary framework, the primary structure, the primary institutionalization, the primary language of love in our society?" It's marriage.

I thought if we could claim that language of marriage, as well as that legal freedom, it would serve as this engine of transformation that would advance everything else. On that basis, I decided I was going to write my third-year paper on why gay people should have the freedom to marry and why we should fight for the freedom to marry.

THE DAY THE EARTH MOVED

After law school, I moved to New York. I began work as a prosecutor. By night, I was volunteering at Lambda Legal, pro bono, writing briefs on yellow legal pads in my

un-air-conditioned apartment. This was a time of terrible challenge and oppression. We were reeling from the AIDS epidemic and, at the same time, confronting the Reagan administration and its outright hostility to gay people.

During that time, I was also putting forward my ideas about how, despite all this terrible stuff coming at us, we ought to have an affirmative strategy. And marriage, to me, was the central element—a strategy for changing hearts and minds and lifting us beyond these immediate challenges.

There were two different sets of resistance to the idea of marriage. One was basically ideological. Many people thought marriage was the wrong goal, the wrong philosophy. Marriage was a bad thing to fight for. Other people didn't necessarily agree with that but simply thought that with this onslaught of AIDS and Reagan and discrimination and Jerry Falwell and the so-called religious right and so on, that fighting for marriage now was premature, dangerous, risky, and so on.

Evan with Vice President Joe Biden in 2009

During that period, a local activist in Hawai'i had begun pulling together a group of couples, saying, "Let's bring a challenge here in Hawai'i." They had heard that there was this guy in the national movement who actually believes we should be fighting for marriage. So they came to me. I in turn brought the proposed case to my colleagues at Lambda, which absolutely refused to take the case.

We fought very hard about this, very intensely. It sometimes felt really personal and ugly. In the end, I was denied permission to take the case. What I was allowed to do was to help them from behind the scenes—which turned out to be the luckiest decision of the

'80s, because what it meant was that the couples, instead of getting a lawyer from Lambda Legal, "outside agitators," they went local and they found this nongay lawyer named Dan Foley. And Dan agreed to take the case, not because he actually thought they were going to win, but because he felt as a nongay man, who was he to tell them they can't have what he has in his life, a wonderful marriage? So he said, "All right, I'll do it."

Dan and I completely bonded. It would be years before we actually physically met. Our work was all by phone and by fax. There was no internet and so on. But we saw strategy and politics and the bigger picture very much the same way. Early on, we agreed that

Evan with his marriage equality map in 2015

he would be the lead, the primary person navigating Hawai'i politics, trying to block attacks in the legislature, trying to set up a government commission to make a report that would buttress our case, standing in front of the judges, and so on, with all his savvy and Hawai'i credibility. And then my job was to think about, "What are the implications nationally? How do we leverage this for the movement? How do we prepare the rest of the country for what was going to happen?"

May 5th, 1993, was the day the earth moved—the day that the Hawai'i Supreme Court, unlike all the other courts that had previously heard this question, said that we were entitled to our day in court. They weren't going to say we should have the freedom to marry. But they did say that denying the freedom to marry is indeed discrimination, and unless the government can show a sufficient reason for that denial, it needs to stop.

That epic ruling, May 5th, 1993, changed everything.

Are we in an immensely better place because of the work we did and the progress we made and the transformation we achieved through winning the freedom to marry? There's no doubt about it. This is shown not only through just the obvious historical momentum and the more than one million gay people who have gotten legally married, and the inspiration it's given to battles around the world where we now have 1.1 billion people living in a freedom-to-marry country, but it can also be seen in the report of the *Journal of the American Medical Association of Pediatrics* that studied where we had won the freedom to marry, and reported that where we had won marriage, the rate of teen suicide has fallen by 14 percent. Now why is that? It's not because those teens are getting married—they're teens. It's because the message and the dignity and the hope and the freedom and the dream and the affirmation that's being sent to young people lifts them up and encourages them to go forward.

Apart from the actual victory he won in the realm of marriage equality, what is undeniably inspiring about Evan is the steely, tireless commitment he used to accomplish it. Whatever quest we embrace as individuals and a community, let us all be Evans in the devotion we bring to the fray.

LORAINE HUTCHINS

AUTHOR, PROFESSOR, BISEXUAL ACTIVIST

WASHINGTON, DC

Loraine Hutchins was born in 1948 in Washington, DC. Growing up during the 1960s and getting involved in both the gay rights and women's movements, she realized that she herself was bisexual, which made her persona non grata in the two communities she cared most about. Thus began a lifelong, uphill battle to alter this reality. Loraine co-founded BiNet USA to spread bisexual awareness, share resources, and build community, ultimately serving on the group's board of directors. She also spearheaded the founding of a direct-action group called the Alliance of Multicultural Bisexuals (AMBi). In 1993, she led BiNet's media campaign for the March on Washington for Lesbian, Gay, and Bi Equal Rights and Liberation, and in 1998 she became the first bisexual grand marshal for the Washington, DC, Pride Parade.

In 1991, Loraine coedited *Bi Any Other Name: Bisexual People Speak Out* with fellow OUTWORDS interviewee Lani Ka'ahumanu (p. 207). In 2011, she coedited her second anthology, *Sexuality, Religion and the Sacred: Bisexual, Pansexual and Polysexual Perspectives*. Loraine's efforts have been recognized by the Bilerico Project, the National LGBTQ Task Force, and the Rainbow History Project of Washington, DC.

I don't remember the first time I heard the word "bisexual." I know that I was in the women's movement, and I became attracted to women that I was working with and organizing with. I know that some of these women were lesbian, and some were heterosexual and bi. The first time I made love with a woman, we were competing over a man and seeing which of us could get him in bed first, and we kind of decided to take him to bed together so we wouldn't have to fight that out. I realized that I not only enjoyed being in bed with her and him, but that I would also enjoy being in bed with her if he wasn't around. That makes me bi, I think.

We had a magazine for many years called *Anything That Moves*, and we did it purposely as a conversation opener to raise the question, "Are bisexuals attracted to 'anything that moves'?" Well, no. And what's wrong with it if we are?

I don't think that the kind of sex or the amount of sex I have says anything about my worth as a person. I tell my students,

Photo of Loraine by Douglas William Neal, for the National Coming Out Day Photo Project, 1992

have no sense of discrimination. Thirty years later, I am tired of fighting the same fights. It breaks my heart to see young people having to fight those fights that I thought we had fought and won, and we haven't won. It'll take many generations.

The fights are so hard to win because heterosexuals and gay people alike are both invested in denying the middle ground. Heterosexual people mostly want to think that they're completely heterosexual, and gay people a lot of time would like it to be a simple world of "We're just the opposite of you," rather than seeing that the spectrum of human sexuality is amazingly diverse.

As long as we have a power-imbalanced world with male supremacy, white supremacy, and rich people having a lot more power over poor people's very lives, I don't think we're going to make it safe for people to be bi or any kind of sexual minority or diversity, because there's just too many power imbalances that benefit from pitting people against each other and denying complexity.

That's why I became a bisexual activist, and it's why I worked to help found BiNet USA nationally, to coedit *Bi Any Other Name: Bisexual People Speak Out* in 1991, that just got re-released last year as a twenty-fifth anniversary edition. It's why I worked with other people to start AMBi, the Alliance of Multicultural Bisexuals in DC.

One of the things that we get criticized for is, "You don't have a bi national organization and office in DC." Why would we create another bureaucracy, when bi peo-

you can have a lot of sex and know nothing about it. You can have no sex and be a virgin and be very wise about sexuality. Holding the contradictions in dynamic play is how I reconcile it.

INTEGRATION

I don't have any trouble being out as a bisexual activist, and I've certainly helped put the B in LGBT and helped create the LGBT movement politically. Over the years, there's a lot about how bisexuals are over-sexualized and stigmatized as being more sexual than we are, the thought that because we're attracted to more than one gender, that that means we

Loraine in 1986, dressed up as "Wonder Woman With a Hard-On" (note the dildo in her tights), about to become the first out bi participant in the Washington DC Pride march

ple are everywhere in every group? Out bi people are integrated with other social justice groups around sexual liberation, and rights of women, and rights of people of color, and health and healing. I don't want to create a separatist bi movement. Never have.

MORE GENEROUS AND OPEN

Young people give me hope. There are research studies now showing that the majority of teenagers and young adults in the United Kingdom and the United States no longer identify as heterosexual.

That's huge. That's historic. Will that sustain under a more right-wing dictatorship or political system that may or may not be in our future? I don't know, but I know the reality is underneath.

Over the past three to five years, I've noticed a relaxation and a shift in my classrooms, with people being less homophobic. Not everybody, but people in general being more generous and open. I'm not talking only about people from suburban Maryland,

who grew up here. My classroom has people from Ethiopia and Senegal and Malaysia and Ecuador, all in the same classroom.

I'm not saying that there's not a lot of resistance and fear and misunderstanding and homophobia and fear of women's power. There certainly is, and I feel it's changing. I feel that people's understanding and generous spirit about sexual diversity is growing, and that gives me hope.

If I didn't go to class and teach, I would be somewhere hiding under the blankets, wailing, depressed. My students, the eighteen-year-olds especially, give me hope.

PAT HUSSAIN

ACTIVIST, CO-FOUNDER OF SOUTHERNERS ON NEW GROUND (SONG)
ATLANTA, GEORGIA

Pat Hussain was born in Atlanta, Georgia, in 1950. After twice marrying men, she came out as a lesbian in her late twenties. A few years later, she met Cherry, a fellow Toys "R" Us employee. The two became partners, jointly raising Cherry's two kids.

Over a lifetime of activism, Pat stuffed envelopes for the NAACP, cofounded the Atlanta chapter of GLAAD, helped the Gay and Lesbian Task Force prepare for the 1993 March on Washington, and was grand marshal of the first Pride parade in Knoxville, Tennessee. At the 1993 National LGBTQ Task Force conference, Pat joined five other women to found Southerners on New Ground (SONG).

In recent years, due to ongoing PTSD and clinical depression, Pat has had to step back from active organizing. On the upside, she and Cherry are now grandparents and recently celebrated their thirty-year anniversary together.

I was a queer kid and I didn't know it. I was a little pale, and that could be a problem. They skipped me a grade. A year means a whole lot. So I lived in the library because I didn't really fit in with my schoolmates.

In 1963, there was going to be a sit-in at a Krispy Kreme Doughnut, which was on the corner of what was then Lee Street and Gordon Road. I heard about it from some friends at school. I asked my parents could I go, and they said no. And then I went.

We took over the lunch counter, and the police were already there. And this man came in and bought a cup of coffee and poured it down a girl's back, and everything went quiet and I turned red and I started shaking. I wanted to jump on him and bite a hole in his throat, I was so incredibly angry. But I knew that if I lashed out, everyone would go to jail and potentially be beaten also. I got up and I walked out, and I walked down the street feeling like an absolute failure. I was too weak for nonviolence, and I was so ashamed of myself for not knowing how that was going to end and not being there and not participating. And I moved as far back as I could from organizing, from trying to be involved. I'd stuff envelopes or answer phones or do something like that. I knew that I was a danger going into the street because of my temperament, and I was very ashamed of that.

BLUE FORD VAN

Growing up, I never felt anything for a man. When my girlfriends were in tears over some guy, I'd say, "Get another one, it's a lot of them out there. What is the problem?"

When I was twenty or so, I talked to my brother. I told him I thought maybe I'm gay; I don't feel this love, this longing, this intimacy for men. His wife, my sister-in-law, asked me what was I going to do, and I said, "Well, I think I'm going to go to a gay bar and see about meeting some women and seeing what I find." I went to a gay bar called Numbers, a twenty-four-hour bar.

I got out of my car and went to go in the bar, and I started sweating and I started shaking. I felt nauseous. I ended up sitting outside on the curb, shaking; my legs had just given out. I did that dance for a couple of hours every Friday and Saturday night for maybe six months and never made it inside.

One night my sister-in-law asked, "Did you meet anybody?" I said, "No, not tonight." She got her keys and a purse, and she said, "Come on, we're going." Took my hand and we walked in the bar. We got a drink. She said, "Are you okay now?" And I said, "Yes." And she left.

There was a woman there. We were dancing on the floor, and she whispered in my ear that she wanted me. I knew exactly what she meant. I did hesitate. Finally I said, "My van is outside," and she said, "Well, let's go."

My van was a blue Econoline 150 Ford van. Once we were in the back of that van, I didn't need anything else to cross my mind. I understood all at once why my girlfriends were crying about these boys, that there could be something that you could feel so deeply in here that you didn't know existed. It's attached, it's with this person, and I was really clear in that moment: "Oh yeah, Pat."

SONG

When Southerners on New Ground began, it was a convergence at the Creating Change Conference by the National Gay Lesbian Task Force, and it was held for the first time in the South. There were activists who were saying that the queer struggle for freedom was the same as blackness—with no context to understand that I never had to come out to my parents over the dinner table. They knew I was a black child. And that those of us who were women and people of color didn't have the opportunity to hide.

And then six of us—Pam McMichael, Joan Garner, Mandy Carter, Mab Segrest, Suzanne Pharr, and myself—came together as southern organizers, and we're talking about a way, rather than subdividing, rather than choosing different areas, that I would bring my whole self to an issue, not subdivide. And that is the issue. A different way of organizing. We didn't want to engage in random acts of senseless diversity. We wanted to be deliberate, intentional, and to break up narratives.

SONG exists in part because, growing up, when I was doing my envelope stuffing and all that work, if I went to NAACP, we were working on issues of race. If I went to NOW, we were working on issues for women. It was rare that I'd find anything that was about economic justice.

Even in the context of Dr. King, who was killed in Memphis, you almost never hear that he was there because of a sanitation workers' strike, which came about after two sanitation workers climbed into the back of their truck, taking a nap or escaping the rain, or maybe both, and the truck activated and they were crushed and killed. But that's not talked about because it's economic.

When I walk through a door, I bring my race, I bring my ovaries, I bring whatever is in my wallet, and the love of my wife, Cherry, all with me. At SONG, we're seeing how we can organize and hone a justice search that's about not leaving our folk out and not having to check parts of ourselves at the door. And being fabulously sexy while we're doing it.

SONG's office is located in Atlanta's West End, where Pat grew up. This is where Pat wanted her OUTWORDS interview to take place; for this neighborhood and this mission are home to her.

ERIC JULBER

EARLY ALLY FOR LGBTQ RIGHTS

CARMEL, CALIFORNIA

Eric Julber was born in 1925 in New York City, but his family soon moved to Southern California. After graduating from Hollywood High School and Loyola University Law School, Eric embarked on a long career as a lawyer.

In 1953, Eric was put in touch with the publishers of *ONE* magazine, one of America's earliest gay rights publications. *ONE* considered itself a "serious" magazine, eschewing erotic photos and sex ads in favor of printed content about gay people's lives, work, and aspirations. (One issue even discussed the topic of "homosexual marriage.") But in August 1953, Los Angeles postmaster Otto Olesen declared *ONE* obscene and refused to deliver it. Eric heard about the case, offered to take it pro bono, filed a federal lawsuit, and pursued justice all the way to the Supreme Court. In 1958, *ONE* emerged victorious. "For the first time in American publishing history," the next issue declared, "a decision binding on every court now stands . . . affirming in effect that it is in no way proper to describe a love affair between two homosexuals as constitut(ing) obscenity."

ONE v. Olesen was Eric's only trip to the US Supreme Court.

After college, I tried to get a newspaper job because I had worked on the school newspapers and so on. But there weren't any jobs, so I went to law school. I thought at that time that I would like to practice civil liberties law—freedom of the press and freedom of speech and so on—which was a very noble ambition, but there weren't any jobs doing that, so I got what work I could find working for other lawyers. But I circulated among all the people that I knew that if anybody knew of a civil liberties case, I'd like to take it. And amazingly enough, one came along right off the bat.

These people were the publishers of a little magazine, eight or ten pages, called *ONE*. It was subtitled *The Homosexual Magazine*, which was very daring in those days. And the postmaster general in Los Angeles at that time, a man named Otto K. Olesen, was refusing to transmit their magazine through the mail. He said it was obscene, though I looked at the magazine and there wasn't anything sexy about it.

So these people needed a lawyer to sue Otto K. Olesen and try to get the federal court to order him to transmit this through the mail on grounds of freedom of speech.

So that's how it started. I filed a case. It was called *ONE v. Olesen*.

My argument was, they have a right to discuss their problems and their aspirations like anybody else does. But the district court and the first court of appeal that we went to disagreed. The court of appeal, the judge there found a phrase in one of the articles that appeared there, a humorous poem, about someone who got into trouble with the law. The line was, "His ins and outs with various Scouts had created a mild sensation." The judge pointed that out as an obscene reference to homosexual conduct.

I couldn't see it, having no experience with the subject, really. But I was sure that if we ever got to the US Supreme Court, where the judges would be more sophisticated, we would win because it was such an obvious free-speech situation.

In those days, in order to file a case with the Supreme Court, you had to personally go back to Washington and enter the bar of the Supreme Court, and then you could file a case. So I went through all that.

In my luggage, I carried with me about twenty copies of *ONE* magazine. And when I got to Washington, I went to the Supreme Court building and asked to see the law clerk for the most liberal justice on the Court, William O. Douglas. Law clerks are very influential on the judges that they work for. So it's very important to get them on your side.

A young man came out, and I said, "Hello. This is a little outside of the formal law, but I've filed this case involving this magazine that they

claim is obscene, and I thought I'd bring all these extra copies for you. If you're interested, you may want to show them to other law clerks here." So I got sort of a little advance push on the case by doing that. And there's nothing wrong with that. You're just bringing an exhibit, as it's called in law. That was pretty clever, if I do say so now.

In my case, I asked the Supreme Court to order the lower court to order Otto K. Olesen to transmit this magazine through the mail. To my great amazement, about three or four months passed and all of a sudden in the mail I got a notice that the Supreme Court was ordering Mr. Olesen to transmit the magazine through the mail, which was a total victory. It's what we had started out to do. So it was a big surprise.

I think the *ONE* case was the first crack in the iron curtain. There really was an iron curtain until that time over anything to do with homosexuality. And this was the first crack in the curtain, and it's gone on, multiplied since then. We're in a much different era now.

BRADLEY PICKLESIMER

DESIGNER, DRAG QUEEN

MEALLY, KENTUCKY

> Bradley Picklesimer was born in 1958 in Lexington, Kentucky. His dad owned a motel/cocktail lounge, a mobile home park, and a set of Tennessee walking horses. From early on, Bradley enjoyed dressing up in elegant and/or flashy outfits. By seventh grade, he was out exploring Lexington's underground gay scene. At twenty, he opened his first club, which featured shows from art to drag to rock. He took a turn as lead singer in a punk band but soon transitioned to drag, appearing at his own and others' bars and clubs and performing for charity fundraisers.
>
> In 1991, Bradley got sober and moved to California intending to record music and perform cabaret; but when he volunteered his design skills for an AIDS fundraiser, a local designer grabbed him and put him to work. Before long, Bradley was running his own company, with A-list clients from Elton to Barbra to Ellen. On the side, he designed sets and did makeup for porn flicks.
>
> In 2016, Bradley purchased forty acres in Meally, Kentucky, and moved home. He still enjoys producing parties and events and—of course—dressing in drag.

My full name is Bradley Harrison Picklesimer. Is that not the most awesome name ever? Now picture being a little boy in first grade when they get you up in front of the class and everyone has to say their name, and you say your full name. And the whole classroom just burst out laughing. It was fabulous. And people, when I was young, used to say, "Honey, you've gotta change that name." I'm like, "Are you kidding me? This is incredible!"

Honestly, that's why I never really had a drag name. People would come up with ideas and stuff, and it ended up just being Miss Bradley. Because honey, there isn't anything better than real.

WE NEED TO TALK TO YOU ABOUT BRADLEY

When I was growing up, my dad would walk my youngest sister, Elizabeth, and me across Winchester Road on Sundays to go to Trinity Baptist Church. And then we would walk the rest of the way. I had a camel hair suit and my little shoes. My little sister had her full dress, patent leather purse, patent

Bradley performing at Club Au Go Go in Lexington, KY

who wouldn't go to the woods and smoke pot with me anymore.

Because of that bunch of clothes thrown out in the street, I started wearing women's clothes. I became acutely aware of the power of drag before I even knew what I was doing or what was happening. It was very powerful. A very powerful medium. You could stop entire groups of people. I walked into seventh grade with my David Bowie haircut, my eyebrows shaved, a pair of platforms, bell-bottoms, and a Nik-Nik shirt from Chess King. People in the hallways just stopped and went to each side, and I just walked through.

It was very hard in those days, dressing up. Carloads of rednecks or country people would just stop and go, "Fucking faggot!" You either stood your ground or ran. I

leather shoes. And then the phone would ring, and it would be the church. They were like, "Mr. Picklesimer, we need to talk to you about Bradley." And he's like, "What?" "Well, he has Elizabeth's purse again, and he won't let go of it."

Another time, a woman's possessions had been put into the street, and my little sister came home and said, "Let's go down there. It's all in the garbage." Well, they were incredible 1940s' gowns with padded shoulders and these big, giant coats with fur cuffs. Just unbelievable stuff. So I got as much stuff as I could and started dressing up and wearing things to parties after school, and then word got out. Because the next day at school, all of a sudden, there were people

Bradley and his sister, Elizabeth, on their way to church

Bradley with drag icon Chi Chi LaRue in Cannes, France

wasn't about to run. I'm not saying that I won every fight, because I didn't. But I won a lot of them.

When I arrived in LA, I probably had about $120. And I was happy. I was free. I had no keys, no responsibility.

There was a wonderful organization there called APLA, AIDS Project Los Angeles. And they used to have these big fundraisers. I volunteered because I wanted to help out, and I ended up doing flowers at a big event for them, and I happened to be standing next to, unbeknownst to me, one of the biggest designers in the business. And we were just making fun and cutting up and laughing about the celebrities and stuff. He was like, "God, you're really fast." I was like, "Yeah, so are you, Papaw." You know, we're laughing. And he was like, "Well, you should come and work for me."

I end up working with him, and he sent me to all over the world, to Paris and Jamaica and all these places to do these events. I was doing these amazing parties and making really good money, and then I decided to go out on my own. I was still clean and sober. I have been ever since. I got involved with some really good people out there, and word of mouth went from one to the next to the next, and I ended up doing all the fabric for Barbra Streisand's wedding. I ended up doing Elton John's 2005 Oscar party. I did Ellen DeGeneres's fiftieth birthday party at Warner Brothers. I did many parties for Sharon and Ozzy Osbourne, and three parties for Tim Burton. For a little boy from Kentucky, there were some amazing moments where I literally had to pinch myself. Elton John introduced me to Elizabeth Taylor at his party. That's unbelievable. From where I came from. So I'm a very fortunate girl to live off of my art and to be able to have had such an amazing life that I have lived in this world.

My very good friend Chi Chi LaRue, who is a porn director, hired me. I ended up being in the porn industry for about twenty years off and on. I did set design and I did makeup and was in some nonsexual roles in the movies. Did gay porn, tranny porn, straight porn, all kinds of porn. That was also a big childhood dream.

Finally, I had been in LA for twenty-five years. Every day in Los Angeles, the concessions that you make to live there mount up before you even realize. Every thirty days, I needed X amount of money. And honey, that wasn't a new pair of eyelashes or a party dress. That was the bare basics. When one thing would go wrong, you could see quickly how someone could actually end up on the streets.

I had bought a piece of family property in eastern Kentucky in 2000. I know I don't look like it, but I'm a gardener. And I love to garden. I wanted something real. I wanted peace. I wanted some tranquility. I wanted some quiet. I knew I would never grow old in LA. I knew that I wanted to be the crazy old queen in a pair of frilly panties and a pair of overalls with a ZZ Top beard, on my porch with a loaded shotgun.

I have forty acres. I have incredible mountains. The Appalachian mountains are the oldest mountain range in the world. They're older than the Himalayas. I consider them a sacred, mystical, magical place. I feel so fortunate to have escaped LA and to be able to have my little farm for this moment in time.

Bradley with RuPaul

SPIRIT

TROY PERRY

FOUNDER OF THE METROPOLITAN COMMUNITY CHURCH

LOS ANGELES, CALIFORNIA

Rev. Troy Perry was born in 1940 in Tallahassee, Florida, the first of five sons. When Troy was twelve, his dad died and his mother married an abusive alcoholic. Troy ran away from home, ending up with his Pentecostal aunt and uncle in Georgia. He started preaching at thirteen, and by fifteen he was a licensed Southern Baptist preacher. He came out as gay to his pastor, whose solution was for him to marry the pastor's daughter. (You can't make this stuff up.) Two kids soon followed. Troy moved his family to Southern California, but he couldn't escape his attraction to men. His marriage failed, and he lost his job. After a failed suicide attempt, Troy had a simple, stunning revelation: God loved him as he was.

In October 1968, Troy convened the first meeting of the Metropolitan Community Church in his apartment's living room. Today, the MCC has 222 congregations in thirty-five countries around the globe. Presidents Carter, Clinton, and Obama have invited Troy to speak at the White House. Troy's autobiography is called *The Lord Is My Shepherd and He Knows I'm Gay*.

As a young kid, there was something about church that excited me. I knew somehow I was going to be in the ministry. Don't ask me how. But I did. It was just there in my head. I couldn't get away from it.

My aunt Bessie had a little church. She said, "Troy, I feel like God has called you to preach. What do you feel?" I was thirteen by this time, and I shook my head yes, I felt like I was called to minister. She said, "I want you to come to my church and preach next week." So at thirteen years old, I preached my first sermon in the Pentecostal Church. At fifteen, I'm licensed to preach in the South-ern Baptist Church. At sixteen, I'm conducting revivals. But I'm still wrestling with my feelings. I knew I loved men. I knew that I was different. But I thought I was the only one in the world.

At age eighteen, I finally go to my pastor and tell him. He looked at me and said, "My Lord, all you do is you just marry a good woman."

So I married his daughter. Both of us at age eighteen. I crawled into bed as a virgin. I'd never gone to bed with a woman in my life. I tried my best for three years. But I was still wrestling with trying to go to bed with

just my wife. You know, it catches up with you if you're gay.

Finally, we moved to California, my wife and I and our two kids. One day I walked into a bookstore in Santa Ana, California, and for the first time in my life I saw *Physique* magazine. Then, as I looked around, I saw a little magazine called *ONE*. [See Eric Julber profile, p. 126.] I picked it up and I couldn't believe it. It used the word "homosexual" in it. When I read that magazine, I knew without a shadow of doubt they were talking about me.

Ultimately, I resigned from my church. My wife and I separated. I didn't know it would be seventeen years before I saw my kids. There is a price to be paid when you come from a church background and you come out of the closet.

THE JOY OF MY SALVATION

At the age of twenty-five, I received my draft notice from the draft board in Mobile, Alabama. They said, "Uncle Sam needs you." I spent two years in the military. Served with distinction in Vietnam. When I got back home, there was something that ate me alive.

It was the thing around church. I knew I was dying and going to hell. There was no changing that.

A few months later, I fell deeply, madly in love. He was a cowboy from Wyoming who was also a school teacher. Six of the best and worst months of my life, I always describe it. One day he said to me, I just can't live with you. He walked out of my life, and two weeks later I climbed into a bathtub, cut both of my wrists, and just hoped I would die.

My roommate found me and rushed me to County General Hospital. A woman came in. She might have been a nurse; I never found out for sure. She said, "My God, I don't know why you've done this, but this is crazy. You're too young for this." I was twenty-seven years old. She said, "Isn't there somebody you can talk to? Can't you just look up?" I broke down, just sobbing.

The next morning, at home alone, I lay there thinking about everything that had happened. Suddenly, I experienced a joy, what we Christians sometimes call "the joy of my salvation." I said, "Wait a minute. This can't be you, God. This can't be you. The church has taught me you hate me. This can't be you."

Then I heard what we Christians call "that still, small voice." God spoke to me and said, "Troy, don't tell me what I can and can't do. I love you. I don't have stepsons and daughters."

At that moment, I knew beyond the shadow of a doubt that I could be a Christian and I could be gay. Over time, I became convinced that if God loves me, then God has to love homosexuals too. If God loves me, then God loves everybody.

THE PATCH

After I tried to commit suicide, I started dating a young man named Tony Valdez. We heard about a gay bar called The Patch in a part of Los Angeles called Wilmington, down by the docks. Tony and I went down there. The bar owner, Lee Glaze, told us, "As you know, it's against the law for two men or two women to dance together. You can dance next to each other, as long as you don't touch."

The problem was, The Patch had plain-clothes cops in there. At one point, a friend of Lee's named Bill Cummings slapped Tony on the rump. The cops came right over. They pulled out their badges and said to Bill and Tony, "Come outside with me." They arrested them for lascivious conduct.

That's when Lee Glaze basically got fed up, and he rallied us to march up to the police station to get Bill and Tony released. We bought flowers on the way. Lee marches us in and says, "We're here to bail our sisters out of jail." The cop looked at him real strange and said, "What's your sister's name?" He said, "Bill Hastings and Tony Valdez." Next thing we know, we've got all these cops around us. We would not go away. We stood there. It took us four hours to get them out of jail. But we waited. We got them bailed out of jail.

This is what sparked my church. Two months later, I took out an ad in this gay little newspaper called *The Advocate*. Gave my home address in Huntington Park with a photograph of me. My roommate had a heart attack. "My God, you've taken out an ad in a homosexual newspaper, giving our home address? Are you crazy? The police are going to be here, scooping them up in nets."

The first service was October 6, 1968. Twelve people showed up in the living room of my home. We went from there to where we have churches in thirty-five countries now. I have continued to carry the Good News for almost fifty years now to all the world.

A man with a crackling smile and dancing blue eyes, Troy Perry lives today with his husband, Phil, in the Silver Lake neighborhood of Los Angeles.

SHARON DAY

INDIGENOUS PEOPLE'S ACTIVIST, WATER-WALKER

MINNEAPOLIS, MINNESOTA

> Sharon Day was born in 1951 in northern Minnesota. Her parents were enrolled members of the Bois Forte Band of Ojibwe.
>
> After a fractured childhood, Sharon ended up in recovery for alcoholism at the age of twenty-one, which led her to study chemical dependency and administration at the University of Minnesota. When her brother Michael tested positive for HIV in 1987, Sharon discovered the total lack of HIV education or prevention for Native Americans. In response, Sharon helped create what became the Indigenous Peoples Task Force (IPTF), serving as the group's executive director since 1990. In addition, Sharon is a water-walker, artist, musician, and writer. She edited the anthology *Sing! Whisper! Shout! Pray! Feminist Visions for a Just World*.
>
> Sharon has been honored with numerous awards, including the Red Ribbon Award from the National Native American AIDS Prevention Resource and the Alston/Bannerman Fellowship to honor and support longtime activists of color. In 1988, the governor of Minnesota, along with the mayors of Minneapolis and Saint Paul, proclaimed an entire day in Sharon's honor.

I was born in Little Fork, in northern Minnesota. Both of my parents are enrolled members of the Bois Forte Band of Ojibwe, which is located six miles south of International Falls. My Ojibwe name is Nagamoo Mahingen, Singing Wolf.

I have thirteen siblings. Two of us are gay. My younger brother, he's four years younger than me. He always knew. It wasn't quite so clear to me.

When my parents went to town, they would be gone for maybe six hours. While they were gone, me and my brother, we would dress up in our parents' clothes. I would wear my dad's suit and tie and be Elvis, and he would be Diana Ross. He wore my mom's clothes. My little sisters would all be the Supremes.

I didn't really figure things out until I was in my late twenties. When I did come out, it was as a political act. I was working for the state of Minnesota and was involved in politics and had been a delegate to the National Women's Conference in Houston. I think it was around 1977. I met a number of lesbians then, and I managed the softball team at a halfway house that I worked at. One day I looked around, and half of the team were dykes, and I was like, "How did that happen?"

I called up my older brother and asked him, "What was the Ojibwe word for lesbian?" He said, "I'll call you back." He called me back in about half an hour, and he said it was *Dikanidikwe*, which translates into "a special kind of woman."

I thought about it. I asked myself, "Could that be me?" It really was a very inward journey. When I did make the decision to come out, I had a party. I was going to live my life in solidarity with my lesbian sisters.

LOVE IS THE HEALING GRACE

In 1988, my brother told me he had AIDS. I remember crying because, back then, if you had an AIDS diagnosis, you were dying. That's all there was to it.

At the time, I was working for the state's chemical dependency program. A lesbian woman, Carole LaFavor, came to me around that same time and said, "I have AIDS. What are you going to do about it?" I discovered there were no services, no prevention services, let alone any direct services like housing or case management, for Native Americans.

So I and three other people created the Minnesota American Indian Needs Task Force, which later became the Indigenous Peoples Task Force. I took a two-year leave of absence from my job to get it going. I just never went back.

At the start, we created a housing complex for people living with AIDS. In 1990, I created a youth theater program. We knew nothing about theater. We just knew that storytelling was an important part of our culture and was an important way to get the message to youth, especially about HIV prevention.

We had to go back and think, what is healthy sexuality in our community? How can we grieve our losses in a way that's part of our culture, as opposed to Kübler-Ross or anybody else? We had to do all this research. There are many spiritual elders in the community who worked with us and helped us along that path. We have curricula for our garden program, for the theater project, and for our women's programs. We tried to incorporate our cultural teachings into them. Most of our work has been experiential. We've learned as we go.

Our youth theater program, I think, really exemplifies our experiential approach. We don't spend a lot of time talking to the youth about the problems in the neighborhood. They see it every day. What we do is we help them to become people who are the solutions to the problems. In our early years, I traveled to twenty-seven states with these kids. We did performances everywhere.

Carole LaFavor died two years ago, but not from HIV complications. My brother is still alive and healthy. They both were doctored by Native medicine people. Never took any HIV drugs. That's the miracle that some people have been able to be blessed with.

THINK INDIGENOUSLY

We have seven teachings among the Ojibwe: to be loving, to be kind, to be truthful, and to be humble and courageous and generous and respectful. If we're not practicing those teachings, we're practicing the opposite.

If there's anything that I wish to live as a legacy here, it will be that the Indigenous Peoples Task Force is a cultural agency. I tell my staff, if we want to be like everybody else, if we want to be the Minnesota AIDS Project and do things the way they do them, there's really no need for our existence. I tell them, think indigenously. Our spirituality, those seven teachings, they need to be at the core of what we're doing. They need to be at the center because at that center, love is the healing grace.

I identify first of all as an Ojibwe woman. Secondly, when I die, I would like it to say on my marker, "She was a good old dyke."

OUTWORDS interviewed Sharon during a heavy snowstorm with high winds. At times, the interview had to pause for the sound of tree branches striking the window—a beautiful contrast and complement to Sharon's calm presence and her testimony about the healing power of love.

RICHARD ZALDIVAR

FOUNDER OF THE WALL LAS MEMORIAS PROJECT

LOS ANGELES, CALIFORNIA

Richard Zaldivar was born in Los Angeles in 1952. Richard's family was Catholic, and early on Richard developed a deep relationship with God that evolved as Richard changed and grew.

From a young age, Richard felt drawn to the sometimes-dirty work of politics. He served as field deputy for Los Angeles councilman Art Snyder and community liaison for Los Angeles city attorney and future mayor James Hahn, while organizing youth and senior citizen support groups and coproducing a local radio talk show. At twenty-eight, Richard was chosen as one of the youngest appointees ever to the Platform Committee for the Democratic National Convention.

Through these professional successes, Richard was waging a personal battle with alcohol. After getting sober in 1989, Richard was ready for the biggest challenge of his life.

In 1993, Richard organized the first annual Noche de Las Memorias (Evening of Memories) for World AIDS Day. At the event, Richard shared his vision for an AIDS monument to memorialize those lost to AIDS and to provide a place of remembrance and healing for those still here. Ten years later, The Wall Las Memorias AIDS Monument became a reality—the first publicly funded AIDS monument in the United States and the foundation of a grassroots, culturally attuned HIV/AIDS service organization that is still growing and evolving today.

Richard's HIV/AIDS advocacy has been recognized in Los Angeles and beyond. In 1997, *Out* magazine named Richard one of the one hundred most influential gay or lesbian people in the United States, and in 2013 he received the LGBT Pride Recognition Award from the California State Legislature.

When I was twenty years old, I saw an injustice in the community. A year earlier, I had been president of a chapter of the Junior Knights of Columbus, a Catholic group for young people, right here in Northeast Los Angeles. I would organize drug awareness nights and community meetings. Nobody had trained me; I just did it. I invited elected officials, and one of the elected officials who actually responded was a German Irish politician who was a Republican serving on the Los Angeles City Council.

Richard presenting an award to the parents of Freddie Prinze at the Beverly Wilshire Hotel in 1978

His office responded to a lot of our concerns. Within that time frame, there was a lot of change in the political landscape. Hispanics were trying to gain more ground. There were several attempts to recall this politician, and the reality is it was all based on race. As much as I was and continue to support people in my community, I also thought that was racist, and I thought it was unfair to the democratic process.

I went and I volunteered my time, and we won a recall election, and he made me an assistant. I became a field deputy. I was there thirteen, fourteen years. I had a great job. I was a delegate for Ted Kennedy, worked on the Democratic Platform Committee with

some really incredible, powerful people at the time, so I was really active.

During those years, I was not out. It really became problematic. Although extremely successful, I also was an active alcoholic. At the same time, my best friend and former partner disclosed he was HIV-positive.

Something in me wanted to do something more for people like me. I knew what gay Latino men were going through, and I didn't want anybody else to go through that.

WALK FORWARD, FREE OF INTIMIDATION

In 1993, I was overseeing the city's summer youth employment program, where nonprofits would get jobs for disadvantaged young people. Many of them were very creative, and they painted some of the greatest murals on the east side of Los Angeles.

I thought Latinos didn't understand or accept the fact that HIV/AIDS was their issue. It was always "white gay men from the west side of town". I figured they needed to own the epidemic. What better way than to create an opportunity for artists to paint murals from the community, so that the community participates and develops their own idea of what HIV/AIDS is, and have a greater conversation about it?

The idea was to paint a large mural of the Virgin Mary somewhere on the east side of Los Angeles, and then have two hundred names of people who died from AIDS. I brought together a committee, and it included a few Catholic priests, and one of them said, "Richard, you don't need one wall. You need a monument, and you can do it, and the community deserves it." In 1993, on World AIDS Day, we founded the organization. Within months, there was an architectural rendering for the monument. I said, "Okay, I don't know how to do this, but we're going to do it."

We organized the community, which included faith folks, people from churches, politicians, union leaders, LGBTQ people, residents, Hispanic celebrities. One of the first organizations I went out to was a group called the Mothers of East LA. I knew the president of the group. I went with Ron Castillo, one of my board members at the time, to meet with their board. Ron was living with AIDS. We sat down and we gave them HIV 101. Ron talked about his situation as a person living with AIDS, and then I asked them for their support.

I'll never forget. We're meeting at a dining room table, and on one wall was a picture of the Virgin of Guadalupe. I saw all these women, and I thought, "I know I want to do this, but what happens if there's any rejection? How do I respond to that?" One of the older women kept on nodding her head as we were talking about this, and I said, "Oh my God, she's really going to shoot us down. She's probably getting really angry."

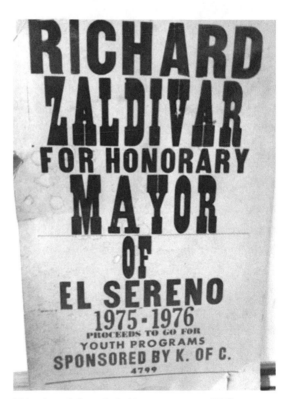

Richard was twice selected honorary mayor of El Sereno, the Los Angeles community where he grew up. In 1976, he spearheaded the construction of a flagpole to raise the American flag in the middle of El Sereno, in commemoration of the United States Bicentennial.

She was the first one to say, "I support this. I learned about HIV/AIDS because I watch *The Cristina Show* all the time."

The women voted unanimously, and with that I went to all the other churches and other institutions and said, "The Mothers of East LA support us on building an AIDS monument here on the east side of Los Angeles. Will you?" That worked. That worked so well. We had a few death threats. It was a painful time and a challenging time, but it was also a great time because it taught us how to walk through it very focused. Just walk forward free of intimidation, because we knew what we had to do.

CHANGING COMMUNITIES

The challenges that Latino men face, they're multilayered because we're talking about different subgroups of Latinos. You could be someone who's Mexican born in Mexico, or you can talk about first-generation or second-generation Mexican American, or you can talk about Central American. If you're Cuban or Puerto Rican, you may have a different attitude when it comes to sexuality. The same holds true when you deal with countries in South America, whether you're from Venezuela or Colombia, Argentina.

The role that machismo plays in Mexican culture is still very heavy. The perception that gay men are effeminate doesn't hold well with the father, even though the father is absent in the home. The tremendous pressure that mothers put on their children to have grandchildren. We've had men talk about those pressures.

There's difficulties for Latinos coming out of the closet because of proximity to their family. They don't move outside their state. They don't move outside their region. Other communities, it's easy for them to leave the family, go across the state, from one part of the country to the other, and all of a sudden be out of the closet. We don't do that as Hispanics. Gay men stay close to mom. They feel a responsibility to keep an eye on her and watch over her.

We become conflicted. It's a struggle. We ask ourselves, "Are we good enough? Are we the good son?"

How do we provide leadership skills to these men? They're not only dealing with sexuality but all of the other parts of their life that make them whole. Addressing where they live, addressing housing, getting active and engaged in systems that they feel that they can change, because that's part of whether men use condoms or PrEP. If you're using a condom or PrEP, you're an activist, because you're taking action, so we would like to be able to expand that interpretation of activism so that they change the communities in which they live. We're always constantly trying to figure out how do we support those men in their lives.

A PLACE AT THE TABLE

I think it's important to address the spirituality of our community, whether it be gay or bisexual, transgender or lesbian. Our job is to try to connect that, to fill that void by connecting the spirit or the higher power to the individual folks, and then help them develop that kind of relationship.

There are a lot of wounded Catholic LGBT Latinos. A lot of our conversation around that has been, "We can still be who we are, but how do we heal from those wounds of abandonment and rejection? At the same token, how do we become activists?"

I have to remind them of a question someone posed to me. "You're a gay activist, but yet you're a Catholic." I say, "Yes, and I go to church every Sunday with my partner, and we sit in the front row of the cathedral in front of a conservative archbishop." I tell them I'm also political because I know that when I abandon that seat, then I have no power.

I remind them there was a time when the Democratic Party banned a gay caucus. We didn't leave the Democratic Party. Or when the world banned homosexuality, we didn't leave the earth. We changed it. I think that our job is, if we really believe in our faith and we really believe that we deserve a place at the table, we don't leave the table. We change it.

Richard and his life partner, Joselito, live in downtown Los Angeles. Every chance they get, they slip off to Chavez Ravine, a couple of miles away, to watch their beloved Dodgers in action.

Richard oversees the installation of the five-ton steel arch that anchors The Wall/Las Memorias AIDS Monument in East Los Angeles.

SUSAN GRIFFIN

WRITER, ENVIRONMENTALIST

BERKELEY, CALIFORNIA

Susan Griffin was born in Los Angeles in 1943 and attended UC Berkeley during the 1960s, aligning herself with the free speech and civil rights movements. She ended up earning her bachelor's degree at San Francisco State University, returning to Berkeley to earn her master's. Along the way, Susan married, had a daughter, divorced, and came out as a lesbian.

Susan has published twenty-one books in nearly every genre. In 1975, she won an Emmy Award for a televised production of her play, *Voices*. She was a Pulitzer Prize finalist for her 1993 book, *A Chorus of Stones*, received two additional Pulitzer nominations, and has been honored by the Guggenheim and MacArthur Foundations.

Susan's 1978 book, *Woman and Nature*, connected society's denigration of women to a broader devaluation of the environment and helped inspire the ecofeminism movement. Susan's later works include *Wrestling with the Angel of Democracy: On Being an American Citizen* (2008). In 2011, she coedited *Transforming Terror*, a collection of essays from sixty-four countries that brings together Jewish, Christian, and Islamic perspectives on the effects of terrorist violence and strategies for responding to it.

In the summer of 1963, I lived in this fabulous building at Grant and Greenwich in North Beach [Editor's note: North Beach is a neighborhood in San Francisco. In the 1950s and '60s, it was the epicenter of the beatnik subculture. In 1964, the Condor Club, America's first topless bar, opened there.] The apartments were kind of run-down. The kitchen wallpaper was done with Chinese newspapers. But the kitchen had this back area that was almost completely unfinished. Almost like a deck, but enclosed. It looked out on this beautiful view of the city. It was sort of rough and unfinished but had these amazing features.

The building I lived in was once inhabited by various members of the Beat Generation. I think Allen Ginsberg lived there. Denise Levertov I know lived there. Lawrence Ferlinghetti was there. City Lights bookstore was wonderful, as it still is. There were coffeehouses, which didn't exist other places in the United States, but North Beach had them. Lots of them. It was just a great kind of place to seed yourself as an artist, to begin to develop as a writer and an artist.

I met my ex-husband through his mother. She was sponsoring a kids' drama program I was teaching in. She invited me to a New Year's party and I went, and I met her son John. He had been in Peru with the Peace Corps. He was also a poet and loved poetry. I was very attracted to him. I felt he was a soul companion. In fact, one of the ways that we first really connected was we both could recite lines from Gregory Corso's poem "Marriage." [Editor's note: Corso's poem expresses the author's disgust with the concept of marriage as a hopelessly middle class institution.] Then we ended up, of course, marrying.

North Beach, San Francisco, 1965

The first years of our marriage, I was supporting him. I was working at *Ramparts* magazine. Then I stopped and had a child. The women's movement was just getting started. I was much more conscious of women's issues. I was becoming aware of my attraction to women. All of that was going on. I left finally.

I didn't have a traditional coming out. It was a much more subtle process for me. I had a small child, and even though I respected my in-laws and I thought my ex-husband would be okay, I couldn't fully trust that, if I were out, I wouldn't lose custody.

That was a constant fear that one had. Sometimes women who came out as lesbians would win custody battles. But sometimes they would lose. In most cases, the complication was that a woman had left her husband and he wanted her back. He didn't want the children. He wasn't even concerned about the children. He wanted to get back at her. He wanted to force her to come back to him. He wanted control.

About two or three years after my divorce, it felt safer for me to come out. The movement for lesbian rights was stronger, and I felt safe that I could write as a lesbian.

A PRESS OF ONE'S OWN
Soon after I left my husband, I was caught up in this huge women's revolution. Part of that was we had our own poetry readings and our own presses. There was a press called Shameless Hussy Press. The publisher was Alta. Alta used just that one name. She was the publisher, editor, typesetter, and everything. Alta lived out in San Leandro, which is a suburb in

Susan, Alice Walker, and Whoopi Goldberg after being arrested in an apartheid protest in 1985.

the Bay Area. She lived in a tract house. It was absolutely typical suburban life, and here's this very radical woman living out there with a mimeograph machine in her garage.

These books were produced on the mimeograph and then folded up and stapled. If you had a book published by her, then you'd drive out there and work in her garage. The books didn't have spines, which is important because a lot of bookstores would not carry a book with no spine. I'll always honor Fred Cody, who owned Cody's Books in Berkeley. Fred accepted books without a spine.

Having presses like Shameless Hussy was extremely important. In those days, we didn't have the internet, so you couldn't go on social

media and post a rant or a little mini-essay. You couldn't have a website. These presses were our chief means of communication. Virginia Woolf talked about having a room of one's own, but she also talked about how only a woman who is her own publisher is really free to write what she wants. Virginia Woolf did that. She had the Hogarth Press. She could write this very experimental stuff and didn't have to worry about what an agent or a publisher thought. Because they tend to go by what is already selling.

Alta wrote in ordinary women's speech about ordinary women's lives. Writing about menstruation and sanitary napkins and having affairs with younger guys. Then she started being with women and writing about that. This is all stuff that other presses might've censored or just not published because they were afraid. Or were turned off by it.

We also had these huge readings. They were combination readings, social gatherings, parties. It wasn't unusual for there to be several hundred, sometimes a thousand people at these readings. There were several poems that became anthems of the movement. Judy Grahn had an epic poem called "A Woman Is Talking to Death." Everybody remembers when they first experienced that poem. It was like a ritual, like a ceremony to hear that poem read in a large group of women. It was an incredible, emotional experience.

THE SPIRIT/MATTER SPLIT

One of the highlights of my childhood was to go to a Girl Scout camp in the High Sierras.

In the Sierras, I learned to feel the presence of trees as beings, not as things. The idea that everything in nature had a soul, had a spirit, seemed self-evident just from my direct experience living there in the woods that way. I've never lost that feeling.

I love material life. I love taste, literally eating, I like to eat. I like beauty. I like being out in trees, and I like the feel of earth.

When I started writing *Woman in Nature*, something I noticed early on is the split between matter and spirit. The polemic our culture establishes between matter and spirit is really disastrous. It has disastrous results for all of us. It's leading now to the possible destruction of the earth as we know it.

Of course, the earth is not going to be destroyed. It's a planet. It's going to keep rolling around the sun. It's not going to disappear. But human life on earth will be destroyed. The beautiful earth that we love, that is our home, will be destroyed. Our capacity to deny that, to continue to destroy the earth and deny its demise, relies on this split between matter and spirit. There's some unconscious belief that our spirits will somehow survive the death of the earth. That kind of craziness comes out of a culture that makes a split between spirit and matter.

We're in a struggle. We're in a titanic struggle for the survival of the earth. The struggle to save the earth is not separate from the struggle for human rights. We often think of it as separate, but it isn't separate. One of the underpinnings of the prejudice against women is that women are associated with the earth. We give birth, we menstruate, we raise children, we clean up the dishes, we clean up the shit, we're in charge of the garbage. Therefore, we're of the earth. We're material. Then men can think of themselves as closer to the spirit, and in this category of spirit, they can escape the consequences of how we're living now and destroying the earth.

The illusion underneath that is that the male gender, by dominating women, can dominate the earth and, therefore, dominate mortality. When in fact the opposite is actually true. Mortality wins over everything in human life.

As we arrive at Susan's home in the Berkeley Hills, the material and spirit realms seem perfectly balanced: dense oak trees cradling the house on the outside, and on the inside, books everywhere.

JULIE NEMECEK

TRANSGENDER BAPTIST MINISTER

SPRING ARBOR, MICHIGAN

Julie Nemecek was born John Nemecek on March 28, 1951, in Chicago. The oldest of four children, John sensed early on that he was female, and he often prayed he would wake up as a girl.

John became an ordained Baptist minister, married, and had three sons. After pastoring three churches, he served as associate professor and assistant dean at a Christian university. In November 2003, John came out as transgender to his wife, Joanne. After much conversation and many tears, Joanne resolved to stay with her spouse, whatever path she chose. John transitioned to Julie and was quickly fired for conduct "not in keeping with biblical principles." After filing a federal discrimination complaint, Julie eventually settled with her former employer.

Like many gay, lesbian, transgender people, I thought getting married would make it all go away. It didn't, and it doesn't. I kept my true nature a secret from my wife, Joanne, for many years.

I was coping. I traveled a lot, and I coped by cross-dressing when I was traveling, a kind of splurge-and-purge thing that transgender people often engage in, where I would buy a lot of things and get rid of them quickly. I didn't understand it, but being able to dress as a woman, I found a sense of comfort, a sense of release, a sense of being me.

In 2003, I told Joanne. She had gone away on a trip. While she was gone, I had gone on the internet and described all the things that I was dealing with, and had found that there

was a name for it, which was kind of good news, bad news.

The good news was that there are other people like me. The bad news was that it was a pretty serious thing. So I shared it with Joanne. The next six weeks there were a lot of tears, a lot of prayers, a lot of hugs. At night I would read to her from books that talked about transgender and what transgender was. She would ask questions or make observations. At the end of those six weeks, Joanne said, "Well, two things. If it's a sin, it's God's job to convict, not mine. And I love the person and not the package." That allowed us to go forward.

We found a group of people who identified as cross-dressers. Went there and found

Michigan State Capitol, 2013

some support. But eventually, I knew that my being transgender was about much more than cross-dressing. Eventually, the internal pressure to transition became quite strong, and the inability to keep living a lie was very difficult for me.

"WE DON'T WANT YOU"

Probably one of the hardest transitions was leaving the Baptist church that we had been a part of for a number of years.

After I had begun my transition, I called the pastor, and we had him and his wife over for coffee, and the pastor and I dialogued back and forth by email mostly for eight months, and then we talked with the elders of the church.

The head of the elder board had a lot of difficulties with my transition. We were talking one time, and I told him about how difficult it was for transgender people and how much higher the suicide rate was for transgender people. He said, "Well, so you say." Kind of in an offhand way, but that hurt.

One day, when we came back from vacation, we received a letter from the church. It basically said, "If you're going to follow this route, you're no longer welcome to use your gifts. We don't want you as an elder." They made it clear that I would no longer be able to teach, no longer be able to preach, no longer be able to use the gifts that I had. In other words, they said, "Well, you can come, but you can't be a full member."

I didn't want to do that. I didn't think it was right. I wanted to be in a place where I was accepted fully for who I was. To be able to worship there and be able to use my gifts there.

So we began looking for another church.

THE RIGHT PATH

I asked many times, why am I like this? Why am I different than so many other people? Studying the Scriptures, talking to others, reading all I could get my hands on, I came to the conclusion that being transgender is part of the rich diversity of God's creation. We're all a little different, and some of us are different in ways that are more evident and obvious than others. But God's creation really is diverse, and if we don't honor that diversity, we deny who God is, because God made us that way.

The process of coming out as transgender deepened my faith in ways that surprised me very, very much. It was just a profound sense of God's presence that sounds weird to other people and is difficult to explain. A sense that I was on the right path, I was doing the right thing, and coming out was a way of being authentic, and that's really what God wanted.

The first time I was able to worship as Julie was a very moving experience for me. I was crying softly through much of the worship service because being able to be authentic and worship was just an overwhelming experience for me.

Today, Julie is a public speaker, Presbyterian church elder, and proud grandmother. She served as executive director of Michigan Equality and on the boards of Soulforce (whose tagline is "Sabotage Christian Supremacy") and PFLAG. Julie and Joanne have been married for nearly fifty years.

ALVIN "AL" BAUM

URBAN PLANNER, PSYCHOTHERAPIST, PHILANTHROPIST
SAN FRANCISCO, CALIFORNIA

It's almost impossible to sum up Al Baum's many careers and passions. Born in Chicago in 1930, he served in the Army, graduated from Harvard Law School, helped save San Francisco Bay, restored various Victorian buildings, became a therapist, founded the Gay and Lesbian Task Force of the Jewish Community Federation of San Francisco, served on countless boards, including the ACLU of Northern California and the Lambda Legal Defense and Education Fund, and in 2013 was honored as the Lifetime Achievement Grand Marshal of the forty-third annual San Francisco Pride Parade.

Today, Al still loves to travel. He is married to the interior designer Robert Holgate.

After graduating from law school, I passed the bar in the first try, but I went three months without a job. Eventually, I got a job because I knew someone. And I was there five years, and they weren't happy years. I didn't like being a hired gun, so to speak, a gladiator, or whatever. I thought most of the work that we were called upon to do wasn't very important. I just couldn't get into it.

I had always loved maps, and I love architecture. So I went and I got a degree in city planning at Berkeley, and then in 1965 I got a job with the San Francisco Bay Conservation and Development Commission, the BCDC. And I was there for six years and used my law background well and was very happy.

During this time, prior to 1975, I still wasn't out. I was very closeted. I would go to the parks and pick up somebody and have

sex, but I never told them my name, or if I did, I gave them a fake name. And then in 1972, Jim Foster became the first out gay man to address the Democratic National Convention. [Editor's note: In his speech, Foster said, "We do not come to you begging your understanding or pleading your tolerance. We come to you affirming our pride in our lifestyle, affirming the validity of our right to seek and to maintain meaningful emotional relationships, and affirming our right to participate in the life of this country on an equal basis with every citizen."]

That was a turning point in this country. And Jim Foster was a friend of mine, and that changed me. I started going to therapy. And I went for a year and that paved the road, so to speak.

Then, in 1975, I had a friend who was one

of a group of ten men who started something called Lavender University, which was an informal night school. They were all gay. So I asked a gay friend of mine, who was the education reporter for the *San Francisco Chronicle*, if he would be willing to do an article about the university. He said, "Of course." So I made a plan to bring two of the ten men to him. I was going to introduce them and then leave, but what happened was only one of them showed up. So the reporter asked me to give some quotes about the university. And then he said, "Your quotes are really good. I want to quote you in the article. Would that be all right?"

And I can remember—you know they say when you're drowning, your whole life passes before your eyes? Well, it was like that. But I had been telling people, friends, that they

should come out. And I said to myself, "You have to be willing to do it yourself, or you're just being hypocritical." So I said, "All right."

Two weeks later there was a story in the newspaper with a picture of me, and a story that made it very plain that I had a personal interest in this Lavender University, and that was it.

A NEW BOTTLE OF SCOTCH

I smile always, still, when I use the word "philanthropist" to describe myself, because I refused the label for years and years and years and years. And to be honest, long after I had the wherewithal to give more than most people can, I didn't. And I finally got into it because I was shamed into it by a gay Catholic friend of mine named Patrick.

One night Patrick gave a party, and it was

a bring your own bottle party, and I brought a half-consumed bottle of Scotch, because that was still my drink of choice at the time. And a couple of years later Patrick started kidding me about that. Why didn't I bring a new bottle of Scotch, an unopened bottle of Scotch? And that struck me as a very strange question. The thought had never occurred to me, and it was sort of against my principles.

But Patrick worked on me, and worked on me, and worked on me. He said, "You can do it. Just do it. There's so many good causes around, and you know some of them already. Just give a little more." And gradually, gradually, gradually, I started giving more.

One year, maybe ten years ago, I made a list of how many charities I gave to in a year. And there were 138. Some of them were larger amounts, and some of them were in the $100 category. Ever since, I've been trying to reduce the spread and increase the average amounts. That's not easy to do because once a group becomes used to you giving a certain amount, they expect you to give the same amount every year.

But it feels good. Philanthropy has become part of my life. And being the age that I am and having had the health issues that I've had, I've had to think about what happens when I die. You can't take it with you.

A MITZVAH

I never liked to be pigeonholed. I didn't like to be pigeonholed as a Harvard man. I didn't like to be pigeonholed as a Brain with a capital "B." I didn't like to be pigeonholed as a Jew.

My family was not very observant. In fact, they were pretty nonobservant, and that's the way I was raised, and that's the way I still am. I'm not a believer. In the past five years, I've gone to service maybe once. Not even for the High Holy Days.

From time to time in my lifetime, I have thought that those who have a faith to sustain them are fortunate. I just don't.

So I used to say I was a bad Jew, and then people, rabbis and other people, would say, "No, you're not," and they would go through the litany of things. They said, "But you do so much else for the world and for people who don't have," and so on, and that's true. That is part of the Jewish religion. It's a mitzvah, and it's true, I do that. I admit that. It doesn't feel spiritual to me, but I think in terms of what people mean by the word, perhaps it is.

An unfailingly courteous, clear-sighted man, Al talked both comfortably and introspectively about his life during his OUTWORDS interview in May 2017. At several points, he broke into gentle tears, for reasons understood only by him. Al's tears suffused his interview with a sense of poignancy and let us know we were in the presence of a bighearted man.

GARY, MILLIE, AND CRAIG WATTS

FIFTH-GENERATION MORMONS AND THEIR GAY SON

PROVO, UTAH

Gary Watts was born in 1940 in Logan, Utah, into a committed Mormon family. After serving a two-year mission in New Zealand, he married Mildred "Millie" Cragun (born 1941), his sweetheart since middle school. Over the next fifteen years, Gary and Millie had six children while Gary went to medical school and became a radiologist.

Just before Christmas 1989, Gary and Millie's second child and first son, Craig, told Gary he was gay. Gary and Millie vowed to stand by their son. When the Mormon Church excommunicated Craig three years later, Gary and Millie made the painful decision to leave the church altogether. Soon thereafter, they became deeply involved with LDS Family Fellowship, which supports Mormon families with LGBTQ members and friends. They have also served on the board of PFLAG. In 1997, their daughter Lori came out as lesbian.

Today, Gary and Millie's thirteen grandchildren, including five from Craig and Lori, are the light of their lives.

MILLIE: In 1989, around Christmas time, we had a lot of Gary's family here for a big family dinner. They were all in the living room. For some reason, Craig and Gary were out in the family room in this deep, deep discussion.

GARY: I don't know what prompted Craig to choose that time, but he called me aside and said, "Dad, we need to talk." I could tell he had something serious. We sat down and he said, "Dad, I'm gay." It was a complete surprise to me. I thought for a minute, and I think the first question I

asked him was, "How gay are you?" His response was, "Pretty gay."

CRAIG: To me, coming out to my parents was ground zero of the universe. It was the scariest thing I could have ever imagined, because I thought the world would explode.

The conversation with my dad was the beginning of me getting on my feet to see that I could talk to someone, and then also to feel that they were with me on this. They weren't going to abandon me. My dad was as worried as I was, and maybe there was a way we were going to get through this. I had glimmers of that in that first conversation. Up until then, nobody was on my side. It was me against the universe.

GARY: What was interesting was that, two years before, I had read an article about homosexuality in *Dialogue*, which is a journal of Mormon thought. It was written by a Mormon psychiatrist in Salt Lake City. For some reason, the article resonated with me. It made sense. I couldn't think that people were choosing to be gay. I said to Craig, "Let's call this psychiatrist and have you go see him," which is what basically happened.

I should interject here. We were having this conversation in the family room, and my family were in the living room. Millie was wondering—

MILLIE: I kept coming in here and saying, "Get in the other room!"

That night when we got in bed, Gary told me what Craig had told him. I said, "Oh, that's ridiculous." I didn't know any gay people. Or I did, but I didn't know they were gay. My perception of gay people was they were in San Francisco or New York City. Very promiscuous. Craig was Mr. Perfect. He was a good kid. I thought, "How can a good kid be gay?"

GARY: This Mormon psychiatrist, Dr. Stout, later told us that Craig was the fifth student body president that he had in his practice who had come out as gay.

I had always wondered, "What makes Craig so great?" It was the way Craig

Gary and Millie with the family

conducted his life. Part of the reason that people liked him so much, he always took time to talk to the underprivileged and the kids that might not be the most popular. He just had this empathy, and I think part of it was due to what was going on in his own persona. So I had an immense respect for him. It was just a matter of, how are we going to deal with this as a family?

COAT OFF, GLASSES OFF

GARY: In April of 1993, we saw an announcement in the newspaper about something called the Intermountain Conference on Homosexuality. So we signed up and went to the conference. About the first person I ran into was a cousin of mine who was a social worker and had come to get some information. I said, "Ann, what are you doing here?" And she says, "Gary, what are you doing here?" So I came out to her, and then we met other people.

MILLIE: We started to meet other parents, and gay people. I found out they were good kids too. You know? I found out there was a whole world of wonderful gay people that I hadn't known about before.

GARY: So that was kind of the genesis of this group, Family Fellowship.

MILLIE: It was kind of a Mormon PFLAG.

GARY: And it wasn't very long before they asked Millie and me if we'd be willing to chair the organization. So then we became the co-chairs of Family Fellowship, and we were the co-chairs of that organization for thirteen years. And we also continued this Intermountain Conference on Homosexuality. That first one had like four hundred people that came to it, just out of the blue. We decided that we'd build on that, and so every other year we had a conference. They were successful, and they were fun, and they got us acquainted with a lot of people.

MILLIE: There were a lot of parents still in the closet. We had one friend who came to one of the conferences, and she had a coat on and a hat and dark glasses because she didn't want to be recognized by anyone, you know? And then at the end of the conference, her coat was off, her glasses were off, and you know, she was proud, proud to have a gay child.

On the day of their OUTWORDS interview in April 2018, the mountains behind the Watts family home were dusted with snow. The mountains and snow seemed to indicate that in times of trial, some things will fade away, but the most important values will endure.

SHANNON MINTER

LAWYER

WASHINGTON, DC

> Shannon Minter was born in East Texas on Valentine's Day 1961.
>
> After graduating from the University of Texas at Austin, Shannon attended Cornell Law School. In 1996, he began his transition from female to male.
>
> Shannon has devoted his career to the quest for LGBTQ legal equality in a wide variety of cases. In 2001, he successfully defended the right of a lesbian woman to file a wrongful death suit after a neighbor's dog killed her female partner; in 2003, he defended the custody rights of a transgender father; and in 2008, he was lead counsel for same-sex couples in the case that ultimately instituted marriage equality in California.
>
> Shannon's accolades have piled up. In 2005, he received the Ford Foundation's Leadership for a Changing World award. In 2009, *California Lawyer* named him one of their California lawyers of the year. And in 2015, Shannon was chosen by President Obama to interview and recommend candidates for senior White House staff positions. After President Obama left office, Shannon secured an injunction to block his replacement's proposed ban on transgender people in the military.
>
> Today, Shannon serves as legal director for NCLR, as well as on the boards of Faith in America and the Transgender Law and Policy Institute. He lives in Washington, DC, with his wife, Robin.

I was born in 1961 in Texas, a rural part of Texas, east Texas. My parents are both from the same very small town, and both of their parents are from the same small town. That was my experience in my early years, and it was really awesome. It was really wonderful. I had this great extended family. I had a really happy, happy childhood. It was a great place to be a kid. We went around in the woods, hunting and fishing with my dad. I was born a female. No one really cared about me being a tomboy. But, you know, they're conservative and Christian. Not fundamentalist or anything like that, but definitely devout people.

Sorry, it's an emotional topic [*crying*].

I didn't know that I was transgender. I couldn't really figure out what was going on, but I knew that I was attracted to girls. I thought I was lesbian. I came out when my parents found out that I had a girlfriend when I was seventeen. That was just a real bad experience. They were very upset and had all the mistaken information that a lot of people had then, that some people still have, I guess. They thought I was doing something wrong and sinful. That I was choosing to do that and trying to be rebellious and hurtful to them. They were very rejecting, and it was devastating to me because I love them.

Sorry about that [*crying*].

I loved them very much. I struggled with feeling cut off from my whole family. I really love my grandparents and my great aunts and uncles. It was just really hard to feel so alienated from my whole family. I tried to hide being queer. I struggled for a long time like a lot of people do. Eventually, I went out to college and cut myself off pretty much from my whole family.

I figured out that I was transgender when I was about thirty-five. I was hoping that my parents would deal with that better than with me being lesbian. I don't know why, I just thought maybe they would.

That was wrong. They were even more upset when I transitioned. At that point they told me that I should not come home anymore. That if I came to see them, that they would have to move. Because you can't hide being transgender. Everybody would know. Especially because they live in such a small town. That went on for about seven years. I didn't see any of my family during that time.

MR. JACKSON

I had a high school government teacher, Mr. Jackson. His name was Larry Jackson, and he's passed away now. He was a very devout Christian and kind of a fundamentalist Christian actually. He saved my life because he and I had been close. He had already taken an interest in me. I was kind of a nerdy, smart kid. He already was trying to give me some extra help. Then I came back after the summer when my parents found out that I was lesbian, told him what was going on. He had me check in with him, like, every morning. He would just make sure I was okay. He was really good. He told me that even though, based on his beliefs, he thought that being gay was a sin, he said it was not any worse than a lot of things he did. He just had a great intuition, I think, about how to talk to a gay kid.

Shannon with his mom in a recent photo. Broken families can heal.

COMING HOME

About seven years after I got married, a cousin of mine, who knew why I wasn't coming home and that I was transgender, he just thought it was terrible. He told my grandmother that I was transgender and tried to pave the way for me to be able to come back and see her. So I did.

I still remember very vividly seeing my grandmother for the first time after all those years. She was very happy to see me. I spent a lot of time with her after that. I came back a lot after that. It was great to see everybody again. People could not have been more loving or accepting.

So then that helped my parents also become more accepting. A few years later, my father was diagnosed with cancer. My sister and I spent the last month of his life with him. I was really happy to have that time with him. He was trying really hard to be more accepting.

My mom is still living. I spend a lot of time with her now. Just a few months ago, my wife and I were able to buy my grandmother's old farmhouse in that little town. I've been spending a lot of time there. I hope I'll be able to retire there, if I can talk my wife into it.

Everybody there has known me since I was a kid. It's been a really wonderful experience. There's been a lot of pain along the way, but I feel we're really lucky to have been able to reconcile with my family and this place, this town. I think it's pretty great and a pretty amazing experience, actually.

SURVIVAL

MARIANNE DIAZ

COMMUNITY ACTIVIST, FOUNDER OF CLEANSLATE

LOS ANGELES, CALIFORNIA

Born in 1959 in a poor neighborhood near LAX, a gang member at thirteen and sent to prison at eighteen for attempted murder, Marianne Diaz found a way not only to heal her own life but to help countless others do the same.

Upon her release from prison, Marianne got a job doing gang-prevention work for Community Youth Gang Services in Los Angeles. Over the next decade, she rose to the position of deputy regional director. In 1995, Marianne founded CleanSlate. Beyond offering affordable tattoo removal for former gang members, CleanSlate helps gang members, felons, and survivors of domestic violence confront and resolve injustice in their lives through therapy, conflict resolution programs, and other services. Since 1998, Marianne has also been the director of outreach services at the Southern California Counseling Center. She also works with LGBTQI youth in the Watts community in Los Angeles.

My family is from Mexico. My father was an immigrant. Came here looking for a better life. Eventually he started working for the railroad. He moved us from a Mexican neighborhood to a white community, the Lennox Hawthorne area of Los Angeles. His intention was to give us a better life. He felt the schools were better in white communities, which I'm not sure he was wrong. But what he didn't factor into it was that we were going to be Mexicans in a white community.

The neighbors actually watched us move in. I was five at the time. I remember wondering why they were coming to our house and telling us to get the fuck out of there, and how many kids do you have. Like, thirty? Making those kinds of comments.

My father tried to be nonviolent as long as he could, and I'm just going to be honest, he was a violent person. He was an angry man. The final straw was when our neighbor across the street saw us bring cats. The man made it clear he hated cats. Within a week our cats were dead.

My father saw me and my sister crying, and he said, "That's it." He went across the street and he beat the hell out of the guy across the street. The whole community shifted in relationship to us. They feared my father. We feared our father too. I think that was my first taste of how you create power in a situation where all you have is

Marianne (center) with members of her gang, Las Comadres

violence. It's a way to equalize the deficit, and it worked. That continued to work for me most of my life.

GANG SEXUALITY

My sexuality is really complex. I remember one day being at my cousin's house, and I was probably nine or ten years old, and I remember my older cousin must have kept some of his girly magazines in some cupboard in there. I remember being nosy and finding them and looking at them and feeling something. It kind of made me nervous. I would go in there often and look at these pictures, and I'd be like, "Wow, something is happening to me." I was only nine or ten. I didn't know what it was at all.

Then as I grew older I started knowing there was something different about me. I would help my dad change brakes or help

him do the yard. I wasn't into, like, hanging out with my mom like my sister was.

My homeboys always told me they thought it was really strange that I could sleep with one of them and never call them or never follow them or try to hook up with them again. I said, it just wasn't that great. You aren't all that, homey. I didn't hate it, but it wasn't something I wanted to pursue.

In the gang, the less feminine you are, the more respected you are. Girls like my sister who were really pretty and cute and tiny and feminine and stuff were seen as toys or relationships, where I was seen as a soldier. There was a different kind of respect. It was like a respect that I guess men might feel for each other.

Me and my homies would hang out, and they'd say, "Hey, you like that girl? She's cute, right?" It was like a game they didn't have any problem with. But if a guy were to come out, different story, different story. I think because a gang is so macho that they can relate to macho women, and they'd rather deal with macho women than an effeminate guy who I think really scares them.

I saw a couple of the homeboys get their asses kicked in public in front of us, just for the suspicion of being gay. It had to be in public. It had to be at a gathering for it to mean something. Another homeboy, he just got ostracized out of the hood, and then what does he do? Whether or not he was, they decided he was. They kicked his ass and banished him, and then what does he have? He gave everything for the hood. I know a few homeboys who were so violent and crazy, and they are gay. They're violent and crazy because they had to hide. They didn't know how else to deal with their truth. And now they're in prison.

It isn't just that you have to hide. Your own humanity is gone. The human part of you has to shut down in order to survive.

"I CAN'T PRETEND I'M NOT BROWN"
I have an LGBTQI group that I run in Watts, which is the first one they've ever had. I run it there with men who are around eighteen to like twenty-four. Some are transgendered, some are just cross-dressers; they call themselves queens. They've survived that community being who they are, and a lot of the homies know them and they're cool with them, but they've been beat up a lot on the way.

We're trying to open up dialogue about that in Watts, which hasn't been easy. I hear this one guy tell me, "Why do you tell people you're a lesbian?" He is an African-American guy. He was like, "Why do you tell people you're lesbian? Who would know?" I go, "I know." He goes, "You're already brown. I'm black. If I'm gay, I ain't telling anybody because I got enough shit." I said, "Me too, but I can't live my life pretending I'm something I'm not. I can't pretend I'm not brown. There is no way I can do that. You can't pretend you're not black. I don't like pretending I'm something else that I'm not."

That's important to the people coming up after me, the kids. There's been so many times in groups of teens I work with, where I'll say, "I'm a lesbian." Then somebody in there will say, "I think I'm bisexual," but they wouldn't have said that if they didn't feel safe. They know I'm going to take care of them in that group.

OUTWORDS interviewed Marianne in the summer of 2016 at the home she shares with her partner, Roxanne. Funny, wry, and a little world-weary, Marianne clearly believes in the fundamental capacity of each person she meets to heal, change, and grow.

JOHN JAMES

FOUNDER AND PUBLISHER OF *AIDS TREATMENT NEWS*

PHILADELPHIA, PENNSYLVANIA

John James was born in 1941 in Brooklyn, New York. After graduating from Harvard in 1963, he got a job with the National Institutes of Health (NIH) in Washington, DC.

On July 4, 1965, a consortium of gay rights groups operating under the name East Coast Homophile Organizations (ECHO) staged the first Reminder Day march in front of Philadelphia's Independence Hall. Originally conceived by activist Craig Rodwell, the event was designed to "remind" people that millions of queer Americans were denied their inalienable rights of life, liberty, and the pursuit of happiness. John risked his job and career to join thirty-eight other people at that seminal march. [For more about Reminder Day marches, see pp. 13, 15–16.]

But John's most important work was creating and publishing *AIDS Treatment News* from 1986 to 2007. *AIDS Treatment News* was part of an underground information network that people with AIDS, doctors, researchers, and even the federal government turned to for the latest information about the disease. As a result, drug companies gradually became more responsive, doctors started treating HIV-positive people as partners, and people with AIDS seized control of their own health. Every other week for twenty years, John and a team of six researchers put *AIDS Treatment News* together in John's tiny San Francisco apartment. By 1991, they had five thousand subscribers. The *New York Times* later called *AIDS Treatment News* the most influential of the AIDS-era underground publications.

I was a nerd all my life. I was not interested in people and socializing. I was interested in ideas and science, things like that. I did have some friends but very much would be called an introvert.

I was concerned when I went to the demonstration at Independence Hall for gay rights that I would likely be fired if my employer, the National Institutes for Health, found out that I was there. I don't know for a fact that I would have been. The people I worked with were happy with my work. They would not have wanted to fire me, but their hands might have been tied. I just didn't know. So I asked not to be photographed in the demonstration.

John James, in dark suit on the left, protesting in front of Independence Hall in Philadelphia.

I didn't know I had been photographed until about a year ago. I found out about it because at the National Constitution Center in Philadelphia, there was an exhibit on the history of gay rights and how it relates to the US Constitution, and there was a press conference at the beginning and one of the pictures that happened to be projected on the wall was this picture with me in it. I asked the person who organized the show, I said, "Hey, I think that's me. What year was that photo taken? Was that the first July 4th Reminder Day demonstration in 1965?" He said he thought it was, and I looked again, and it certainly was me.

The most important part of my story is my work in AIDS. I published a newsletter called *AIDS Treatment News*, a newsletter for twenty years, and wrote most of it.

The way it began was that I was living in San Francisco and had some chronic fatigue. This was in the early days of AIDS, before the HIV virus had been identified. It was widely suspected that AIDS was caused by a virus, but that wasn't known at the time so there was no way to get tested, and so I figured the chances were good that I had it because so many people in San Francisco did.

EMPOWERING THE AIDS ACTIVIST MOVEMENT

As it turned out, I didn't have AIDS. But I started thinking, what would I do if it turns out that I do have it? I figured there must be some things you can do, maybe diet and lifestyle-wise, that would either help or hurt in progression of the illness, and that the best guidance on this would be to look at the scientific research that was being done, and see what was known, and then just put together whatever one can put together for oneself.

At the time, I was working as a programmer for a small medical research company, and while working there one evening, I noticed a book from a company called Dialog. In those days, there was no World Wide Web, but you could dial up Dialog and get on to various databases, and they had dozens of different databases, and you only paid for the information you used. So I would look up things that people were interested in about medical treatments and such, and then I decided to make it into a newsletter. I put a low price on it, and much lower for people with HIV, which quickly changed to much lower for people "with financial difficulty" because we couldn't have any information about HIV status on my mailing list, which of course we kept very confidential for people's privacy. For that reason also, I didn't use volunteers on the newsletter, only employees, because I didn't want to have a lot of people around where the list could have gotten taken.

I didn't realize that *AIDS Treatment News* could have a really great importance until later on, when I realized that it just might. The real importance was to help organize and educate the early AIDS activist movement so that people in the movement would know as much or more about the subject as federal officials or pharmaceutical company employees. The scientists might know more about their special areas, but as far as how the information fit into the bigger picture, the AIDS activists ended up knowing more.

At times, activists had to be the go-between between different scientists who were rivals, or between drug companies and the FDA, because the people didn't communicate on their own due to rivalries and exclusivity or they wanted to be the big deal. Activists became the glue to talk to the different people and get them on the same page when they should have been all along. *AIDS Treatment News* contributed to that.

John's Philadelphia apartment is extremely bare—so much so that for his OUTWORDS interview, he had to sit on a $2 folding chair from the local AIDS thrift store. John has devoted his time, energy, and formidable intelligence to what matters most: saving people's dignity and their lives.

NANCY NANGERONI

TRANSGENDER RADIO HOST, EDUCATOR, ACTIVIST

ALBUQUERQUE, NEW MEXICO

At her birth in 1953 in Milton, Massachusetts, Nancy Nangeroni was designated male. She graduated from MIT in 1976 with a degree in electrical engineering and computer science, moved to California, became despondent about her gender issues, and nearly died in a motorcycle accident. The accident helped move her from despair to determination.

After transitioning, Nancy began volunteering with the International Foundation for Gender Education (IFGE), serving as its executive director from 1997 to 1998. She founded the Boston chapter of Transexual Menace, wrote extensively about gender issues, and coedited and published *In Your Face*, the first periodical to document hate crimes against transgender people.

In 1995, Nancy founded the radio program *GenderTalk*, which aired weekly for over eleven years, attracting an international audience. She led gender diversity training workshops for corporations, academic institutions, and nonprofit organizations. Along the way, she fell in love with Gordene MacKenzie, a feminist professor and gender activist from New Mexico. Together, Nancy and Gordene produced a music video about the 1998 vigil for Rita Hester, a transgender African-American woman who was murdered in Allston, Massachusetts. Rita's murder and the ensuing controversy over disrespectful press coverage helped spark Transgender Day of Remembrance (TDOR), which is held every year on November 20.

In the 2000s, Nancy served for six years as chair of the Massachusetts Transgender Political Coalition, while leading Boston's TDOR event for over ten years. While *GenderTalk* no longer airs, GenderTalk.com continues to serve thousands of visitors monthly though its archive of past shows.

I went to MIT. When I got there, I was hit by the awareness that my father had been such a hardworking person. He would confide in me about his life being just about working, working, working, going to sleep, get up, work, work, work. I grew up promising myself I would never work that hard. So I didn't develop good study habits, and I really struggled academically. Even though I have a facility with technology, I lost my love of it.

Nancy and her wife, Gordene, recording their groundbreaking radio program *GenderTalk* at KUNM (University of New Mexico) in 2001

I lost my excitement for it. It became something that I do well, but it was no longer a passion.

At the same time, I had this other burning issue in my mind. I was waiting to graduate so that I could start working on my gender issues. I needed to get out there on my own, so that I'd be free of family and finally be able to figure out how in some way I was going to live the second half of my life as a woman, which is what I promised myself when I was younger.

There are some kids who are just very clear, "I'm a boy," "I'm a girl," contrary genitals notwithstanding. They have that clarity, and they always amaze me. I have one friend, a trans man, who says, "I always knew I was a man." That always amazes me. I never knew I was a woman. I just knew I needed to live as one, and that's different. It's just one of the many different flavors of being transgender that are out there.

When I came out to my parents, I figured that as a guy transitioning to living as a woman, that this would be very difficult, very embarrassing for my father. He was a saint. Not only did my father express just unreserved acceptance, but he asked me what I was going to do with it. He challenged me to do something, to be an activist about it. I thought that was just wonderful, just an amazing, amazing level of support.

"WHO KILLED MY CHILD?"

In 1995, a young trans man named Brandon Teena was murdered in Falls City, Nebraska. At the time, Riki Wilchins and I had just met, and she was looking for some kind of activism to work on. We flew out and organized the first nationwide demonstration on behalf of transgender people in Falls City. We didn't know if we were going to meet with baseball bats. The only example we had to draw on was back when people had gone to the South to protest discrimination against African Americans in the South, and some of those people had been met with terrible violence. We did our homework, we consulted with the Falls City police beforehand, and we had a very good experience, a very empowering experience.

Just a few months later, Chanelle Pickett was strangled to death in the apartment of a young computer programmer in Massachusetts. I led a series of demonstrations at the courthouse in Middlesex County around Chanelle's death. During those demonstrations, a newspaper reporter interviewed a trans woman named Rita Hester, who said,

"I'm very disturbed by this. I'm afraid that this will lead to open season on transgender people." Well, a year and a half after that verdict, Rita Hester was herself murdered in Allston, Massachusetts. She was stabbed more than twenty times in the chest.

In the wake of Rita Hester's murder, we called for a community meeting. About thirty to forty people showed up, which was a really big turnout at that time, and people wanted a vigil. So we organized a vigil in Allston, and about 200, 250 people showed up for it. Rita's mom, sister, and brother were there. I led the vigil with Rita's mom on one arm and her sister on the other arm. We walked through the streets of the city with candles. Her mom was very open in her grief. She wailed out into the night, "Who killed my child?" It was the most moving thing I've ever experienced.

A transgender activist in San Francisco named Gwendolyn Smith picked up on this, and she declared that from then on November 20th would be the Transgender Day of Remembrance. In my great wisdom I thought, this will never catch on, but it did. I ended up leading Boston's Transgender Day of Remembrance event for ten or fifteen years.

Transgender people are a very small fraction of the population. Yet the violence done against us is way out of proportion to our small part of the population. Trans people of color are the most victimized people in our culture, as far as we know. Yet at the same time that transgender people suffer terrible violence, we're used by the media to attract attention. The television networks use transgender content to attract viewers. So the culture at large has an interest in us, and yet at the same time, it has this cognitive disconnect. It has an intense interest in people going beyond gender norms. At the same time it feels terribly guilty about it. And that's where the violence comes from.

LUIGI FERRER

BISEXUAL ACTIVIST, HIV/AIDS EDUCATOR

MIAMI, FLORIDA

Luigi Ferrer was born in 1958 in Ponce, Puerto Rico. At 27, Luigi was living in Florida and working on a PhD in oceanography when he was diagnosed with HIV. Believing he had only a few months to live, he decided to dedicate his remaining time to battling AIDS. More than thirty years later, he's still battling.

Luigi's first post was as executive director of Miami's second-largest AIDS service organization, Body Positive. He later worked for several national HIV-specialized pharmacies, was president of Florida AIDS Action (now the AIDS Institute), and served on the boards of the AIDS Action Council and the National Association of People with AIDS. In 1996, Luigi played a key role in the first reauthorization of the Ryan White CARE Act. In subsequent years, funding for the CARE Act's drug-assistance program increased tenfold, from $52 million to $528 million.

Luigi is one of six founding board members of BiNet USA. In 1998, to help counteract media portrayals of bisexual men as "the ultimate pariahs" of the AIDS epidemic (*Newsweek*, October 1987), Luigi helped organize the National Institute on Bisexuality HIV/AIDS Summit, hosted by BiNet USA.

I was infected with HIV by my first boyfriend in 1979, before we knew anything about HIV or AIDS or GRID. Several years later, I was three years into my PhD in oceanography at the University of Miami when I was diagnosed with HIV formally. At that time, you were diagnosed and you died within six months. I had already been working at the Body Positive Resource Center here at Miami as a volunteer, and because of my expertise in grant writing, I was offered the position of executive director. So I left my oceanography program and became executive director at the Body Positive Resource Center.

At that time, we were doing a lot of palliative care, watching our friends die, coming together as a family to help each other in those difficult times. Our lesbian sisters were amazing. I spent twelve years of my life as if I only had another two years to live.

I was on AZT monotherapy, which was horrible. I would take my medications and go lie down, because I knew within five minutes, that punch in the stomach was coming. I

Self-portrait, 1995

would roll in bed for about twenty minutes, and then it would pass. I was spending three to four days in bed just to be able to function marginally during the other three to four days, but I did remain employed during that whole time, so I had good insurance.

When my T cells finally dropped down to zero, I said to my doctor, "So I've been taking this medication that makes me feel horrible to keep my T cells up. Now I have zero T cells. What does that mean?" He says, "Your guess is as good as mine." "Could I stop taking this medication?" "Sure, stop."

So I spent about three years with zero T cells, but I was able to get intravenous immunoglobulin, IVIG, every two weeks. It costs about $1,200 a dose. Essentially, I would get an immune system in a bottle every two weeks. That, I believe, is what really kept me alive. When protease inhibitors came on the market, I started taking a protease inhibitor. Within a month, I had twenty T cells, which was remarkable because we didn't really know at that point that the immune system could be reconstituted. Nowadays, I have almost eight hundred T cells, which is almost normal.

At age thirty-nine, realizing I was going to turn forty pretty soon and that I had no savings, I decided to buy a home with a thirty-year mortgage. I realized I wasn't going to go anywhere. So it was a real shift in my attitude, wanting for the first time to make long-term plans and settle down and figure out what I was going to do in my old age.

"ARE THOSE YOUR SHOES?"

My most vivid incident of biphobia was meeting a guy through the personals in the newspaper, because we didn't have online dating yet, and going out on a first date. We went to a nice Thai restaurant, took our shoes off, and sat down at a little table. We had just ordered and we're talking. And I said that I was bisexual, because it wasn't anything that I was embarrassed about.

This guy just got up and left. He didn't say a word. He just got up and left. So I finished the meal, paid. And as I'm walking out, the waitress says, "Are these your shoes?" The guy was in such a panic and in such a hurry to get out of there that he had left his shoes.

SEAT BELTS

One of the issues that we're having here in Miami-Dade County today is the fact that our teenagers in high school live in the jurisdiction of the country that has, and has had for the past six years, the highest HIV rate in the country, the highest number of new HIV infections in the country. And they don't get any sex education in school. That is unconscionable. The school board has said nothing to address this issue, although we've asked repeatedly.

There are several factors that contribute to the high rates of transmission. The fact that we're an immigrant-majority city. Fifty-seven percent of the people in Miami are foreign-born. That means they come from a different cultural context. The sexual silence that we won't talk about it. Then, all the *machista* culture. When people don't have the information they need to make good, informed decisions, they can't make them. It's not to say that if they had the information they needed to make good decisions, they would make the right decisions. But if they don't have the information, they just can't make those decisions.

What passes for sex ed in our high schools right now is abstinence-based, abstinence only, and extremely heteronormative, and our queer teens complain about it all the time. I think parents don't realize the danger their kids are in. If they did, they'd be up in arms demanding comprehensive sex ed in our high schools. HIV prevention and using condoms isn't 100 percent effective. Neither are seat belts, but we still expect people to use them,

right? I didn't have that information when I was eighteen, when I was twenty, and that's one of the reasons why I'm HIV-positive today. I do the work that I do because I don't want any other young people to have to live through what I lived through.

DIANA NYAD

OCEAN CONQUEROR, SEXUAL ABUSE SURVIVOR
LOS ANGELES, CALIFORNIA

Diana Nyad was born in 1949 in New York City and grew up in Florida. She began swimming seriously in the seventh grade and soon was dominating her sport, winning three Florida high school championships in the backstroke. Diana seemed a shoo-in for the 1968 Olympics until a rare heart condition slowed her times and canceled that dream. Undaunted, Diana looked for new challenges—like parachuting out a fourth-story dormitory window at Emory University. That stunt got Diana kicked out of Emory and ultimately changed the course of her life, because she next enrolled at Lake Forest College in Illinois, where she was introduced to long-distance swimming by Buck Dawson, director of the International Swimming Hall of Fame.

Diana's first distance race was in July 1970, a ten-mile swim in Lake Ontario. She set a women's record for the event. Five years later, Diana swam around Manhattan Island. But that was just a warm-up compared to her next challenge.

In 1978, Diana mounted her first attempt to swim from Cuba to Florida, a distance of one hundred and eleven miles. No one had ever done this unassisted (including no shark cage). Diana's first attempt ended after forty-two hours in the water. In 2013, at the age of sixty-four, thirty-five years after her initial attempt and on her fifth try overall, Diana accomplished the feat.

My father was Greek. People used to think he looked like Omar Sharif. He was larger than life.

On my fifth birthday, my dad called me into the den, and he had a big, fat unabridged Webster's dictionary open. He had his hands on the pages and tears in his eyes. He said, "Darling, I have been waiting for this day for you to turn five, because today is the day you are going to understand the most important thing I will ever tell you. Come here. Your name, my name, the name of my people, darling, my people, it is in the bold black and white, in the important book, the dictionary. 'Nyad: girl or woman champion swimmer.' Oh my God, this is your destiny, darling!"

I tell that story with a little bit of, what would you call it, "latter-day poetry," because truthfully do I remember every word he said?

No. But I do remember being dragged in. I do remember my name being in the dictionary. I do remember asking friends if their names were in the dictionary. I do remember thinking, "Wow, this is who I'm supposed to be. What I'm supposed to be."

I started walking around with my shoulders high. I start telling everybody I met, "I'm a champion and I'm supposed to be champion, that's who I am. That's what my name means." Now it turns out that my name is an apt eponym, and I became this champion swimmer. So it was all, if not destiny, it was a delightful connection or circumstance.

IN PARALYSIS AND IN SILENCE

I was touched without my will when I was young. And like a lot of kids who go through sexual abuse from a parental figure, a priest, a coach, a stepfather, a mother's boyfriend, an aunt, I was confused. I felt humiliated. I felt terrified.

This was my hero. This was my coach. I had him on a pedestal. I wasn't close to my

After fifty-three hours in the water, Diana completes her historic swim in Key West, FL, flanked by best friends Bonnie (left) and Candace.

parents and didn't talk to them about everything, and reveal myself, and ask the difficult questions. They weren't available for that. My coach was. He was my confidant, my everything. I didn't know about sex. It's so confusing to a kid who is told by that parental figure whom they adore, that this is right for them. My coach used to say to me all the time, "I know you don't understand this, but one day you will. I'm an adult and I need this, and you know this is our special thing. This is our special moment."

I think that one of the shameful aspects of sexual abuse, especially in pedophilia for boys and girls, is that they feel that they should have stopped it. I was a strapping, strong, fit fourteen-year-old when I was first attacked by my coach. I was bigger and stronger than I am now. I could have thrown him up against the wall and said, "Don't you ever come near me again. I'm going to the principal at school. I'm going to the police." But I didn't. I suffered through it in paralysis and in silence, because there was something in me that said, "This must be love. I don't get it, but he must love me so much because he said, 'This is our special thing.'"

It's taken me years to work through that. I think I've largely done that and gotten out to the other side. But there's a remnant of that wound. That little girl who was terrified and humiliated, who's still there.

THE OTHER SHORE

People have been trying to swim from Cuba to Florida since 1950. They call it "the Mount Everest of the earth's oceans." The most challenging, most obstacle-ridden swim on earth. It is the particular species of sharks. The particular venomous species of jellyfish, the box jellyfish. Most people have died who have been hit by one of those. The Gulf Stream going sideways six times faster than you're trying to swim. The chances of getting all that right at one time are close to impossible.

Way back when I was twenty-eight years old and first tried the Cuba–Florida swim, it was already called impossible. Most people in the marathon swimming world said, "That is one swim that will never be done by anybody of any era, any gender, any age. It just has too much going against it to get it all right in one two-to-three-day period." And I found that to be true four times. After the fourth try, even people on my own team would say, "You went fifty-one hours last time. We weren't even close to the shore."

I said, "It's the age-old debate: is it the destination, or is it the journey?" My team felt that we were on a journey that was rocking us with inspiration. Not one of them got paid a penny, but adventure, history, discovery, friendship were driving us. I asked one of our kayakers, Bucko, I said, "Bucko, would you be willing to step up a fifth time?" He said, "Diana, I've discovered more about myself paddling next to you than I have working my job in Key West. I'm in. Let's go another time."

We all knew that we might never reach the other shore, and it was still worth the journey.

Diana is—to put it mildly—intense. She doesn't speak words; she launches them like rockets. But when she paused at the conclusion of her OUTWORDS interview to be photographed, she became very calm. Her eyes turned warm. In that brief moment, we glimpsed the deep, patient wisdom Diana found in the water—a wisdom she shares generously and vibrantly with the world.

KARLA JAY

ACTIVIST, AUTHOR, EDUCATOR

NEW YORK, NEW YORK

Karla Jay was born in 1947 in Brooklyn, New York. She attended Barnard College and received her PhD in comparative literature from New York University.

In 1970, she became the first female chair of the Gay Liberation Front. She was also active in Radicalesbians and participated in the Lavender Menace action to interrupt the Second Congress to Unite Women. In 1972, Karla coedited *Out of the Closets: Voices of Gay Liberation*, a compilation of manifestos and personal accounts from early leaders of the gay and lesbian liberation movement. She would ultimately write, edit, and translate ten books, including a memoir, *Tales of the Lavender Menace*, published in 1999. She has appeared in many documentaries, including *She's Beautiful When She's Angry* and *The Question of Equality*, and has won many awards, including the Bill Whitehead Lifetime Achievement Award for lesbian and gay writing and a Lambda Literary Award for Dyke Life. Karla's essay "When Darkness Falls: A Journey into Visual Disability" was nominated by the *Chronicle of Higher Education* as best essay of 2006.

There are women who romanticized the bars from the 1960s, but I didn't find them pleasant. There were men who were let in by the Mafia who owned places like Kooky's and the Sea Colony. They would stand around the edge of the dance floor and jerk off. We called them "dyke daddies."

Kooky was a Mafia moll who had probably been a prostitute. She had blonde hair in a beehive that looked as if it had been sprayed into place in 1950 and left there forever. She had carmine nails and lipstick. She always had a cigarette between her fingers, and she would patrol up and down the bar, and she would make you order another drink. She had a thick Greenpoint accent. She would say to us, "Girls, this ain't no church. If you want to talk, go to church and talk in the pew." Then she would take her cigarette and hold it under your chin and order you a drink just to show you who was in charge.

It was very unpleasant in there, but it was the only place we had. We didn't have coffeehouses. We didn't have groups. We didn't have any place that we could meet.

I was afraid of being busted in a bar and my life being ruined. The problem was even if the police let you go, which they generally

Karla at the 1976 Pride Rally in Central Park, where she served as master of ceremonies

did, they would notify your school, they would notify your place of employment, they would notify your family, they would notify anybody they could that you had been in a lesbian bar. Without benefit of a trial or even a formal arrest, your life could be completely ruined. You could lose everything—your children, your job, your family—just because you had been in a bar.

THE LAVENDER MENACE

On May 1, 1970, there was a conference called the Second Congress to Unite Women, organized by Betty Friedan. Betty Friedan had famously called lesbians "the lavender menace." She said if lesbians were let into the women's movement, we would destroy the women's movement. On the program for the

congress there was nothing about lesbians, working-class women, or people of color. We had had enough.

We got together with lesbians from the women's movement. We were calling ourselves various things, such as GLF [Gay Liberation Front] women and Radicalesbians. We got together in various apartments and wrote a document called "The Woman-Identified Woman," which has become a classic document and begins by stating, "A lesbian is the rage of all women condensed to the point of explosion." It was truly a collective document.

We put this document together, we mimeographed it, and we silk-screened T-shirts that said "Lavender Menace." We ran off the T-shirts with dye in a bathtub. These were the tools of the revolution. Then we headed to the congress.

The Congress to Unite Women started. We had cased the place. One of us went behind the stage and pulled the plug on all of the lights. The whole place went dark, and the mics went out. When we turned the lights back on a few minutes later, the audience was completely surrounded by lesbians. There were lesbians with signs like, "Take a lesbian to lunch," "We are your worst nightmare," "We are your best fantasy," and so on.

Rita Mae Brown stood up and said, "Who wants to join us?" A plant in the audience said, "I want to join you, sisters." Rita Mae Brown pulled her T-shirt off over her head. Women in the audience were just gasping in horror, but she had a Lavender Menace T-shirt on underneath.

I was in the audience. I stood up and said, "I'm tired of being in the closet in this movement." I ripped my blouse off, and I had a Lavender Menace T-shirt on underneath. We got up on the stage and said, "Look, this is not going to go on as usual."

The congress did change things. We put lesbian issues, of social class and race, onto the agenda of the women's movement for the first time. They did not come off after that. It was really a significant victory in the women's movement.

THE TIGER AT THE GATES

One of the things that I think is different between my generation and young people today is that if, heaven forbid, I had been in the Pulse Nightclub, I would have expected that violence to happen. I always expected people to come in and shoot us at meetings, at demonstrations. When we went to Albany to protest for civil rights, people in the crowd threw things at us. I was shot at three times over the years.

I think that younger people today are maybe a little naive, and they think they are safe now that marriage is legal. I think we are in a very dangerous political moment. I believe very strongly that all of the rights that we think we have now can be taken away tomorrow, such as the right to marry. I think that we could see camps in the future. They would be different. They might be for Muslims instead of for Japanese Americans. I think that lesbians and gay men might go underground and live in fear or might have to move to Canada. I think that the Christian right in this country advocates stoning us to death. I think that if the right-wing forces in this country got their way, things can always go backwards. I think that the tiger is always at the gates and that you always have to stand guard at the gates to keep the tiger from eating you alive.

The late 1960s and early 1970s were fun. We certainly risked being arrested, and some people were arrested. You risked being persecuted at some future time. My phones were tapped. But we took political action anyway and disregarded the potential personal cost. Gandhi said something to the effect that there is no change without action, and if you don't take action then there'll be no change. That's the conundrum of life—that if you want something to happen, you have to do something.

Karla lives today in Manhattan with her spouse, Karen F. Kerner, a retired emergency room physician, and with the constant companionship of her guide dog, Duchess.

JAMES CREDLE

DECORATED VETERAN, UNIVERSITY ADMINISTRATOR
NEWARK, NEW JERSEY

James Credle was born in 1945 in Mesic, a small town on North Carolina's eastern shore. While serving as an Army medic in Vietnam, James was wounded yet still managed to help evacuate his fellow soldiers. He was subsequently honored with a Purple Heart. After Vietnam, James attended Rutgers University and later served as the school's assistant dean of students from 1976 to 2005. He also held multiple veterans' leadership positions, including vice chair of the Agent Orange Commission for the state of New Jersey. He helped found the National Association of Black and White Men Together and the Newark LGBTQ Center and served on the board of the Newark Pride Alliance.

On October 21, 2013, the day same-sex weddings became legal in New Jersey, James and his partner, Pierre Dufresne, were married at Newark City Hall by Newark mayor and future US senator Cory Booker.

Growing up in Mesic, North Carolina, the church was the center of our lives. Mount Olive Baptist Church. I grew up singing in the choir, which a lot of young men did at that age and that stage in our lives. For me, though, early on I knew I was gay. There was no such thing as gay, but I knew I had feelings for men or boys that was different than for girls. In fact, I would often hang out with the girls, and we would talk about how cute the boys were.

But I knew there was something in church that I learned early on, that man does not lie down with man and that was an abomination. I had problems with that notion because it was natural for me. It was just natural that

I felt that way about men or boys. It's just a natural affection. So I had problems with the idea of that, that something was wrong with me if I had these feelings.

I also had a problem with the church in the sense that we would go to church and we were being told that, as far as blacks were concerned, as far as our status in life, we accept and work through where we were at. To just accept that and do the best you can. Then you would get your rewards in heaven if you were a good Christian. I had problems with that because I knew that there was a rich white family that lived on land right across the river from my family house. I often wondered, well, they can be rich and all of that

James in 1992, on a trip from his hometown of Mesic, NC, to New Orleans

and they will go to heaven; why do we have to wait? Why do we have to wait to get our salvation and they can do both, they can be rich here and go to heaven as well?

I also had a problem with the fact that, in the black church, there was this white Jesus. I had real problems with the fact of, why would there be a white, blue-eyed Jesus? Why was that also something that we would look up to, when we looked around us and whites were treating us as less than human?

I didn't have the audacity to ask anyone about that. Growing up in Carolina at that time, there was always the sense of not rocking the boat. My real thought was, how do I get out from this situation? How do I get away from this small town, get away from this racist situation, and allow myself to grow?

BAD PAPER

After Vietnam, I enrolled at Rutgers. While I was there, I started working in the Office of Veterans Affairs. I later became director of the office. That began my major work with working with veterans.

A lot of minority veterans were given "bad paper" during the Vietnam era. Bad paper is a less-than-honorable discharge. That means you do not get any veterans benefits at all— none for housing, none for education. When you apply for a job and people learn that you got a less-than-honorable discharge, they automatically think of you as a bad person and a bad risk.

What happened a lot of the times was that, if you were drafted, you did your year in Vietnam. When you came back to the States, you had three or four more months to serve. That's when you might decide that all that stuff about spit shine no longer applied. Black veterans might decide that they wanted to wear an Afro. They might not have their boots shined and their clothing in condition that was viewed as Army ready. Their commanding officer would see that as disobeying an order, and they would be given a less-than-honorable discharge. It was a recipe for 800,000 less-than-honorable discharges.

Later, when President Carter offered a form of amnesty for draft dodgers who left the country, we tried to get him to include veterans with bad paper in that amnesty. We felt that it was unfair that these white guys mostly who went to other countries were given a break, and you can't give a break to veterans who were of color who went to the military. Because they, in their own way, were also protesting the war. But they got bad paper, and you don't give them a break.

That's what I'm angry about.

"I SEE YOUR HUMANITY"

My first husband was Dutch. He worked with the International Lesbian and Gay Association. Although the ILGA was based in Europe, they spent a lot of time focusing on issues in South America, in Africa, in other parts of the world that were affecting gay people. We worked very closely with the international gay community around what was going on with Simon Nkoli in South Africa. [Editor's note: Simon Nkoli was an anti-apartheid, gay rights, and AIDS activist in South Africa.] We wrote letters to support him as an openly gay man in prison with the ANC [African National Congress]. The result was that when Simon got out and when the ANC rose to power, they made sure that LGBT rights were a part of the constitution of the new South Africa.

Whereas with US gays, it's always been centered around what's happening here in America and not really having a worldview. When you grow up in the US, in a society that has become, in a lot of ways, the biggest, the boldest, the richest ever in history, and it's built on the backs of slaves, we can't even talk about that. We're still in denial about slavery. That if it weren't for slavery, the US would not be the rich, powerful country that it is,

because all of that came out of the ability to build an economy without the cost that goes with it because of slavery.

Hope happens when all of America can come together and say, "Okay, all of America, let's have a dialogue around race, a real dialogue around race and its impact on our society." That's been my disappointment with the gay community, working with whites who don't put humanity up front. What hurts is that, I hate to put it this way but I'm going to put it out there anyway—at some level, white supremacy is in the DNA of America. Unless we as gay people struggle to understand that in everything we do—we've got to examine, where does white supremacy fit into this? And if it does, how do we rip it out? Unless we do that consciously, we're going to subconsciously always include that because it's part of our DNA.

Just a sense that someone can tell you, "I see your humanity." [*crying*] That's all it takes. I can see you are another human being, just like me.

BRIDGES

DONNA RED WING

ORGANIZER, RECONCILER

DES MOINES, IOWA

> For more than thirty years, Donna Red Wing was a national leader in the fight for human rights, civil rights, and LGBTQ equality. A right-wing opponent once reportedly called Donna "the most dangerous woman in America." She wore the title proudly.
>
> Born in 1950 in public housing in Worcester, Massachusetts, Donna cut her activist teeth on 1960s anti-war protests. She soon joined the burgeoning women's movement while running the Child Assault Prevention Project of New England. In the early 1990s, Donna and her partner, Sumitra, moved to Portland, Oregon, just in time for one of America's great gay rights electoral battles: Ballot Measure 9. After Donna helped defeat the anti-gay measure, she was named Woman of the Year by *The Advocate*.
>
> In subsequent decades, Donna played countless important roles in the campaign for LGBTQ inclusion and equality. She worked with GLAAD, HRC, the Gill Foundation, and the Howard Dean 2004 presidential campaign, and she served as co-chair of the Obama campaign's LGBT Leadership Council. She received the Interfaith Alliance's first Walter Cronkite Faith and Freedom Award, and she later served as the alliance's Washington, DC, chief of staff. Not tired yet, in 2012, Donna moved with Sumitra to Des Moines, Iowa, where she served as executive director of One Iowa for four years.

My wife, Sumitra, and I have now been together for thirty years. One day, I said, "Let's move." We chose Portland, Oregon. We subscribed to the *Oregonian* and saw an ad in the jobs section for someone to run the lesbian community project. It sounded like lesbian Disneyworld. There were softball tournaments, and there were parties. Laughingly, I put my résumé on lavender paper. I sent in my résumé, and within a week I had a call. They wanted to interview me. About ten minutes into the interview, they offered me the job. We packed up everything we had, put it in the big van, and drove across country to Portland.

Lesbian Disneyworld did not last very long. The radical religious right had decided to try to pass an amendment to the state constitution. Ballot Measure 9 was their attempt to splay open the constitution of Oregon and create a second-class citizenship for LGBT people. [For more on

Ballot Measure 9, see pp. 260–61.]

If the measure passed, LGBT people could have any state licensure taken away from them. Your stereotypical hairdresser, to a physician, to your driver's license—you would have second-class citizenship. We thought, "Nobody's going to vote for this. This is insane. This is really insane."

We found ourselves front and center with the radical religious right. It was like a war. Sumitra and I were literally attacked by white supremacists and neo-Nazis. We got death threats. Other people were murdered. Churches and homes were burned to the ground. At my office, I had to have police open my mail because of the things that were sent in the mail.

I remember one time driving across a bridge in Portland. The bridges go up and down for the boats. The bridges had gone up and we had to stop, and there was a fellow in a pickup truck next to me, and he leaned over and he recognized me. He leaned down, and I thought he was going to ask for directions or something. I had my window down. He just spit in my face.

I was shaking. I was horrified. I was trapped there. I couldn't go anywhere. This man, all he did is spit in my face, but it was the most disgusting thing.

We won the battle, but not by much. I think it was 47 percent of Oregonians who voted to make us second-class citizens. I think people forget, the LGBTQ movement is not very old. Thirty years ago, we were illegal in almost every state. That gave people permission to hurt us.

THE OUTSIDE AND THE INSIDE

During the battle over Ballot Measure 9, we lived in absolute fear. Do you live in fear and do something about it? Or do you live in fear and just live in fear? I think we decided to just do something about it.

For the first time, I really flexed my political muscle. Not only was I working with the LGBT community, but we worked with people we never thought we could work with before. I started working with the local police department. They were kind and accepting and protected us. We worked with local government. We forged relationships that I think really, really helped us as we moved forward.

At one point, I realized all the power was in the police bureau's budget committee. I'd rather stick pins in my eyes than be on a budget committee, but I got appointed. I got a whole bunch of other people appointed. We designed the police bureau's budget. How much power is there in that? We had women's strength programs, and we had all kinds of things that they'd never even thought of before.

I learned how to navigate both on the outside and the inside. In fact, one of the police officers said that they were always glad to see me because they knew Queer Nation or ACT UP were going to do something extreme, and then they would just pivot to me because as extreme as I was, I wasn't that extreme. Of course, I worked with ACT UP and Queer Nation and all of these groups, and we would plan it. You do this really outrageous thing, and I'll come in and say, "Hey, come and talk to me."

It was life changing, life changing.

YOU'RE BUYING COFFEE NEXT TIME

There's a fellow here in Iowa, his name is Bob Vander Plaats. He's head of the radical right group here. One day, I just walked up to him and said, "Hi, my name is Donna. I'd like to have coffee with you." He said, "Okay, call my office." Afterward, he told me he was stunned. He had no idea what I wanted and what I was up to.

We met for coffee. What surprised me was, I really liked him. He was funny. He was smart. He has a son who's profoundly disabled, and he's an amazing father. The first time we met, afterward I got in my car and I called my wife. I said, "I don't want to like this man. Why did I laugh at his jokes?" Well, they were funny.

That isn't to say, if Bob did something really horrible or stupid, I'd come after him like you wouldn't believe. He would do the same. We're dealing with each other as human beings and not as stereotypes. He had to give up what he thought lesbians were about, and I had to give up a little bit about what I thought right-wing evangelicals were about.

There are people on Bob's side who are really angry that he meets with me. There are people in the LGBT community who are really angry that I meet with him. For me, I think it's the next step. We live in a place and space that we have to share, and we're finding out that we have things in common.

After we won marriage on a federal level, Bob and I bumped into each other at a TV station, and he just gave me a great big hug and said, "You're buying coffee next time."

In 2017, Donna was diagnosed with cancer. Learning this news, OUTWORDS hurried an interview team to Iowa in March 2018. Donna and Sumitra welcomed us with pastries and tea, and Donna bestowed on OUTWORDS one of our most compelling, inspiring interviews. Six weeks later, she passed away.

MARCUS ARANA

TWO-SPIRIT/BISEXUAL/TRANSGENDER AMBASSADOR

SAN FRANCISCO, CALIFORNIA

Marcus Arana was born in Anchorage, Alaska, in 1957, designated female and given the name Mary. He spent most of his childhood with his mom and siblings in Fresno, California. Starting at age fourteen, Marcus lived and worked on a cooperative farm while paying his own way through a private "hippie" high school, where Marcus found a community of like-minded queer kids. At fifteen, still living as Mary, he came out as lesbian.

In 1976, Marcus moved to the "queer paradise" of San Francisco. Two years later, he helped organize against the Briggs Initiative, which would have banned gays and lesbians from teaching in California public schools. The lessons Marcus took from this fight would later aid him as a bisexual, trans, and two-spirit activist.

From a young age, Marcus felt his true identity was male. In his thirties, he finally transitioned. Since then, Marcus has done vital work for the transgender community, including training San Francisco police officers in transgender community awareness, integrating transgender women into women's shelters, and helping draft protocols for the fair treatment of transgender inmates. Marcus also authored two reports for the San Francisco Human Rights Commission.

In 2004, Marcus met two-spirit people for the first time. [Editor's note: two-spirit is the modern English umbrella term for queer identities and gender roles that are part of hundreds of Native American cultures.] This prompted Marcus to reconnect with his Blackfoot heritage, embrace the indigenous two-spirit identity, reclaim key aspects of his own femininity, and strike a deep, spiritual balance to all the different elements that add up to Marcus Arana.

As a toddler, before I even hit school, I knew I was different, and I knew somehow it was something that couldn't be talked about.

When you're a masculine little girl, you get called a tomboy. And I think in the world of kids, it's probably easier to be a tomboy than a sissy, but I think it's only marginally easier because I still got picked on and I got called names and I got boys beating on me and little girls not wanting to play with me. So it was kind of a solitary childhood. I did a lot of reading and flying kites and hanging out with the dog.

At age nine I knew that I was attracted to girls, but also you know at a very early age that that's a bad thing, that's a wrong thing. So even by age nine I knew words like "lezzie" and "fag," and that was in 1966. So I spent my childhood as a little queer kid who has to keep that under wraps. It wasn't until I was fifteen that I finally came to grips with it. And I remember I was sitting in my friend's house and I was lamenting about the problems in my life, and she looked at me and said, "It sounds like you need a good man." I shook my head and I said, "No, I think I need a good woman."

It's one of those moments where something comes out of your mouth and you can't really take it back. So that was my coming-out-as-a-lesbian moment.

LESSONS FROM
THE BRIGGS INITIATIVE

In 1976, I moved to San Francisco. And San Francisco in 1976 was just an amazing place. There was the Center for Individual Responsibility, which was kind of this clearinghouse for gay activities. There was the Stonewall Parade that happened every year. It started in the Castro and it marched to the Civic Center, and it was very political.

In 1978, Anita Bryant and John Briggs were doing their thing, trying to pass legislation in California to ensure that no teachers could be homosexuals. In fact, no teachers could even support homosexuality as a viable lifestyle. It was the Briggs Initiative. [For more on the Briggs Initiative, see p. 237.] It

was a very polarizing initiative because it was couched in a way of, "We have to protect the children. We have to protect the children." Homosexuals were being painted as people who went out and recruited. And that was the whole line that was being given out, that we couldn't possibly procreate on our own, so the only way that we can keep having more gay people is to go out and recruit young people and to turn them homosexual, because that's how it works, you know: we all got turned homosexual.

The Briggs Initiative was the place where I found a greater need for a concerted queer civil rights movement. I'd come out of the anti-war movement. I'd done a lot of protesting in the streets. But that was a point where I saw the efficacy of organizing, of grassroots organizing, of working with allies within a system, of creating equal pressures both within a system and outside the system to create change.

When you're trying to create change, it takes equal pressure on both the inside and the outside to create that change. If all you have are people standing outside of the institution throwing rocks at the windows, people inside the institution are not going to do much. They're going to feel very defensive and very entrenched in their position. If you have people on the inside who have managed to get into that position, and they're saying, "You know, the people on the outside, they actually have some valid points," then you create pressure from the inside and pressure from the outside. And that's when change happens.

Marcus at 25, serving as MC for a Halloween dance in Humboldt County, CA. Marcus writes: "My persona was called Dread Weatherly. I was secretly in love with that tux and tails."

STANDARDS OF CARE

What does somebody do with their gender identity when they're hiding it? Does it ever go away? Does it disappear? I had figured out that I was born as this man inside this woman's body. It never went away, and it was always this nagging sensation that followed me all through my teens, all through my twenties, all through my early thirties. And it wasn't until thirty-seven that I finally came to grips with being transgender, that I even learned the word "transgender."

I was in a staff meeting at work in San Francisco, an organization called Community United Against Violence, and one of the staff people says, "We keep talking about transgender people and offering services to transgender people, but we don't have any transgender staff members, and that's a problem."

All of a sudden my arm shot up in the air and I said, "Yeah, you do. I am that person."

In 1994 and '95, when I first started transitioning, the *DSM*'s Standards of Care

were a lot more stringent. [Editor's note: *The Diagnostic and Statistical Manual of Mental Disorders* (*DSM*), published by the American Psychiatric Association, offers a common language and standard criteria for the classification of mental disorders.] They were based upon this notion if you were transsexual, that you had gender identity disorder. It was actually a psychological diagnosis. And it had funny criteria such as if you were female, you always wanted to stand and pee. Not all of these criteria necessarily fit all of us who were transsexual. Furthermore, I resent and resist this idea that I have a psychological disorder that makes me transsexual. I think that it's a medical condition, not a psychological condition; that for some people, it's a social choice to be gender queer or to transition for gender; for some of us, it's not. There's not this one certain way of being transsexual.

When transsexual people participate in creating the Standards of Care, as opposed to doctors who are not transsexual creating the Standards of Care, we have much more of a humane and approachable way to transition.

APPLES AND ORANGES

When we're talking about bisexuality, there's a lot of misconceptions that people have, that you are incapable of stable relationships; that if you're with one gender and somebody else catches your eye, you're immediately going to go off with the other gender. My relationship with my bisexuality was an understanding that I related to men and women differently, and the things that I explored sexually with them were different. So I tended to have far more emotionally intimate relationships with females. I fell in love with females. I tend to have more vibrant sexual relationships with men. They're easier to have sex with, they're a lot of fun to have sex with, it seems very playful, it's less of an emotional tie to me.

So I enjoy women for their softness; I enjoy men for their hardness. I enjoy women for their "heartness," I enjoy men for their laughs and their fun and playfulness. Just different. Apples and oranges.

AMBASSADOR

In 2004, I went to do a transgender education training for a group called the Bay Area American Indian Two-Spirits. And I met two-spirit people. Two-spirit people are indigenous people who don't fit inside the heteronormative boxes of male and female. That's the best way to describe us. We're outside the box.

How has being two-spirit affected me? It's affected me in so many ways. I'd say probably the most profound thing is this idea that I am an absolute embodiment of masculine and feminine and that I don't have to disavow either one. Because when you transition, somehow there's this idea that you're expected to throw away the gender that you once were. For some people that's really important, and I honor that; but for me that always felt awkward. When I changed my name, for example, I chose the middle name DeMaria, which means "from Mary," because I wanted to carry Mary with me wherever I went. So being two-spirit and coming into the two-spirit community actually allowed me

to reclaim a certain amount of my femininity and to find it to be an appropriate part of the balance of who I am.

I think that, for myself, a two-spirit person who is also transgender, I'm a great ambassador. I'm an ambassador from the Indian world to the non-Indian world. I'm an ambassador between men and women. As a bisexual person, I'm an ambassador between lesbian and gay people. So in many ways I think that two-spirit people are the balancing point. And we're a very important part of the foundation to keep everything in spiritual balance.

Marcus was one of OUTWORDS' first interviewees. He immediately invited us to call him Tío (Spanish for "uncle"). Marcus has battled cancer, physical disabilities, and homelessness. In spite of or perhaps because of these hardships, his spirit, warmth, and wisdom always shine through.

JIM TOY

CAMPUS ORGANIZER

ANN ARBOR, MICHIGAN

Jim Toy was born in 1930, in New York, to a Scotch-Irish American mother and Chinese American father. After Jim's mother passed away, his father moved the family to Granville, Ohio, to be close to Jim's maternal grandparents. After the Japanese launched a surprise attack on the US naval base at Pearl Harbor in December 1941, killing more than 2,400 Americans, Jim's stepmother sent him to school with a sign around his neck that read, "I AM NOT A JAP."

In 1957, Jim became music director at Saint Joseph's Episcopal Church in Detroit and gradually began coming out of the closet. After the Stonewall riots, he helped establish the Ann Arbor chapter of the Gay Liberation Front (GLF). Soon after, at an anti–Vietnam War rally, Jim became the first recorded person in Michigan to publicly come out as gay.

Jim helped create the Lesbian-Gay Male Programs Office (LGMPO) at the University of Michigan—the first staffed university office in the world for addressing sexual orientation issues. Jim later helped pressure the University of Michigan, the city of Ann Arbor and other cities to adopt nondiscrimination policies for LGBTQ people. He continued to work extensively within the Episcopal Church on queer issues, and he also worked as an HIV/AIDS educator and patient counselor. Today, the LGBT center in Ann Arbor is named the Jim Toy Community Center.

In 1957, I got the letter from my former rector inviting me to direct the music program at Saint Joseph's Episcopal Church in Detroit. The letter saved me from my morass of, "Oh my God, what am I going to do with my life?" I was happy to move to Detroit. Packed up. I had a Siamese cat. Put it in a container, got on the train.

During the Vietnam War, Saint Joseph's opened its doors to men who were seeking sanctuary from the draft. The FBI knew very well that Saint Joe's was a "radical" parish. They found out that one of the draft resisters, Tom Sinkovitch, was going to take sanctuary at the church. We knew somehow that the FBI was going to break in to try and arrest Tom, so six hundred people filled the church that night. The FBI broke through the locked door and came to the front of the gathering and said, "Tom Sinkovitch, stand up!" Six hundred people stood up. I still get chills when I think about that.

They had Tom's photo, so they arrested him, and that was the end of that.

I was not yet out of my gay closet, so I married a woman who was a member of the church choir. I said to myself the night before the wedding, "You are bisexual at worst, and this marriage will cure you." Obviously it didn't. After six years or so my wife filed for a no-fault divorce.

In December of 1969, I was typing up the Sunday church bulletin, and on the calendar I see a note that says, "Gay meeting." I went to the priest. We called him Daddy-O. I said, "Daddy-O, what is this gay meeting thing?" He was a great big guy with a big deep voice. He said, "I don't know what it is. One of the guys in the draft resistance group asked if we could have a gay meeting here, and I said, Whatever that is, if we can't have a gay meeting here, we might as well shut this God Box down."

I said thank you from the depths of my closet. I go back to typing. After work, I drive back to Ann Arbor, where I lived. I immediately run down to the local gay bar, and there's my buddy John. "John, there's something very strange going on at the God Box." "What?" "A gay meeting." "What's that?"

We didn't know. There never had been an open, above-ground, advertised, "gay meeting" in Michigan.

For a month, we "ambivalated" about whether to go. "Are we going to go?" "Yes." "No." The night before the meeting we get

together at the bar. "Are we going to go to this meeting?" We looked at each other and simultaneously said, "If we go, that means we're gay."

The next day, we got into John's car, and we drove to the meeting. There we found a dozen other women and men, just as excited and scared and confused as we were. A few months later, we decided to start a group in Ann Arbor.

"I'LL SAY SOMETHING"

In the course of our gay and lesbian meetings in Detroit, all the radical groups in Detroit got invited to march down Woodward Avenue in a radical march and have a big rally at Kennedy Square downtown.

Jim at the historic 1993 March on Washington for Lesbian, Gay, and Bi Equal Rights and Liberation.

We debated. "Are we going to march?" "Yes, we're going to march!" "Who's going to talk?" Some guy whose name I don't remember said he would talk.

We got downtown to Kennedy Square, and the groups began sending their speakers up to the platform. Our guy said, "I'm not talking," and he walked off.

We sat there for a couple of minutes. What were we going to do? I finally said, "I'll say something."

I got myself up to the podium, and this being an anti–Vietnam War rally, something inspired me to give my name, my age, and the fact that I was gay. I said, "My name is Jim Toy. I'm forty years old, and I'm a gay man."

I had not thought about the press. The *Detroit Free Press* and the *Detroit News* were there, and they published articles, and so I was out.

"GET YOUR BUTT OVER THERE"

The group we formed, we called ourselves the Ann Arbor Gay Liberation Front. We registered as a student group at the University of Michigan and started holding our meetings in the Michigan Union.

In 1973, we appealed to the University of Michigan to add sexual orientation as a protected class to its nondiscrimination bylaw. There was no mention at that time of gender identity or gender expression.

One of the regents strenuously objected to the inclusion of sexual orientation in the bylaw. He appealed to his Christian faith as justification for his objection to adding sexual orientation to the bylaw. He used Bible quotations in his pronouncements. He was a favorite with the Michigan electorate and kept getting reelected to the Board of Regents.

In 1992, two liberal regents, Rebecca McGowan and Laurence Deitch, got elected to the board. They asked me to meet with them about this concern, which I very gratefully did.

Two years later, I got a call one morning from a friend. The friend said, "The regents are going to vote on the nondiscrimination bylaw this morning. Get your butt over there." Over I went. Then-president James Duderstadt said, "Our next agenda item is the amendment of the university's nondiscrimination bylaw." Immediately, the opposing regent asked for the floor. He said, "You have heard over the years my objection to this addition to the bylaw. I am repeating it today." Then he sat down.

Regent Deitch was across the table from him. Regent Deitch pounded on the table and said, "The only reason that we have wasted time for twenty-one years on this concern is because of you and your obsession!"

That's language one doesn't ordinarily hear at a regents meeting. Then the regents cast their vote. It was 9–1, I believe, in favor of amending the bylaw.

After the vote, I was euphoric. I don't know what other term to use. After those decades of working for this change, it was an explosion of relief.

Jim was the first interviewee on OUTWORDS' first road trip in July 2016. At nearly ninety years old, Jim has a vibrant voice, piercing eyes, and a sharp memory. Above all, he exudes honesty, kindness, and humble strength.

MARTHA SHELLEY

RADICAL ACTIVIST, RADIO PRODUCER, WRITER

PORTLAND, OREGON

Martha Altman was born in 1943 in Brooklyn, New York, to Jewish parents of Russian and Polish descent. In November 1967, Martha attended her first meeting of the New York chapter of the Daughters of Bilitis (DOB). Because of FBI surveillance, DOB members were advised to take aliases. Martha took Shelley as a temporary alias and ended up keeping it.

Martha helped found the Gay Liberation Front, and in May 1970 she helped organize the infamous Lavender Menace "zap" of the Second Congress to Unite Women. From there, Martha poured her energy into countless media, literary, and journalistic projects. She produced the radio show *Lesbian Nation* on New York's WBAI radio station, contributed to the 1970 anthology *Sisterhood Is Powerful*, helped run the Women's Press Collective, and published many works, including *Crossing the DMZ* (a collection of her poetry) and *Haggadah: A Celebration of Freedom*. Along the way, Martha made time to co-parent two sets of children.

Martha is currently at work on the last novel of her trilogy about Jezebel, queen of ancient Israel.

When I was in middle school, the effects of McCarthyism were still very much with American culture. There was this thing called a "loyalty oath," and in New York State, school teachers were required to take this loyalty oath. I didn't understand all of it, but what I understood was people were supposed to be swearing that they weren't communists and anything related to that kind of "anti-government" stuff. I thought, "This is really stupid. If you are a communist and you want to be a school teacher, you're certainly not going to come out and say it. You're going to swear the oath and keep doing whatever you were doing."

Well, there came a moment where kids were bringing water guns to school and having water gun fights in the cafeteria or outside in the schoolyard. The principal sent around this thing you had to sign saying you weren't going to bring a water gun to class. To me, it looked like a kind of loyalty oath, so I refused to sign it. I wasn't planning to bring a water gun to school or anything. I just thought

Martha reading from her first poetry book, *Crossing the DMZ*, which was published in 1974

it was a stupid thing to do. They pulled me down to the principal's office and kept me there until they got me to sign it. They beat me down. I never forgave them for that. It stuck with me.

SMEARING THE PEACE MOVEMENT

Around 1968, '69, when I was working at Barnard College, I became friends with Stephen Donaldson, aka Bob Martin. Stephen was a student at Columbia University right across the street. I joined him on a peace march at Columbia University, where a number of the other Columbia University students were uncomfortable with having all these out gay people being part of the peace march. It was like we were smearing the peace movement. Like, if you are a communist or a queer, you have to keep it a secret in order to support a cause like civil rights or peace, because your very existence is a dirty name.

So Stephen and I got to be friends. He actually turned me on to LSD, and we would go to gay conferences together. We were actually dating each other, and that upset people because here we were being public representatives of the gay movement, and yet we were screwing around with each other. Of course, we were both sleeping with people of our own sexes as well. We were young, and we enjoyed upsetting people's expectations. A lot of them wanted to be recognized by straight America as, "All we want is to have a nice house in the suburbs with a white picket fence and straight job, and just be accepted like everybody else." On the other hand, some of us were doing psychedelic drugs, and some of us were dropping out, and an awful lot of us were saying, "We don't want that kind of white middle-class America. We don't want to work for the corporation and keep our nose to the grindstone all our lives. We have other ideas of what we want." Stephen and I were part of that young movement. Then, of course, came the Stonewall riot, and all hell broke loose.

CHANNELING ANGER

What made Stonewall different from other riots was, first, that the disturbances continued, and that was because of the peace movement and all of the other things that were going on. People weren't going to take it anymore.

It was something in the air, you might say, the temper of the times, people demonstrating and rioting against the oppression by the police and by the government, and they weren't going to just go home and be quiet afterwards.

The other thing that made a difference was that we formed an organization afterwards. We didn't just let it go. We were sitting in the offices of the Mattachine Society, drinking beer, planning a march to protest what had happened at the Stonewall, and we gave ourselves a name which was the Gay Liberation Front. Some people say that I made that name up, and I swear to God I do not remember using those words, but everybody says I did. What I do remember is, I was drinking beer, it was a hot afternoon, and slamming my hand on the table and yelling, "That's it. That's it. We're the Gay Liberation Front," and then realizing that I had cut myself on the pop-top that was sitting there on the table, and my hand was bleeding.

We started the Gay Liberation Front with a policy of, if you want to do something, go do it. You want to put out a newspaper, go do it. You want to put on a dance, do that. If you wanted to organize a demonstration, you organize it, and everybody who wanted to come would show up. It was a very loose organization. Its problem was that because we were so loose, we didn't have an ongoing structure to continue. It didn't take very long for people to start quarreling. It started off with having separate women's dances, then having a separate women's organization. I joined that organization, but I think it was a mistake. Same thing with a group called the Third World Action Revolutionaries. Because of racism, they decided they needed their own organization. Same with STAR, Street Transvestites Action, and the Gay Activists Alliance that was more politically oriented. We split off into these little factions, and that was not in my opinion a really good thing.

I think that because we are all human, people are going to squabble over power, and people are going to have their personality problems. This is really hard when you're young because everything seems so very important at that time. And when you're part of an oppressed group, you've got a lot

Martha in 1976 at the first Women in Print Conference, which brought together 130 lesbian and feminist publishers, booksellers, and printers to explore how to build a sustainable women's book network

of stored-up anger, and that comes out, but instead of you channeling that anger to fight the oppressors, people fight with each other because they're closest. It's like, your boss yells at you at work, you come home and you yell at your wife or your children. That's a very normal thing to do, but it's something that has to be resisted as much as possible because it's so destructive. I don't know how to get the next generation to resist that. I wish I had that magic wand.

SHARING FOOD FROM OUR GARDENS

If we have differences of opinion about really crucial items, I think the most important thing is to figure out what crucial things we have in common. For example, our next-door neighbors are fundamentalist Christians. They do not approve of gay marriage. They believe that the world was created in six days and God rested on the seventh.

They are also our best friends. They probably pray for us to become converted so that we don't have to go to hell. That doesn't matter. What matters is we are kind to each other, we share food from our gardens. I am teaching their little children martial arts, self-defense. I'm no great shakes as a martial artist, but I know enough to get them started.

What matters is that we are all human and that we have to look after each other and follow the basics. You know, love thy neighbor as thyself; do not oppress the stranger. Real basic stuff. They don't have to agree with me, I don't have to agree with them, we have to look after each other. As long as you are not

coming after me to throw me into Auschwitz, I am willing to work with you. If your core beliefs are so fragile that you can't work with me, I am truly sorry. There's nothing I can do about that.

OUTWORDS interviewed Martha at the red-shingled cottage she shares with her wife in Portland's Saint Johns district. Their yard is designated a Portland Certified Backyard Habitat. Well into her seventies, Martha has found ways to sustain and adapt her activism—to keep it passionate, but also fluid and humane.

GIGI RAVEN WILBUR

INTERSEX AND BDSM EDUCATOR

HOUSTON, TEXAS

Ladyboy Gigi Raven Wilbur was born in 1955 in Houston, Texas. At birth, Gigi's genitalia did not fit the standard definitions for male or female bodies, a condition known as being intersex or a hermaphrodite. Within days, Gigi was operated on to "normalize" her anatomy and define her as male. Today, Gigi identifies as intersex and uses the title Ladyboy to offset the lack of pronouns for hermaphrodites. At Gigi's suggestion, we've used both male and female pronouns to refer to her.

Gigi learned that he had been born intersex during college. Armed with this new knowledge, Gigi chose to come out fully as dyslexic, ADHD, intersex, and bisexual. Since then, she has been an outspoken activist for the bisexual and intersex communities. Gigi coproduces *After Hours*, a radio program that provides information about human sexuality. He has also served on BiNet USA's board of directors and helped create Celebrate Bisexuality Day in 1999 and turn it into an annual event.

Gigi is also deeply involved with the BDSM world. She wrote *The Dominant's Handbook: An Intimate Guide to BDSM Play* and operates Aphrodite's Temple, a modern-day sex temple that provides sex-positive education and a sex-positive sacred play space for adults. Gigi also wrote the essay "Walking in Shadows: Third Gender and Spirituality" about his intersex identity.

During college, I took a sex ed class and I discovered that I was a hermaphrodite. They call it intersex, but I like the term "hermaphrodite."

Basically, I have a penis and testicles, but also I have scarring where, at least as far as I can gather, my pussy was.

I don't know if my parents knew. Back in the '50s, when I was born, they just took the baby to another room, did surgeries, and then brought it back and said, "Oh, you're the proud parents of a whopping boy." My father was a minister and both my parents were very Christian and they didn't talk about those kind of things, so who knows?

I was kind of scapegoated and looked at as the black sheep from early, early on. I'm not as hyper now as I was when a kid, but being hyperactive, and my father coming home from work, all of a sudden here I am all over the place, it was like lighting the fuse, and he'd just take it out on me—all the frustrations and anger and whatever he'd been stuffing all day. He also tried to teach me sports. I remember one day he looked at me in frustration, and he sat down on the curb and he just shook his head like, "It's hopeless."

Somehow in our family, I became this monstrous thing that needed fixing. I knew I wasn't near as bad as what they were trying to propose. It kind of felt comic on one side and yet very awkward and weird on the other side. I mean, my mother was really into the speaking in tongues and the whole Holy Ghost bullshit. She kept trying to get me into that, and I said, "No way."

LADYBOY

In college, I had to come out as being dyslexic and ADHD, and I said, "I'm going to come out all the way." So I came out as bisexual and as intersex.

One of the hard parts of being bisexual is that I've been kicked out of gay bars. I've been kicked out of straight bars. Both sides don't like bi's. I've had gay friends say, "Just get off the fence. Make up your mind. You know you're gay." I said, "No, I'm bi." I always have liked both.

Sex and gender is a complex thing. It's not just hormones. It's not just chromosomes. It's not just body parts. I am a ladyboy. I'm not a male, I'm not a female. I've been at campfires in the pagan community. We run around naked, it's clothing optional, and everybody looks and sees my dick and says, "Oh, Gigi's a boy." I'll say, "No, there are parts missing, hidden. I'm part female." For a long time, even some of the pagans didn't get it. They said, "But you should just choose one or the other." We're so programmed in our culture that there can only be males or females, and if you identify as both, then that doesn't work.

That's why I had such a rough time. Why didn't they tell me? Why did they keep this big dirty secret? Why can't I be what I was born to be? It's nature, natural. I popped out this way. Get over it.

A WORD FOR ME

For about twenty-five years now, once a month, I've been doing a radio show called *After Hours: Queer Radio with Attitude* on KPFT 90.5 Houston. On the show, I talk about everything sexual, from bisexuality to how to improve your love relationship. Everything on techniques. I even did a Taoist genital massage live on the air, and the radio station banned us for a month and a half. I've gone naked on the air. I teach people how to have anal sex and how to do it in a way that's pleasurable, without any pain whatsoever, by starting with a good deep massage and tricking the muscles into relaxing before trying to go inside.

I know that we get a lot of younger people listening in sometimes, sneaking their little radio to bed with them. With sex education in this country being abstinence only, I go out of my way to educate people on where you stick what and how, and how it all works. Abstinence doesn't really work for all of us.

In addition, I teach that in sex, we're not just two physical bodies coming together. We need to form a genital-heart connection. We want to connect with each other at a deeper than just physical level, but we've lost that in this culture. So I bring in some of the tantric teachings, the breathing techniques. It's been a lot of fun doing the show. I'm always getting in trouble. And here's the amazing thing: they keep asking me back for more.

I've also gone on the air many times and talked about being intersex. It's been hard to find other intersex people who are willing to come on the show. So many live in shame and doubt, and they will not come out of the closet. What the medical community has done to intersex people is criminal. I mean, they actually strapped them down and opened their legs up and invited whole teams

of medical personnel to come in and parade and look at their odd, weird, abnormal genitals and make a big spectacle of them. After that happens, it's no wonder they are living in shame and stigmatized and thinking, "Oh, my body is not worthy of love. I'm abnormal. I'm weird."

I think one of the first magical words I found in childhood was "androgyny," "androgynous." When I saw that, I said, "That's what I am." That just resonated deep within me. I didn't know that such a word existed before that. I was so glad to find that word. I embraced it. I must have written it all over my room at the time. "Androgynous." "I love androgynous." "I am androgynous." It was just such a powerful thing to find that word. "Oh, wow. I didn't know they made words for me."

OUTWORDS interviewed Gigi in June 2017 inside Aphrodite's Temple, a standalone, soundproof structure behind her home. Gigi's temple and her life as a whole may be unfamiliar terrain for some within the LGBTQ community, which makes it all the more important that they be witnessed, listened to, honored, and shared.

LANI KA'AHUMANU

AUTHOR, BISEXUAL ACTIVIST

CAZADERO, CALIFORNIA

Lani Ka'ahumanu was born 1943 in Edmonton, Alberta, and grew up in the San Francisco Bay Area. As a member of the Kanaka Maoli (Hawaiian for "true people"), Lani stands with the Hawaiian sovereignty movement. As a mixed-heritage bisexual, she challenges any socially constructed assumptions that prevent us from fully being and expressing ourselves.

Lani married young and soon had two children. During the 1960s her activism bloomed. She became Another Mother for Peace, collected food for the Black Panthers' breakfast program, supported the United Farm Workers, and switched from Mrs. to Ms. In time, she and her husband amicably parted ways; Lani came out as lesbian, helped found San Francisco State's Women Studies Department, and in 1979 she became the first person in her family to graduate from college. Soon thereafter, she realized she was bisexual. In the growing shadow of HIV/AIDS, she cofounded BiPOL, the first feminist bisexual political action group. She also helped launch BiNet USA, the first national bisexual rights organization. For several years, she traveled the United States, using humor and sketch comedy to facilitate sex-, age-, and body-positive workshops, which led *Ms.* magazine to include Lani in their "50 Ways to Be a Feminist" issue.

Along with Loraine Hutchins (p. 120), Lani coedited *Bi Any Other Name: Bisexual People Speak Out*, a groundbreaking anthology whose twenty-fifth anniversary edition (2015) was listed as one of the *Lambda Book Review*'s "Top 100 GLBT Books of the 20th Century." Lani is currently writing her memoir, *My Grassroots Are Showing: Movement Stories, Speeches, and Special Affections*.

In the '60s, I started reading. I watched a lot of talk shows, and they'd have these feminists talking about the women's movement. My friend Kathy stopped shaving her legs, and that was so revolutionary. I changed from Mrs. to Ms., and my father's family was upset with me. It was "so disrespectful," blah, blah, blah. I'm thinking, "Really?"

My husband didn't mind. He thought it was kind of cool. But my consciousness was broken open. I saw the Black Panthers being interviewed on television about feeding kids.

They said, "Kids go to school without food. How are they gonna learn unless they have a hot breakfast?" I thought that made a lot of sense, so I started collecting food for the Black Panther breakfast program. Then the UFW, Cesar Chavez, boycott grapes. I identified with the people. Always with the people.

There came a time in the late '60s, early '70s where I was just crying a lot. I didn't know why. I was a Little League mom, a field trip driver, ran the art corner at my kids' school. I had a full life, an amazing life. But one afternoon I was at a friend's house. She was relaying a really moving story that had happened to her. When it came time for me to go home and cook dinner for the kids, I called my husband and said, "I'm gonna stay with her. I'm gonna stay overnight." I stood up for myself in a way I never had.

Some time later, my husband said, "I figured out why you're crying so much." He goes, "You've never, ever had a life of your own." He said, "You need to leave." As soon as I heard him, I knew he was right. Six weeks later I had an apartment of my own. I was about a mile away from the kids, and that's the hardest thing I've ever done in my entire life was to leave those kids. My hus-

Lani marching with BiPOL in the 1984 San Francisco Lesbian & Gay Pride Parade. Peppered with characters like San Francisco Mayor "Bi-Anne" Feinstein and England's Princess "Bi-ana", BiPOL walked away with the award for Most Outrageous Contingent.

band stood by me. I started going to school full-time at San Francisco State, right when people were organizing to found the Women Studies Department, so I got involved with all that. It was an awakening, an amazing awakening.

PUSH IT ALL

I think it's important that the "B" and "T" got added to LGBT because it represented all the work that had come before. But it doesn't mean that everybody understands B or T at all, and what the connections are, and what the history is—especially the history. Bisexual people have been around.

The two big examples are the first student homophile group at Columbia was founded by a bisexual man, Stephen Donaldson [see p. 201]. Does anybody know that? Does anybody know that Brenda Howard, a bisexual woman, was at Stonewall and helped organize the first march to commemorate Stonewall a month later, and then helped conceive of a yearly parade, and that was the birth of all our Pride parades? No.

There's an erasure that happens. It's overwhelming, makes me cranky a lot of times, and a lot of people burn out. I don't know what the resistance is. We've got to educate and educate and educate. And on the other side, the researchers were only researching gay and lesbian people. There was never any research on bisexuals, and now we have research that is showing in the GLB community there's more bisexuals than gay and lesbian put together. What does that mean? It means a lot of things, but it also shows that

bisexuals' suicide rates are higher because of the invisibility, the mental health issues, drug abuse. The research now is happening, and the education is happening on all the levels that it needs to. And some people are still so stubborn. They're stuck in this either/or kind of thing.

I've never lived in an either/or world in my whole life. My life has always been both/and. The other day I was driving, and I was thinking, it's beyond both/and. It's all/and. It's all/and. There's so many young bisexuals coming up, and transgender people, and pansexuals, and fluids, and whatever you want to call yourself. Yes, do it. Just push it all. Please.

DAVID McEWAN

PHYSICIAN, AIDS ACTIVIST

HONOLULU, HAWAI'I

> David McEwan was born in Manitoba, Canada, in 1946 and raised near Rochester, New York. At the age of eight, he resolved to become a doctor. Five years later he read about Father Damien, a nineteenth-century Catholic priest who cared for people with Hansen's disease (more commonly known as leprosy) on the Hawaiian island of Moloka'i. Inspired by Father Damien, David dreamed of devoting his life to helping marginalized people.
>
> After graduating from medical school in 1972, David set off to hitchhike around the world—but when he hit Hawai'i, he fell in love with the remote island chain. Five years later, David opened his family medicine practice in Honolulu. When AIDS emerged in the early 1980s, David cofounded Life Foundation to provide education to the community and assistance to those affected by the disease.
>
> David has also been involved with many other LGBTQ-affiliated organizations and projects, including the Hawai'i LGBT Legacy Foundation, Names Project Hawai'i, and Marriage Project Hawai'i. He served on the boards of the Susan G. Komen Foundation and Hawai'i Public Television. In 1991, he was awarded the ACLU's Allan Saunders Award for Civil Liberties. Over David's thirty-eight-year medical career, he's been named on multiple occasions by *Honolulu* magazine as one of Hawai'i's best doctors.

A round 1978 I joined a new organization in San Francisco called the Bay Area Physicians for Human Rights. It's the first exposure that I had to an organized gay doctor group. At the first meeting I went to, I was sitting right next to Randy Shilts, who wrote *And the Band Played On* and lots of other amazing books. We were hypothesizing this new disease that people were talking about. Nobody really knew what it was. I went to the washroom, came back, and was standing in the back of the auditorium when a New York physician named Dr. Alvin Friedman-Kien talked about Kaposi sarcoma in gay men. Everybody was like, "Okay. That's interesting. What are you talking about, really?" Towards the end of his presentation, Dr. Friedman-Kien said, "Has anyone else in the room seen this?"

Hands went up all across the room. Kaposi sarcoma was a rare skin cancer that traditionally only occurred in people in the

Mediterranean region of Europe and often in people in the Jewish community. Everybody was looking around like, "What's going on here?" That got the conversation really going. That was my first exposure to what came to be known as AIDS. Within a month or so of that, Dr. Michael Gottlieb, who also became a good friend because we started sending patients back and forth, he made the first announcement of pneumocystis pneumonia that got reported with the Centers for Disease Control. A few weeks after that, I diagnosed this first case of pneumocystis in Hawai'i. I was like, "Whoa. It's coming to Hawai'i too."

I subsequently heard about a doctor in San Francisco who was working on this, who I could send my patient to to get a second opinion. His name was Dr. Donald Abrams. He was a fellow at UCSF Moffitt in San Francisco. I sent my patient to him. About a month or so later, I went over to meet Dr. Abrams to see what I could learn. I'll never forget this for the rest of my life. I went up into his lab. He said, "Let's go look at the lymph nodes of your patient upstairs because I think there's some interesting stuff here." We looked at the lymph nodes and he says, "Right now, I'm doing my research on the T cell leukemia virus that causes leukemia in Japanese people and some other Asian folks as well. We've isolated that virus. My prediction is the lymph nodes from those patients look the same as your patient's. I predict this disease is caused by a T cell–like leukemia virus. It's sexually transmitted. It's terminal. There's no cure for it. Take that with you back to Hawai'i, and see what you can do to save lives."

Dr. Abrams was correct. I came back. I got information from Gay Men's Health Crisis in New York City. I got the brochures from San Francisco AIDS Foundation. Both organizations were about a year old about that time. I got permission to reproduce the brochures. That's basically how I and three friends started the Life Foundation.

THE LIFE FOUNDATION

In the first year of the Life Foundation, in late 1982, early 1983, we were frantically running, trying to make it happen. We knew we were behind the mainland in the epidemic, but people with AIDS would come here, and people from here would go to the mainland and catch it. We were further behind. We had an opportunity.

In other parts of the country, the various AIDS organizations often were in conflict with the local department of health. We made a decision early on that we were going to work with the department of health. We worked with them really closely. We became the first AIDS organization in the nation to recommend that everybody get tested, even though there was no treatment yet.

We had a very simple theme that came from Jack Law, the owner of Hula's bar here in Honolulu. He said it one day. "We will do what saves lives. It may not be politically correct. We will do what saves lives."

We said, "If people get tested, granted it's tragic that we don't have any treatment yet, but there will be treatments eventually. We're going to damn well pass laws here, including confidentiality laws, so that people

DAVID MCEWAN   211

don't get discriminated against." And that's what we did.

Next we had a private school here called Punahou. One of our nurses and myself, we put together a program to provide AIDS education to Punahou kids. The nurses did an incredible job. The department of health eventually came to us and said, "Can we steal your curriculum?" We said, "Of course."

Then the military came and asked myself and a few others, "Could you come over here and teach the marines over at the Marine Corps Air Station in Kaneohe? Please don't tell anyone in the military you're doing this." We said, "Sure." I and another guy went over thinking we were going to speak to maybe twenty or thirty people. There were a couple thousand people there.

Next it became clear that a needle-exchange program needed to be implemented in order to prevent the spread of AIDS amongst needle users and into women who might become pregnant and then into children. The program started at the Life Foundation, then it moved over to the department of health. All we needed to do was get over the bigots and the legislature that would vote against anything AIDS-related. We just overwhelmed them. We just had great people. It got through the legislature. Today Hawai'i has the lowest pediatric AIDS rate in the nation. You can count the number of kids born with HIV on one or two hands. The HIV needle-transmission rate is almost zero because you can get your needles without any problem whatsoever.

The Centers for Disease Control really appreciated what we're doing. We were considered very innovative. We did a whole bunch of those first things.

Those who envision Hawai'i as a conflict-free paradise have never met the state's religious and political conservatives. In the 1980s, they came after David with a vengeance, accusing him of profiteering and having sex with his patients. Fortunately, David is both mild-mannered and very tough. Like Father Damien before him, he served those he was sent to serve.

ARDEN EVERSMEYER

OLD LESBIANS ADVOCATE, ORAL HISTORIAN
HOUSTON, TEXAS

Arden Eversmeyer was born in 1931 in Stevens Point, Wisconsin. In 1932, she moved with her family to Dallas, Texas. She worked as a public school teacher and counselor for thirty years, then embarked on a second "career" building community and developing resources for old lesbians. (Arden prefers the term "old" to "elderly" or "aging," which she regards as euphemisms.) In 1987, Arden founded Lesbians Over Age Fifty (LOAF), a social networking and support group. Eleven years later, she founded the Old Lesbian Oral Herstory Project (OLOHP). Since then, Arden has conducted or coordinated the interviews of 650 lesbians seventy years or older across America, publishing two anthologies featuring many of their life stories. Today, the OLOHP archives are preserved at Smith College in Northampton, Massachusetts.

In addition to her other work, Arden and her late wife, Charlotte, served for fourteen years on the steering committee of Old Lesbians Organizing for Change (OLOC), working to challenge ageism, specifically as it affected lesbians and other women.

I came out in 1948. I was seventeen years old, a freshman in college. I was on the field hockey team, the badminton team, and synchronized swimming. I was right smack in the middle of a mess of lesbians. I met the woman who would become my first lover. She was a senior, and I was a freshman. We had to be very, very careful. We had a dean at the time whose mission, I think, was to discover everybody. My freshman year, a good percentage of the students went home for the Christmas holidays, but then a whole bunch of them didn't come back. Somebody else came and packed their belongings. That's

what was known as a purge. That's when it came home to me how careful you really had to be.

You didn't necessarily have to be caught in a compromising situation. Students would get called into the dean's office, and they would be asked about people. It was kind of, "We won't bother you, if you will help us." Students were terrified if they didn't cooperate.

The second purge was when I was a senior. A lot of students, all the same weekend. Go home for a holiday. Don't come back. The sad part about it was that there were a couple of those girls who were sent away in that

Building the float for the 2012 Houston Pride Parade

purge that didn't have a clue. They were not gay. They were not lesbians. They were not involved with one. But somebody was mad at them, and that's how you got even.

LOOKING YOUR AGE

In December of 1990, Charlotte and I went on the steering committee of a new organization called Old Lesbians Organizing for Change, OLOC. We served in that organization for fourteen years. And the last seven of those years I was codirector with Vera Martin, an African-American woman from Apache Junction, Arizona.

OLOC basically fights ageism. Ageism against women is what we were really concerned with. And not just lesbians, but for the population as a whole. Because we live in a very ageist culture. We're the only so-called modern culture that doesn't revere old women.

We worked with some of the national organizations helping them confront their ageism. The Creating Change Conference, for example. They are ageist beyond belief. A national organization is totally staffed and run by young people who are telling us old folks how it is we are supposed to feel and what it is we are supposed to do. We have done workshops with them on ageism, and they don't get it. It's a big battle, so we do a lot of that kind of work. I still get exercised over it.

Somebody will be talking and ask, "How old are you?" "I'm eighty-six." "You don't look your age." And I'll say, "And what is eighty-six supposed to look like?"

It all goes back to, "You're old. You're decrepit. You're tottering. You're using a cane. You're quivering in your voice." All of this is the picture, not the person. Our culture categorizes women, particularly, as we reach a certain age. The only thing left that we're worth anything for is caregiving, taking care of the grandkids and the great-grandkids. And that's what our role is supposed to be.

So this is what OLOC is all about. Fighting this conception of what age is.

A GIFT OF AGE

About twenty years ago, I started what today is the Old Lesbian Oral Herstory Project.

By now, my wife, Charlotte, and I were both retired, and we had a motor home. Twice a year, we were making trips someplace. When we were planning a trip, I'd check the Old Lesbians Organizing for Change database for women who were seventy or older. I'd create a route going out one way and coming back another way, and I'd look on the route and check the database, and when I found somebody that was seventy or older, I'd get in touch with them.

Today, we've got over six hundred interviews. The oldest woman in the project was a woman born in 1916. Our first book, *A Gift of Age*, came out in 2009. We are actually international. We have stories from Australia and Japan and Costa Rica.

We have interviewers located all over the United States. So if we get the name of somebody, we probably can match them.

We have one in Connecticut, one in North Carolina, and three in Florida. And we've got four women, whose home base is Iowa, who are full-time RVers who are all over the country traveling. And they winter as a rule in Arizona. So we've got this moving group, and we are getting wonderful stories from all over the country.

I did the whole thing for maybe the first ten years. I did probably three hundred interviews. Two years ago, we had ten trips. This year, we've cut back a little bit. Age and health is kind of slowing us a little bit.

I've had a ball with the Oral Herstory Project. I have made some wonderful friendships. Absolutely incredible. So it in a way was self-serving, but it's helped others too, so that's what it was all about.

OUTWORDS interviewed Arden at her Houston home in June 2017. Two months later, Hurricane Harvey decimated the city, flooding Arden and Charlotte out of their home. In an email, Arden wrote, "People are coming together. Stories of heroics and miracles abound." Charlotte passed away in April 2018.

WORDS

CRISOSTO APACHE

NDEISDZAN POET AND EDUCATOR

DENVER, COLORADO

> Crisosto Apache was born in 1971 in New Mexico. His father is a member of the Diné (Navajo) tribe, and his mother is part Mescalero Apache and part Chiricahua Apache. Crisosto grew up with his mother on the Mescalero Apache Reservation in New Mexico. After becoming the only member of his family to graduate high school, he earned his BA in English and Native American studies from Metropolitan State University in Denver, Colorado, followed by his MFA in creative writing in 2015 from the Institute of American Indian Arts.
>
> From 2008 to 2010, Crisosto served as the director of the Two Spirit Society of Denver. In 2011, he founded Two Spirit National Cultural Exchange to promote two-spirit identity and help LGBT Native Americans connect with their tribal and cultural traditions.
>
> Crisosto has published a collection of poems called *GENESIS*, performed his poems in a wide variety of settings, presented his work at academic conferences, and written articles about two-spirit people. He currently teaches at Red Rocks Community College and Rocky Mountain College of Art + Design in Lakewood, Colorado.

I grew up on the Mescalero Apache Reservation in south central New Mexico. Part of my identity is Chiricahua Apache, which is part of the Mescalero Apache tribe. Another part of my identity, on my dad's side, is Navajo.

I grew up mostly speaking English. It wasn't until probably ten years ago that I started to realize how important a person's spoken language is, because it has a huge connection to their cultural ties. It's very important to one's identity.

Finding my identity, learning about who I am, learning where I come from, learning

how that all fits, has been a lifelong journey. I don't think I'm finished trying to find out how I fit, because I have to think about my cultural context. I have to think about my political context. I have to think about my gender context, my sexuality. How I fit in these multiplexes of identity.

THE SWIMMING POOL

Growing up, our house was about eight miles from the town of Ruidoso, New Mexico. I used to hitchhike into town on the weekends or when I had a moment. There was a public swimming pool in town. I used to go there

Crisosto and his spouse, Todd A. Andreff, during the June Gay Pride in Denver, Colorado. Todd owned one of the oldest gay bars in the Denver area.

and sit on the picnic tables and just watch. I used to look at the lifeguards. I used to watch some of the people because they had bathing suits on. That was close enough to satisfy my need to look at the male form without arousing suspicion from others.

One day, I was sitting there, and I noticed that cars kept pulling up and parking in the pool parking lot. There's a small bathroom off to the side. Guys would get up and go into the bathroom. It dawned on me in the back of my head. I said, "That's an awful lot of traffic to go into the bathrooms." The women's restroom wasn't being visited at all. I was maybe fourteen, fifteen. Just out of curiosity, I decided to go in there. I hadn't been in there before. I, of course, naturally found out what they were doing in there. That became my mode of expression. Growing up in a small town, what do you know? Nobody's there to tell you that.

That was about the time when I started hearing about HIV or AIDS. I did unsafe things back then because, what do you know? I went and got tested. I went by myself. Didn't tell anybody. That scared the living crap out of me, to sit there. Back then, you had to wait two weeks, three weeks before you get your result. I remember just sitting there as they drew my blood and just feeling numb and thinking that it's that small vial that could determine whether I was going to live or die. I was fifteen.

DANGEROUS SUBSTANCES

My uncles drank pretty consistently. They would sometimes pass out, and when they did that, we'd always go and steal whatever they didn't finish and run off and drink it. I was probably ten, eleven.

Around the same age, I started smoking pot. Another thing that we did a lot of growing up was huffing. It would be spray paint. It would be gasoline. It would be sometimes household cleaners. It was very dangerous. At the time, you don't know that. You just do it.

In college, I started doing other types of drugs. Cocaine, meth or crystal. Crack is what it was called back then. By that time, you know, you started hearing that people on the reservation that I grew up with are dying. They're getting in car crashes or overdosing and whatnot, suicide, killing themselves. All that kind of stuff. I pretty much grew up with that.

It wasn't until I was twenty-five or twenty-six when I realized that I'm repeating the same pattern as when I was a teenager, this dangerous living. It wasn't with sex this time, but it was with chemicals. I decided I've got to do something about this.

NDEISDZAN

When I was in my early thirties, I was exposed to the term "two-spirit." It was a term that came around in the late eighties. The term is used very loosely. It's a generic term, but it doesn't apply to all Native tribes. A lot of Native American LGBT people use "two-spirit" to identify themselves, versus LGBT, to give them some type of empowerment about how they want to identify, which has nothing to do with the Western world. I thought that that was a good thing. I think it's used by people who may be Native American or of Native American ancestry who live in urban areas, who have been disconnected from their culture. They want to identity with their culture but don't have any clear, direct ties to that culture. "Two-spirit" is the only term that they can come to grips with, to identity who they are.

Later, I learned the word *ndeisdzan*. *Ndeisdzan* means something like male and a female put together. It's the only term that I know of that closely resembles what I am in my mind. I know now we use the word "trans," but I don't necessarily see myself as a woman, and I don't necessarily see myself as a male. Biologically, I'm male, but how I move in my culture, how I move in my identity is very fluid.

There's a poem that I've written about that which talks about this idea. It's something that's been there since the beginning of time,

or the beginning of the existence of male and female, because so much in our culture is defined by that. We have the harsh rains which are male. We have the light rains; that's female. Our ceremonies, they cycle between male and female. There's a moment where we become both male and female. We have to be in balance with that concept in order to fully understand who we are as people.

I do see who I am as a gift. It's a gift for myself and a gift to my family, because of how I chose to walk, how I chose to express myself, how I chose to look at things, look at my environment. I think that if you are able to see that balance and incorporate that balance as you are meant, there's nothing wrong with that. It allows me to incorporate what I've learned into who I am. It allows me to understand myself a little bit better and to build better relationships with people.

TERRY BAUM

ACTOR, PLAYWRIGHT, POLITICIAN
SAN FRANCISCO, CALIFORNIA

Terry Baum was born in Los Angeles in 1946. In high school, she wrote a journalism-themed musical parody of *My Fair Lady*, retitled *My Fair Reporter*, with songs like "I could have typed all night." Over the next half century, Terry's plays addressed more substantive issues, from gay marriage and the Holocaust to religious conversion and queer history. She also founded a community theater in Santa Barbara, California, and a feminist theater group called Lilith in San Francisco, which still exists today.

On the political front, Terry worked for Bill Clinton's first presidential campaign, then joined the Green Party in 2003. In 2004, she ran an upstart write-in campaign to unseat legendary San Francisco congresswoman Nancy Pelosi, ultimately winning 2.9 percent of all votes cast, the largest percentage for any congressional write-in candidate in history.

In 2014, Terry premiered her play *Hick: A Love Story*, based on more than two thousand letters from Eleanor Roosevelt to Lorena Hickok, her intimate friend and, most likely, her lover. Today, Terry continues to create theatrical spaces to give voice to feminist, queer, gay, and Jewish histories.

In my mid-twenties, I stopped falling in love with men. My impression was that men were not interested in me because I was a feminist and so outspoken, but in fact something mutual was going on between me and men. We were drifting apart.

In Santa Cruz, California, this guy and I started having an affair. He was a poet, and he wrote this beautiful love poem on the back of my food stamp application. And I just filled out the food stamp application and turned it in. And he said, "You just turned in my poem with the food stamp application?" "Yeah, I need the food stamps." That was kind of how it was.

Around that time, some women friends came to Santa Cruz for a women's music festival in the Santa Cruz Mountains. The music was incredible, absolutely amazing. And we were all naked, all the time mostly, and we dropped acid. And then it turned out the place where we were having this festival was a motorcycle club, and suddenly all of these guys on big Harleys came up and they wanted to come in, they want to disrupt the whole thing. And I was tripping on acid, and I felt that we should kill them. I had this amazing desire to kill them.

Terry with Alice Thompson II in the original 1981 production of *DOS LESBOS*, written by Terry and Carolyn Myers. Subtitled *A Play By, For, and About Perverts*, *DOS LESBOS* ran for two years in the San Francisco Bay Area and Santa Cruz, CA.

From that experience, I had a desire to write a play about the rage women feel against men. And I knew I was going to start a women's theater. So I left Santa Cruz and I moved to Berkeley, and I started Lilith, a women's theater collective.

I still was not a lesbian. For the very first show, I wrote a monologue about realizing that all the things that I looked for in a man, I could be myself. So in a certain way, I was releasing myself.

LEAVING THE SAFE STRUCTURE OF BELONGING

In 1976, a week after my thirtieth birthday, there was a conference in San Francisco on women and violence. A woman named Sherry and I

were the only people from Lilith who went.

At the conference, the keynote speaker went on a rampage about heterosexual women and how they should be labeled like cigarette packs. It was very inappropriate for a conference on women and violence. I remember thinking, "This is my last day as a heterosexual woman, so this is my last day to stand up for heterosexual women." So I stood up and challenged everything she said about heterosexual women.

After the conference, Sherry took me to the Top of the Mark, which is a good place to take somebody when you want to seduce them. And she said, "How does it make you feel that I'm a lesbian?" And I said, "It makes me want to sleep with you."

We didn't actually have sex that night

Terry in 1989, marching in the San Francisco Pride Parade. "I was a one-woman contingent," Terry writes. "No one would march with me."

because I was very freaked out on some level. I did not want her to touch my genitals. I just wanted her to hold me. In fact, I got very depressed for the first time in my life because I knew I was leaving the safe structure of belonging. I was leaving the straight world and the freedom to walk down the street with your arms around your lover. I found it very difficult that that was over for me, but it was very clear. I'm a lesbian. That's that.

ALL THE WAY WITH RACHEL

As far back as 1974, I've wanted to write a play about women's rage. I've discovered that there

is so little tolerance for the exploration of women's rage. There is no leeway for women to talk about this. Nobody can handle it.

So the play I'm working on now, *Mikvah*, is the play that I've been meaning to write ever since I started Lilith in 1974.

Mikvah takes place in a Jewish women's ritual bath. The play is about a lesbian relationship between the *mikvah* attendant Hava, who is a dyke, and Rachel, a beautiful young woman who has been brought up by her father, who cherished her and educated her, and now she's marrying this rich man and everybody's very happy. And then it turns out that this man is horrible.

Rachel and Hava fall in love. Rachel kills her husband. And then she and Hava leave.

I'm trying to understand why I feel the courage now to express this rage, or the courage to go all the way with Rachel, because Rachel's going all the way. And I think my Buddhist practice has something to do with it, because Buddhism is about being fully who you are. If you're an artist, your path is your path, and that's that.

MARK SEGAL

LEGENDARY "ZAPPER," PUBLISHER OF *PHILADELPHIA GAY NEWS*

PHILADELPHIA, PENNSYLVANIA

> Mark Segal was born in 1951 in Philadelphia. By thirteen, he was marching in his first civil rights demonstration alongside his suffragette grandmother. Shortly after moving to New York in 1969, he took part in the Stonewall riots. It was the birth of a lifelong rabble-rouser, queer activist, and freedom scribe.
>
> Following Stonewall, Mark helped create a new organization called the Gay Liberation Front. Soon thereafter, he formed a radical group called the Gay Raiders to protest the defamation of homosexuals on entertainment programs. The Raiders began staging "zaps" to draw public attention to the gay and lesbian rights movement—events like handcuffing themselves to the Liberty Bell, interrupting a Nixon fundraiser, and perhaps most famously, storming the stage of the *CBS Evening News with Walter Cronkite*.
>
> Mark's most enduring platform has been the award-winning *Philadelphia Gay News*, America's longest-running LGBT publication, which Mark has published since 1976. In 2015, Mark penned his memoir, *And Then I Danced: Traveling the Road to LGBT Equality*.

I liked men my entire life. I never thought that there was anything wrong with that fact. I knew I had to keep quiet. I thought, "It's not something you talk about. It might upset my parents and might cause them embarrassment."

In May of '69, about six weeks before Stonewall, I moved to New York. I was eighteen. My parents thought I was going to New York to join the RCA Technical Institute and learn how to be a TV cameraman. There was no such thing. It was basically made up. I escaped to New York. I wasn't going to grow old in Philadelphia, living in a closet somewhere.

All I knew was that there were gay people in New York. I knew there was this place called Greenwich Village, where all these strange people hung out. Since I'd heard that gay people were strange people, I assumed they would be in Greenwich Village. Eventually I came across Christopher Street. I realized, "There they are: my brothers and sisters."

A typical night on Christopher Street was just walking up and down from Greenwich Avenue all the way down to the Silver Dollar off of Hudson. You go in the Silver Dollar and you have a cup of coffee. Then you walk to a corner and talk to your friends, or you'd sit on a stoop somewhere, and then you'd pop in and out of the various gay bars and clubs that were in the area. That was it. That was what you did every single night. You would pop into the Stonewall. You would pop into the International Stud or whatever it was called then.

NO PROSPECTS

Everybody who was at Stonewall has their own account, and they vary widely. I decided early on that I wasn't going to correct other people. Everybody has their memories, some of us are getting a little older, and I generally suggest to other people that they give their own accounts, not other people's accounts.

For me, it was very vivid. I was in the back of the bar. The lights flickered on. I was wondering what was going on, and someone said, "Ah, we're just being raided." They were very casual. Inside my head, I was scared to death. I'd never been at raid before, and then the police came in. They started to push some people around. They were being really mean to the trans people, who at the time we called drag queens. They were literally extorting men, taking money out of their wallets.

I looked like the boy next door in those days because I had just got to New York. I was of absolutely no use to the cops. They couldn't get money out of me because I didn't have any money. I was one of the first to be carded and let out. That turns out to be very lucky because I got to stand across the street and watch as it unfolded.

One by one people came out, but instead of just dispersing, they started forming a semicircle around the doors of the building. Eventually that crowd became larger than the people left in the bar, which were the police. When that happened, people just started throwing things at the door. I remember people throwing rocks and stones, cans, bottles. I don't remember anyone throwing a Molotov cocktail.

While this was all going on, a man by the name of Marty Robinson walks up to me. Marty said, "What's going on?" I told him, "Some kind of demonstration." He ran off, came back a little later with chalk. He gave us chalk and told us our job was to go around the neighborhood and write on the walls and the street, "Tomorrow Night Stonewall." That was Marty's idea. That was a very smart idea, because what most people are not aware of is that Stonewall was more than one night. It was four. The next three nights, members of the community came together for the first time, I mean everybody from every political spectrum of the community who wanted change, which primarily were people in their twenties and thirties. They gave speeches outside Stonewall.

At that period of time, 1969, you have to realize that women were fighting for their rights. African Americans were fighting for their rights. Puerto Ricans were fighting for their rights. Everybody was fighting for their rights. The only group that wasn't were gay men and lesbian women. They wanted change, but they didn't know what to do about it.

The spark of Stonewall created that. Thank God for the New York City Police raiding that bar! They brought us all together. The most magnificent, incredible thing to watch were those three nights after Stonewall, to watch men and women from our community coming together to speak in one voice. Afterward, a bunch of us got together and created the Gay Liberation Front, which changed the world.

We did something that had never been done before. We created a community. We weren't going to be isolated. We weren't going to be pushed into bars and told we can't go anywhere else. We weren't going to let the police come into Christopher Street, our neighborhood, and do what they wanted. It ended then. It ended.

LIFTING SOCIETY'S THUMB

Prior to the Gay Liberation Front, the primary gay organizations were the Mattachine Society, ONE Incorporated, and the Daughters of Bilitis. For the most part, these groups believed in trying to fit in society. Their routine was to say, "Hey, we're just like you. We even look like you." In their demonstrations, men had to wear suits and ties, and women had to wear dresses. No one under eighteen could march. No one under eighteen could be in their offices. They were afraid of being raided by the police. They wanted to do things by the rules.

We at the Gay Liberation Front, on the other hand, didn't give a fuck. The rules were against us, and we knew it. We were out to

Mark disrupts a Nixon re-election fundraiser in November 1972.

One of Mark's many run-ins with the police.

change the rules. We had no rules. We didn't follow Robert's Rules of Order. When people walked in for a meeting, a stick was thrown. Whoever got the stick, they were the chair of that meeting. There were no officers.

Those early days of the Gay Liberation Front were probably some of the most joyous times I've ever had. We were by far the most dysfunctional organization that has ever existed in the LGBT community, and it was magnificent. It was wonderful to watch. It was wonderful to be a part of. We were creating change. We didn't know what we were doing. We knew why we were doing it—because we hated living with the oppressive thumb of so-

ciety on us. We were going to lift that thumb. We didn't know how, but we were going to experiment until we found the solution.

DISRUPTING THE MEDIA

In the early 1970s, I realized if gay people were going to change the world, we had to change the world's mind about who and what we were. The only way to do that was to reach the world. How do you reach the world? Through the media. Well, but the media censors us. The media doesn't know we exist. How do you change the media if they won't listen to you or meet with you? You disrupt them.

So in 1973, I started disrupting TV shows throughout the country. We called these actions zaps. The first time, I disrupted a local TV station during their live evening news broadcast. I woke up the following morning to discover that the entire front page of the local tabloid was a picture of me disrupting that TV show. I realized, with that one disruption, I've reached 1.6 million people in the Delaware Valley.

So I created the Gay Raiders, and the idea was that every six weeks we did a demonstration of some sort. We did some crazy things, like chaining myself to the Liberty Bell, disrupting a President Richard Nixon re-election fundraising dinner, but the thing we're most known for is our TV disruptions.

At that time, there was a show in Philadelphia called the *Mike Douglas Show*, which was your typical afternoon talk show where they would have celebrities come on and do crazy things or talk about crazy things. One afternoon, they had a professional foot reader reading the feet of the actress Helen Hayes, the so-called first lady of the American theater. I came out of the audience, handcuffed myself to the camera and started screaming and yelling. The police wanted to arrest me, but the producer was nice and said, "What do you want?" I said, "I'd like you to put a gay spokesperson on your show." They said, "Okay."

It all culminated on December 3rd, 1973. Right after the first break of the *CBS Evening News with Walter Cronkite*, I slipped between the camera and Walter's desk and actually sat on Walter's desk, directly blocking the view between Walter and the camera, and held a sign up into the camera which said, "Gays protest CBS prejudice." This was a live broadcast. Walter Cronkite had the largest audience and was the most trusted man in America for many years. His evening broadcast was broadcast to 60 million Americans. The CBS Television Network went blank for seven minutes.

All I wanted them to do was start talking about the subject, even if it was negative, because up to that point there was no discussion, no debate. There was no debate. We were guilty. We were sinners. We were criminals. No debate on all those things. I wanted to create the debate.

Back in the day, the offices of the Philadelphia Gay News *were routinely vandalized.* Thunderbolt, *the national magazine of the American Nazi Party, put Mark on its death list. I asked Mark if he was ever scared. The question actually stunned him. He thought about it, and finally replied, "We didn't have time to be scared."*

JEWELLE GOMEZ

AUTHOR, PAST PRESIDENT OF SAN FRANCISCO LIBRARY COMMISSION
SAN FRANCISCO, CALIFORNIA

Jewelle Gomez was born in 1948 and grew up in Boston. Jewelle is of Cape Verdean, Wampanoag, and Ioway descent and was largely raised by her Native American great-grandmother, who pushed her to develop her imagination, read, and pursue education. Jewelle graduated from Northeastern University and earned her MS in journalism from Columbia University. While in New York, she became involved in activist movements and black theater. Just as importantly, she started writing.

A prolific writer, Jewelle is best known for her novel *The Gilda Stories* (1991). A Lambda Literary Award winner for fiction and science fiction, *The Gilda Stories* takes place from 1850 to 2050, following the protagonist Gilda on her journey from slavery to empowerment, mortality to immortality.

Jewelle was also a founding member of GLAAD, and served as president of the San Francisco Library Commission and on the board of the Astraea Lesbian Foundation for Justice.

I came to live with my great-grandmother Gracias when I was eight years old. She was already in her seventies and worked in a factory in our neighborhood in Boston's South End. In order to receive public assistance for me, my great-grandmother had to legally adopt me because my parents still lived nearby. I watched her go through that whole process and red tape and found it amazing because she was really elderly.

My great-grandmother had been raised on Indian land in Iowa. She was stalwart and steady and was a great counterbalance to the insecurity that I felt. Incredibly loving, although she didn't talk that much.

My great-grandmother and I would go to secondhand sales, and any book she could get for a quarter, she would have a shopping bag and bring them home. She stacked them up beside the couch. She would read them and I could read them, so I grew up reading everything. Detective novels, *The Fall of the Roman Empire*, whatever cost a quarter, I was reading it. That was my major education, I think.

This may seem counterintuitive, but we also watched a lot of television. We read a lot, we watched TV a lot, and we looked out the window a lot. Our two front windows looked

Jewelle with renowned poet and civil rights activist Audre Lorde (1934–1992) during the filming of the 1984 documentary *Before Stonewall*

out on the main street. It was a big street in Boston, Tremont. My great-grandmother would sit in one window, and I would sit in the other. You'd see your neighbors, obviously. People going in and out of the corner drugstore, friends, strangers, people going to church. We saw wild things and normal things. One day I saw a woman drive up in a pink Cadillac, and this was way before the Aretha Franklin song. She got out of the car. She was dressed in all hot pink. Head to toe, high heels, everything, and she had a pink poodle, a miniature poodle who was dyed pink. It was the wildest thing I had ever seen. I must have been ten years old. I said, "Are you seeing this?" My great-grandmother said, "Yeah . . ."

When I was in high school, my great-grandmother wrote out a genealogy for me, going back to Massasoit, who was the chief of the Wampanoag Indians when the colonists arrived. Massasoit was the chief for whom the Commonwealth of Massachusetts was

named. My great-grandmother literally lined our genealogy out on a piece of paper which I still have.

I took two things from my great-grandmother Gracias that still guide me today. One is the need to be independent. Particularly wanting to be a writer, I was never going to sit around and wait for a publisher to show up and do this or that for me. I was never going to wait to become famous. I was going to write, which also meant figuring out how to have a job and write. And the other thing that I carry from my great-grandmother is a sense of how important history is. Because she was so much older, because she carried her history with her, and she wanted to tell me what she knew. I feel like her narratives became my narratives in some level. I think that's part of the reason that most of my fiction is historical. We need to carry our history with us because, oddly enough, it helps show us where the future is.

QUEER SUPER POWER

There's definitely a connection for me between my character Gilda and the queer community. In many ways, her life parallels what we as queer people, certainly queer people of my generation and before, have had to do. That is, develop a community that will sustain us because we can't count on our biological community.

I wanted Gilda to be the kind of person who understands the need to connect, so I created a vampire community that understands that vampires survive because they are connected to mortals. It's not just the blood connection. They need to be connected emotionally to mortals. And I feel that for queer people, connecting with each other is our super power. You can go to any queer community in the world, and it's probably going to include a more diverse group of people than any other community. I know we have issues around clubs that don't want black people in them, and how we have the Latino gay bar over here. That happens because we are also a reflection of the larger culture. However, in most queer activism you will find a huge diversity of people. That is our queer super power, that we can make a connection with just about anybody in the world.

A while back, my spouse, Diane, and I were down in Gulfport, Mississippi. I had some family down there. But needless to say, I don't know anything about the South, so it was really freaky for me to be in Gulfport, Mississippi. So Diane and I went to one of those big box stores to buy some groceries for the family. We're going up and down the aisles. As a Bostonian, a person of color, a lesbian, I was nervous. And you can really tell I'm a lesbian when I'm with Diane, because she's a fabulous butch. It was a little nerve-racking.

Then we looked down the aisle and we saw two white gay men, a little younger than us. Our radar went up, and we started stalking them through the store. I went around to try to get in front of them and I just said, "Hi." They said, "Hello." Then Diane came around the corner, and they realized we were lesbians. Then they said, "Hi! How y'all doing?" [*laughing*] We're like, "Great! How's it going?" We just said maybe three sentences, and we were connected. If we had wanted to know more, we could've talked to them more, but all we wanted was the connection. That wouldn't have happened except that we were queer and we recognized each other, and that was fabulous. That was fabulous.

As a lesbian feminist I see that all the time, and I want it to spread throughout the queer community. If we can bring our ability to connect to a deep political movement, I think it will change the world.

Jewelle and her spouse, Diane Sabin, live in a beautifully preserved California Craftsman bungalow in San Francisco. Fog and sunlight took turns dancing outside the windows on the May 2017 morning when Jewelle sat down to tell OUTWORDS her story.

BETSY PARSONS

ENGLISH TEACHER

MAINE

> Betsy Parsons was born in 1954 in Boston, Massachusetts, and raised in rural Illinois. Each summer, Betsy's parents took her to Maine, where they had grown up. As soon as Betsy graduated from college, she returned to Maine to live and teach.
>
> For many years, coming out at the schools where she taught seemed like an impossibility to Betsy. But in the late 1980s and early '90s, she noticed increasing hostility toward queer kids, especially as HIV/AIDS spawned runaway fear and anxiety in the general public. Something had to be done, so in 1996 Betsy helped found the Gay, Lesbian, and Straight Education Network (GLSEN) of Southern Maine. Two years later, she came out herself, the first teacher in Maine's largest school system to come out and keep his or her job. Over the next fifteen years, Betsy helped Maine students form gay-straight-trans alliances (GSTAs) across the state, also supporting the faculty advisers who stepped up to guide the nascent groups.

I can remember feeling different in some way that I shouldn't talk about as early as four. Certainly, I was wildly in love at fourteen. There was no consciousness of LGBT relationships among the people that I was surrounded by. There was also no way to really understand or talk about the intensity of that. My girlfriend and I were "best friends" for four years.

Through my twenties, I threw myself into learning and then into teaching. I tried dating men, didn't enjoy that very much, and didn't know why. It was really not until I fell in love at almost thirty that I said, "Oh. I guess I was looking at the wrong half of the human population."

There was a rightness about this relationship that was both wonderful and blissful and ecstatic but also deeply problematic because I was a public school teacher. It was 1984. There was no history of any public school teacher surviving being outed, at least here in Maine. To be outed as a lesbian at that time meant the loss of career. Usually, it meant you had to leave the state, in addition to loss of family and faith community and friends.

HESTER'S WAY

By the mid-1990s, I'd been teaching for twenty years. I still loved teaching. Yet these

Betsy (in baseball cap) marching in the 1998 Portland Pride Parade. Betsy writes: "We had just lost our second statewide referendum on LGBT civil rights, and the climate was extremely ugly. High threat of violence and job loss. No protections."

shifts were happening around me. There was this preoccupation with HIV/AIDS, this level of fear and actually terror around HIV/AIDS, and this new level of unbridled harassment that I had never seen before.

The most prevalent form of hate language in the school was anti-gay language. Constant ridicule and verbal harassment coupled with physical harassment, shoving, tripping, kicking, punching. It happened in the hallways and even sometimes in classrooms. Teachers would not typically intervene because to target LGBT people was acceptable.

At the start of a new semester, a young man entered my junior English class who had been outed halfway through his fresh-

man year. For a year and a half, he had been targeted continuously with the most severe and constant anti-gay harassment that I had ever seen to that point. This was a very bright guy, but his PTSD and depression were so severe that he really couldn't function in my class at all. He couldn't remember anything that he read. Even a pretty simple American novel, he would try to read it and he couldn't remember any of it.

This young man had supportive parents who accepted him and who advocated for him with the school. But the school's disciplinary procedures were just completely ineffective. There was very little will to follow up on what was happening to him.

About the same time, a former student came back to visit me. She was a college grad now. She was a young lesbian. She told me that during her freshman year of high school, when she was my student, she had been on the brink of suicide the entire year.

I had thought her life looked perfect. She was brainy and beautiful and athletic and musical. When I heard eight years later what that had really been like, it was just shocking for me. I asked what I could have done to make that year less painful and less frightening. She said, "You could have been out."

That moment, along with everything else that was going on, was a point of no return for me. I was going to have to either leave public school teaching or find a way to keep teaching and come out.

By this point, it was my legal right to come out. That right had been affirmed and reaffirmed by both the city council and the school board. Even still, there was a lot of pressure for me not to do it. Eventually, my principal and I agreed that I would wait to come out until students actually asked about LGBT issues. Then I could use that moment to cross the line.

It took a whole semester. But one day in my class, we were having a discussion about Nathaniel Hawthorne's *The Scarlet Letter*. The discussion was all about stigma and judgment, and how communities respond, and the moral choices that individuals have in the face of mass community stigma.

Finally a student said, "This is like gay people. We do this to gay people all the time. We're just like these Puritans judging people and saying terrible things about them." That gave me the opening to say, "Well, I know something about that. I'm a lesbian. In the novel, we see how different people respond to stigma. And we see Hester's decision to live openly and turn her energy into something healing for her community. I am now changing my way to Hester's way. What way will you all choose?"

We had one of the best discussions of my entire career. It turns out, unsurprisingly of course, there were LGBT students in that room who were closeted, who came out to me later, for whom that was a major liberating moment.

In April 2010, President Obama traveled to Portland, Maine, to speak about the Affordable Care Act, which he had signed into law one week earlier. At the event, Betsy and fellow LGBTQ activist Jim Bishop were invited to sing the national anthem. Although not allowed to speak (only sing), Betsy and Jim made sure to wear rainbow-colored triangle buttons emblazoned with the Statue of Liberty and the words "with liberty and justice for all."

FENTON JOHNSON

WRITER, CULTURAL CRITIC

TUCSON, ARIZONA

Fenton Johnson was born in Kentucky in 1953, the youngest of nine children in a bourbon-making family. He earned his BA in English at Stanford and an MFA in creative writing at the Iowa Writers' Workshop.

Much of Fenton's writing grapples with the slow-motion cataclysm of the AIDS epidemic, especially during the 1980s. His novel *Scissors, Paper, Rock* was among the first novels to present openly gay characters and to deal with AIDS in rural America. After his partner, Larry, died of AIDS in 1990, Fenton explored his and Larry's love in his award-winning memoir, *Geography of the Heart*.

In *Keeping Faith: A Skeptic's Journey among Christian and Buddhist Monks*, Fenton described his experiences living in community at the Gethsemani Abbey and at various branches of the San Francisco Zen Center. Fenton's 2015 essay "Going It Alone: The Dignity and Challenge of Solitude" (Harper's) pondered the contemplative life and what it means to be single and celibate in middle age. In 2018, Harper's published Fenton's essay "The Future of Queer: A Manifesto," in which Fenton suggests that gay marriage has robbed gay culture of its power to challenge cookie-cutter societal expectations and norms.

Fenton is the recipient of a Guggenheim Fellowship as well as fellowships in fiction and creative nonfiction from the National Endowment for the Arts. He teaches English at the University of Arizona in Tucson.

As a kid, I was a bookworm. My mother said of me at one point, "You were the quiet one. I never knew that you were there, and then one day I turned around and you were gone." I was in hiding from very early on. I was maintaining a low profile. That was my survival mechanism. I think any number of LGBT people would be very sympathetic with that point of view.

There were two ways to achieve power in the culture where I grew up. One was through threat and violence, and the other was to be able to tell a good story. If you could command a room, if you could tell a good story, you earned some respect. The guys were out in the driveway talking about guns and cars. What did I care about guns and cars? I sat in the room next to my mother's bridge club and listened to them talk about human nature. That was what I was interested in.

My father was a maintenance worker for Seagram's. Seagram's had a scholarship for a son or daughter of a Seagram's employee that paid everything anywhere you got into school. I got that scholarship. Stanford University sent a catalog filled with pictures of hunky guys lounging in Speedo's under the palm trees by Lake Lagunita, and I thought, "That's where I want to go to school."

Sitting on the floor of my dorm in freshman year at Stanford, people would trade stories in the way that they did. Everybody grew up in mostly the sort of background you'd expect from kids at Stanford. I would tell the stories of my childhood. Deer hunting, gutting deer, deer roast every Sunday, moonshining, all this kind of stuff. These stories would just kind of ramble on, of course. Finally, I remember somebody saying, "Would you get to the point?" I was genuinely puzzled. I thought, the point? The point is telling the story. The story doesn't have a point. It just rolls on and on and on.

A BEACON

Anita Bryant was a half-Cherokee from Oklahoma, and she was Miss America. [For more on Anita Bryant, see pp. 27, 254–55.] She was also the poster woman for the orange juice campaign out of Florida. In 1977, Miami-Dade County had passed an early gay rights protections legislation. Anita Bryant was really an innocent country girl. But pushed by her husband, she launched this campaign to have that initiative overturned. That campaign was successful.

Inspired by Bryant's success, in 1978 a man named John Briggs, a state representative in California, proposed an initiative statewide in California that was even more draconian. [For more on the Briggs Initiative, see p. 193.] Homosexuality could not be mentioned in the high school classroom. If there was any mention of homosexuality, the teacher could be fired. Forget about hiring anyone who was gay and lesbian.

I had just seen Peter Adair's documentary *Word Is Out*, which really galvanized and radicalized me. Seeing one's self, one's stories, up on the screen, or in writing, there's no substitute for that. Then the Briggs Initiative was so draconian that it really left us no option. It didn't matter whether we lost or not. If we lost, we lost, but for us not to do anything was not an option.

This statewide grassroots coalition rose up of gay and lesbian people, and people who love them, fighting that initiative. Harvey Milk and Sally Gearhart made their names by traveling around the state debating fundamentalists, debating anybody who would debate them on local television stations, on local radio stations. I got involved in a local way, duplicating that role. We would go and stage debates. We were spat upon.

What dominated our consciousness at that time was our awareness that what we did in San Francisco really mattered, that everybody was watching us. There was a sense, and it was true, that San Francisco was at that point unique in the world. There was only one place in the world at that point where one could have a professional career as an out gay man. That

Fall, 1998: Fenton and Larry on a whale-watching expedition in Half Moon Bay, CA

was certainly not true of Washington, Hollywood, or even to a great extent New York.

There was very much a sense that anything you did was possibly going to end up being seen by the farm kid in rural Kentucky or Kansas, or the kid in the Orthodox Jewish community in the Bronx, or whatever. There was a sense of being a beacon. It was a privilege to be able to participate in that.

At the beginning of the summer that year, the polls were 68 to 32 in favor of the initiative, and we ultimately ended up winning by a pretty comfortable margin. There was such joy and celebration.

And then three weeks later, Harvey Milk and George Moscone were assassinated.

[Editor's note: On November 27, 1978, San Francisco Supervisor Harvey Milk, arguably the most important gay politician in history, and San Francisco Mayor George Moscone were assassinated at San Francisco City Hall by former supervisor Dan White. The murders and White's subsequent conviction for voluntary manslaughter devastated, enraged, and forever galvanized the queer community in San Francisco and beyond. In 1985, a year after his release from prison, Dan White committed suicide.]

GEOGRAPHY OF THE HEART

I'm the ninth of nine children of a bourbon maker and moonshiner from rural Kentucky.

My lover, Larry Rose, was the only child of Holocaust survivors.

The three years that Larry and I were together, I felt like I was living out an opera. I felt like I was living *La Traviata*. He was HIV-positive. I found that out early on. He was a lover of books. He was a lover of me. He had the impossible seduction that accompanies somebody who has nothing to lose. Plus, he was really handsome and really smart, and he had many gifts to give me. I was a wild man by his standards. Larry took me to Europe several times and taught me French. To give a continent to someone, to give a language to someone, that was a fantastic gift.

Larry wanted to die in Europe because he did not want to die in the presence of his parents. In October 1990, I carried him around to the grand monuments of France. Literally carried him around, in some cases. Finally, it got too desperate, and I drove him at breakneck speed from Tours to Paris, to the American hospital. At first, they didn't want to see him because he had AIDS. Then when he was checked in, they wouldn't let me see him. I sneaked around, tried coming in through the emergency doors. They threw me out again.

Larry died. I was alone in France with him being dead, and I certainly got a chance to use the French that he had taught me. I arranged for the cremation. There was only one crematorium at the time in all of Paris. Amazing, but it's Catholic country. They weren't doing many cremations in those days. That crematorium is in Père Lachaise, which is the cemetery where everybody who's anybody is buried. Jim Morrison. Oscar Wilde. Collette. It's where the Communards were shot in the 1871 Revolution. There was something really right and wonderful about taking Larry to the crematorium at Père Lachaise.

This is the subject of my memoir, *Geography of the Heart*. It's not surprising that three HIV-negative men came out with memoirs virtually simultaneously. Mark Doty's *Heaven's Coast*, Bernard Cooper's *Truth Serum*, and my *Geography of the Heart*. I thought memoirs were something that you wrote when you were seventy-five. Your last book, if you were publishing books. I felt compelled by a historical moment. I thought, "I'm a writer. I'm a witness. I have to tell this story." And the story demanded to be told.

OUTWORDS interviewed Fenton at his Tucson home in February 2018. His low-slung adobe cottage felt just how a writer's home should feel. Books everywhere, loosely yet tidily organized; a sense of each one being known, respected, and treasured.

KITTY TSUI

POET, BODYBUILDER

LONG BEACH, CALIFORNIA

Kitty Tsui was born in Hong Kong in 1952 and spent her childhood there and in London before moving with her family to San Francisco in 1968. While studying creative writing at San Francisco State University, Kitty established the Third World Poetry Series, featuring poets like Roberto Vargas, Victor Hernández Cruz, and Jessica Hagedorn, and studied with feminist and activist Sally Gearhart.

In 1981, Kitty helped found Unbound Feet, a female performance group that aimed to upend stereotypes about Asian women. Two years later, she published her first book of poetry and prose, *The Words of a Woman Who Breathes Fire*. It was the first book ever published by a Chinese American lesbian. Kitty's second book, *Breathless: Erotica*, came out in 1996 and won a Firecracker Alternative Book Award. Her third book, *Sparks Fly*, was written by her alter ego, Eric Norton, a gay leatherman living in pre-AIDS San Francisco.

Kitty has won two women's physique medals at the Gay Games, and she is the first Asian American woman ever to appear on the cover of the lesbian erotica magazine *On Our Backs*. Through the years, her poetry and prose have been collected in dozens of anthologies. In 2016, she received the Phoenix Lifetime Achievement Award from APIQWTC (the Asian Pacific Islander Queer Women & Transgender Community).

THE EARTH MOVED

I grew up straight, you know? My parents were my role models. I had good relationships with men. When I was twenty-one, I think, I started feeling something for women. It was strange. It was totally alien to me.

I had a good friend who was bisexual, and she was married to a bisexual man. So they would take me to gay clubs like Bojangles on Polk Street. The first few times I picked up women, it was like nothing happened. I didn't know what to do. I thought, "Oh, let me go back to men."

Then my friend Diana called me one night. It was Halloween. It was a Tuesday night, and she said, "Let's go to Peg's Place. It's Halloween. Come on." I said, "No, it's Tuesday night. I have to study." She said, "Come on." So we went to Peg's Place. There were a lot of people there. A lot of people were dressed up. We saw this Asian couple come in, and we thought, "Boy, are they in the wrong place,"

because it looked like a man and a woman. So we were kind of chuckling and laughing at them, and then the man came over to ask me to dance. Well, it wasn't a man, it was an androgynous woman, and she became my first lover. When we made love, the earth moved, so I knew I had found the right woman.

DATES, BUTTER, AND HASH

San Francisco in the '70s was a great time to be a lesbian. There were bookstores, there were coffeehouses, there was women's music, there were readings—lesbians love their writers. I did feel colored. It was a very white movement at that time. So I felt that I was exoticized and eroticized because of my ethnicity, but other than that, it was a great time.

We Asian Americans had a lot of issues around coming out to family, bringing your partner to family gatherings. But you know what united us? Food. We were very famous for our potlucks. Because if you think about it, we had Japanese Americans, Korean Americans, Chinese Americans, Thai Americans. Our gatherings would all be centered around food. We would kind of laugh at white women whose potlucks consisted of, like, cheese and crackers and carrot sticks, and we would have all these amazing ethnic dishes. So that's certainly something that united us: our love of food and being able to talk with like-minded women about family or work or our partners.

I remember one time, one of our bisexual members, Kay, she brought dates, butter, and hash. We pitted the dates, we melted the butter, we melted the hash in the butter, and put it inside the dates. It was a large gathering of Asian women, right? We played spin the bottle. The straight women left. That's all I remember.

"Nice Chinese Girls Don't"

nice Chinese girls don't
swear, sing, or shout out loud.
nice Chinese girls
talk with their eyes averted,
sit with legs crossed
and laugh with hand in front of mouth.

nice Chinese girls don't
drink, smoke or talk too loud.
nice Chinese girls
sip their tea slow,
use umbrellas in the sun,
wear skirts and perm their hair.

nice Chinese girls don't
get divorced or become dykes.
nice Chinese girls
marry nice Chinese boys,
have sons, stay home,
and keep dinner warm on the stove.

nice Chinese girls don't
question, argue or complain.
nice Chinese girls
suffer in silence,
endure with a smile,
use chopsticks
and speak fluent Chinese.

nice Chinese girls don't
make waves or talk back.
nice Chinese girls
smile without showing their teeth,
speak only when spoken to,
and learn young to turn the other cheek.

nice Chinese girls don't
stay out late,
or take the subway alone at night.
nice Chinese girls
get straight A's,
never tell lie or say what they mean.

I was born a nice Chinese girl.
good thing it was a phase
I soon outgrew.

my heritage as
a nice Chinese girl
forced me to rebel.
I grew into
a different breed of Chinese girl.
visible, vocal, and proud to be
a different breed of Chinese girl.

TRUTH TO
POWER

ELIZABETH COFFEY WILLIAMS

ACTOR, TRANS COMMUNITY ADVOCATE

PHILADELPHIA, PENNSYLVANIA

Elizabeth Coffey Williams was born in 1948 in Brooklyn, New York, and grew up in Philadelphia. Assigned male at birth, Elizabeth knew she was a girl from an early age, and despite attending a Catholic school, she presented as female, wearing her hair long and going on dates with boys.

At twenty-two, Elizabeth moved to Baltimore, where she met rising film director John Waters. Elizabeth went on to appear in Waters' iconic films *Pink Flamingos* and *Female Trouble*, in which she worked alongside legendary drag queen Divine. In 1972, she became one of the first women to participate in Johns Hopkins University's groundbreaking sex reassignment program. She later married and moved to Rockford, Illinois, where she raised a son, became a professional quilter, and served on the board of the Rockford AIDS Care Network and as a facilitator of the Names Project AIDS Memorial Quilt.

Today, Elizabeth lives back in Philadelphia, where she co-facilitates Transway, a trans and gender-nonconforming support group.

MAKING THE JOKE (INSTEAD OF BEING THE JOKE)

I first met John Waters in a church basement in Baltimore, at the premiere of one of his earlier films, which was called *Multiple Maniacs*.

He didn't single me out as someone new, but there were a lot of heavy hitters in that room, with Divine and Cookie Mueller and Mink Stole and Pat Moran. They're a tough crowd. Pat Moran is John's casting director. She's this tiny red-headed spitfire with so much energy, and I just remember thinking, "Man, I want to be like that. Okay, so I'll be a five-foot-ten-inch version." Pat was very strong, and if I can use an invented adjective, she was sort of un-fuck-with-able.

For *Pink Flamingos*, John came to me and said, "I have an idea," and he told me about a scene where there was a flasher and that I would ultimately be a flasher.

We're going back far enough that the word "transgender"—I'm not even sure if it existed at the time. Even though my looking good and acceptable helped as a form of armor, one could still be the brunt of some jokes. But what occurred to me with what John was doing was that, instead of being the joke, I got to make the joke. I got to win, and that appealed to me.

The other thing that appealed to me was that John's really funny, and he thought it up. I was happy that I got to do it, and I was lucky enough to be surrounded by these amazing, smart people, who were rather unlike the films, of course. Everyone thinks that people who do something in a film are like that off-camera, which they're not. They were just a pack of delightfully crazy bohemian-type hippies living down on the docks in Baltimore, so I had all these friends.

A PLUMBER, NOT A SHRINK

I don't know if Johns Hopkins was the first place in the country to be doing gender reassignment. But I heard about it and figured, "Well, cool. I'm already good, so I may as well just take care of 'that.'" This was in the early 1970s.

Being relatively casual, a member of the arts community, and I guess what you'd call

Elizabeth in John Waters' 1972 comedy *Pink Flamingos*.

a hippie at the time, I just marched through those big doors at Hopkins in a little blue jean miniskirt and tank top and my flip-flops, and my hair up in pigtails, and a big old pair of sunglasses, and said, "Hi! I'm here. I'm here for . . . this is where, like, you do that, right?" They said, "What?" I said, "Well, you know, like, fix up somebody's, like, genitalia." I figured I'd use a proper word.

They said, "Oh, well, it's actually this whole big process," which really kind of surprised me, because I had no clue. I said, "Well, you know, I'm not sure what you're all about, but I'm not here for a shrink. I just want a plumber. Can you help me?"

This was in a boardroom with all of these doctors—I suppose they were all doctors—who were scrutinizing me. They were kind of shocked by me, but I was kind of shocked by them too because they were running this groundbreaking program, and they were so uptight you couldn't pull a pin out of their ass with a tractor.

What they were really looking for were people with double-processed blond flips who wanted to be Stepford wives and had enormous aspirations to be a dental hygienist. Not that keeping your teeth in good order is not a good idea. It just wasn't something that particularly appealed to me.

They told me that I was inappropriate. "No, no, no, dear. You are not what we may consider to be a suitable candidate because you are most likely unstable and you are not part of mainstream society. Anyone who would choose to be a woman . . ." At which point, of course, I said, "I didn't choose to be a woman. It just turned out that way. It's just who I am, and I'm already a girl. I came here for you to help me."

When I look back on it, I think it's understandable to have an issue or have a concern about someone's "stability." But being judgmental about a person's lifestyle just seemed really in left field to me. It was like, what do you care if I wear blue jeans or J. Crew? What's it to you?

They still made me go through this whole tedious, tedious audition, where I met a lot of people who didn't have a clue, but it was their program. It was really weird to keep going back and forth between this prestigious institution and dancing all night on the bars down on the waterfront in Fell's Point in Baltimore, which was heaven. It was more fun than anybody should have.

AUTHENTICALLY AND UNAPOLOGETICALLY

I think there comes a time when we realize that we're really all very different and there is no typical or stereotypical story. Everything doesn't have a name, and everyone is different. Because of that, everyone's story is different. There may be similarities. There are places where the bumpers of our boots may touch. But we don't overlap.

Genuine diversity is just what it is. It's not contrived. It's not created. It's just an expression of authenticity, and I think at the end of the day, no matter who we are, no matter who we love, no matter what we eat, no matter who we fuck, when you put all of those things together, I think what's most important is that

we do it authentically, and that we unapologetically live our own truth. That has been a survival mechanism for me, and a healthy mechanism for a lot of people I've known.

We all need to be exactly who we are, rather than some societally created contrivance of gayness or "lesbiterianism" or transgender sexual binary queer. Personally, I don't care what you call me, as long as you call me Elizabeth.

Video excerpts of Elizabeth's interview are featured on the seminal LGBTQ storytelling site I'm From Driftwood. To watch, please visit imfromdriftwood.com/elizabeth_coffey_williams.

ALAN STEINMAN

RETIRED ADMIRAL, US COAST GUARD

OLYMPIA, WASHINGTON

> Alan Steinman was born in Newark, Ohio, on February 7, 1945. He graduated from MIT in 1966 and went on to receive his MD from the Stanford School of Medicine in 1971. He subsequently joined the US Coast Guard, ultimately earning the rank of Rear Admiral and serving as the Coast Guard's chief medical officer and chief safety officer.
>
> In 2003, the tenth anniversary of "Don't Ask, Don't Tell," Alan came out publicly in a *New York Times* op-ed denouncing the policy. At the time, he was the highest-ranking military official ever to have come out. Alan campaigned tirelessly against DADT until its repeal in 2011. He subsequently coauthored an article entitled "Medical Aspects of Transgender Service," arguing for the rights of transgender people to serve in the military. Alan's involvement in the issue was instrumental in the American Medical Association's decision to officially endorse transgender military service.

In 1992, President Clinton was elected. And he had promised as one of his first acts to repeal the ban on gays serving openly in the military. He was opposed by a massive amount of congressmen and senators and chaplain corps, and unfortunately was forced to retreat, and we ended up with this so-called compromise called "Don't Ask, Don't Tell."

I decided to retire in 1997 because I wanted to live my life as a gay man, who I was, who I knew I was since I was twelve or thirteen. I mean, fifty years was enough. That's more than enough.

Because I was an admiral, I knew when I retired that I could make a contribution, certainly in the military gay world, to getting "Don't Ask, Don't Tell" repealed. I would have a certain amount of authority in the minds of the people who had to make that legal decision in the legislatures. "Here is a senior officer who is gay, and it's not a big deal."

In November 2003, we came up on the tenth anniversary of "Don't Ask, Don't Tell." The Servicemembers Legal Defense Network, SLDN, proposed that the anniversary was an excellent time to come out and make a state-ment. And so basically that's what we did. I came out in an op-ed in the *New York Times*.

It was a huge news story everywhere. The commandant of the Coast Guard at the time was not pleased at all that I came out and was overheard to say that I was a disgrace to the Coast Guard and a disgrace to the nation.

To hear that was very hurtful, particularly after I had given so much of my life to the Coast Guard. But I understood that this was not the prevailing opinion for the entire Coast Guard. Certainly, the people I knew in the Coast Guard didn't care. The flag officers who I served with, they shrugged. They knew who I was, and it wasn't a big deal. So even though the comments were hurtful, it didn't stick with me.

THE SUBMARINER'S TESTIMONY

General John Shalikashvili was the chairman of the Joint Chiefs of Staff at the time "Don't Ask, Don't Tell" became law in 1993. Ultimately, he retired and moved to a little town called Steilacoom, Washington, which was about thirty miles from where I was living. We had a mutual friend, and I asked the friend whether he could introduce me to General Shalikashvili. So General Shalikashvili and I met in his living room, and we had a great conversation about "Don't Ask, Don't Tell" and gays in the military. When I left, I asked the general if we could meet some more, and he said sure.

At the time, I remembered that General Shalikashvili had said that one of the reasons that we'll never be able to repeal "Don't Ask, Don't Tell" is submarines. "You can't be gay on a submarine. It's just too close quarters. The other submarine sailors aren't going to want to interact with an openly gay sailor." So a few months later, I took some

gay former service members to meet with the general, including a former submariner. General Shalikashvili was interested in all their stories. But he was particularly interested in the submariner. He leaned forward in his chair, and for thirty minutes he and the submariner talked about life on a submarine. This submariner, this big bulky muscular guy, said, "Everybody on that boat knew I was gay. They didn't judge me by who I slept with on my off-duty time. I was judged by how well I did my job, and kept all of us alive, and protected our nation."

A few months later, in January 2007, General Shalikashvili wrote an op-ed in the *New York Times*. He mentioned our meetings in his living room, and he specifically men-

Alan's official Coast Guard photograph following his 1993 promotion to the rank of Rear Admiral and position of Director of Health and Safety (equivalent to the Surgeon General in the other branches of the Armed Forces)

tioned the submariner as helping to change his mind. And he concluded, "I think the time has come for us to revisit this issue."

That was like a nuclear bomb going off on the issue. The former chairman of the Joint Chiefs of Staff saying we can repeal this law.

General Shalikashvili has passed away, but I wanted his family to know and the nation to know what role he played, how important he was in getting the law repealed.

THE WILL TO SURVIVE

I've been asked if there are any similarities between people going through a sea survival situation and the quest for LGBT equality. And I would say, yes there are.

One of the most important things about surviving, whether it's sea survival or land survival or anywhere, is mental toughness. The will to survive, the will to carry on and persist. People who give up too quickly usually die. And the people who are willing to fight, they survive. Usually, it's their family. They're thinking about leaving their loved ones and how horrible that's going to be. They didn't get to say I love you, or say goodbye. The survivors I've interviewed, that's one of the strongest motivators, is doing it for their family.

And so it is with the LGBT community. As a community, we came to the conclusion, "We don't want to be persecuted anymore, to be discriminated against anymore." And we found some success when we began to get straight allies, when those allies found that they had gay and lesbian or bisexual or transgender family members or friends or cowork-

ers. I think that's the key factor on how we in the LGBT community have managed to progress in this nation. And there's no going back. You can't just suddenly disown your family members or your friends or your coworkers. We have persisted in our fight for equality for many, many decades and are succeeding. And I think we'll continue to succeed.

Today, Alan lives with his husband, Dallas, a former Navy enlisted man, in a wood-and-glass home overlooking Puget Sound. Alan, Dallas, and Dallas's sister Nicole are jointly raising Nicole's son, Ethan. Alan remembers legally adopting Ethan as one of the greatest days of his life.

KAREN CLARK

POLITICIAN

MINNEAPOLIS, MINNESOTA

Karen was born in 1945 in Oklahoma and grew up on a farm in Edgerton, Minnesota.

In 1980, Karen was elected to the Minnesota House of Representatives in District 62A (South Minneapolis), the lowest-income district in Minnesota. Over her nearly forty years in this position, Karen championed LGBTQ rights, workers' rights, and social, economic, and environmental justice for low-income people, Native Americans, and communities of color.

One of Karen's greatest political achievements was the 1993 passage of an amendment to the Minnesota Human Rights Act, coauthored with gay legislator Allan Spear, to include gays and lesbians. In 2011, Karen helped defeat the GOP-controlled Minnesota Legislature's attempt to ban gay marriage, and in 2013, she authored the bipartisan House bill to legalize same-sex marriage in Minnesota. That year, President Barack Obama honored Karen as a Harvey Milk Champion of Change. Karen retired in 2018, having become the longest-serving out lesbian legislator in United States history.

In 1993, we passed a law here in Minnesota that added those really dangerous words, "sexual orientation," to the Minnesota Human Rights Act. My mom and dad came to march with us that June. They were carrying a sign that says, "OUR HOMOSEXUAL CHILDREN SHOULD HAVE THE SAME RIGHTS AS OUR HETEROSEXUAL CHILDREN." When I met up with them afterwards, my mother said, "I just cried all the way through. People were so wonderful to us. They were so happy."

Years later, the little town where my parents lived, a little village of ninety people, had a centennial celebration. My mother made sure that marching sign was there to be seen along with the other things from our family. That's the kind of development that can happen, and it's part of the basis for my understanding how people here can change.

A POSSIBILITY (MAYBE EVEN A DUTY)

I was working as an OB-GYN nurse practitioner at Hennepin County Medical Center, and I had come out. I was part of the lesbian feminist community. I thought, "I got to figure out what I'm doing with my life." I decided to take a break and go to this feminist retreat that was in Vermont.

Elaine Noble came and spoke one day. She was the very first openly lesbian person who'd gotten elected to office in the US. She was in the state legislature at that time in Boston, and she talked about her district, and it sounded a lot like my neighborhood at the time, a diverse community, racially diverse, lots of older people, and she talked about how she had worked with a lot of the elders in her community. And she talked about how lesbians should think about running for office.

She was so powerful in just saying, "This is a possibility. It's maybe even a duty that some of us should consider going forward." She was just so positive about it that it planted that seed of possibility.

THE MOST RIDICULOUS THING

My dear friend Janet Dollum and I started something called the Lesbian Feminist Organizing Committee, LFOC. One of the things that we did was look at the issue of, should LFOC get involved in electoral politics, or is it too dirty for us? We organized a forum

With Karen looking on, Gov. Mark Dayton signs the bill to legalize same-sex marriage in Minnesota in May 2013.

at the women's coffeehouse, which was in a church basement at Plymouth Congregational Church. We had a couple hundred people there. We took a vote and decided yes, we will start a committee on electoral politics, and so we did.

What we did was organize lesbian feminists all over the state to go to precinct caucuses. We put together a twenty-two-item agenda of what we stood for and took it to the caucus, and when we did that we drew incredible attention from other progressive groups. "Whoa, who are these lesbian feminists? They have everything from fair prices to farmers, childcare, racial issues, housing, environmental issues. Who are these women?" Out of that LFOC was invited to become part of an organization called the Farmer Labor Association, FLA. I became the delegate from LFOC to the FLA.

A few years later, in 1979 or 1980, some people from the Farmer Labor Association approached me. They said, "We would like you to run for a state legislature." At the time, we were talking about the Senate, and I just laughed. I thought it was the most ridiculous thing I'd heard. I'm much more comfortable organizing in the street and behind-the-scenes with my lesbian feminist community.

After I got done laughing, I said to them, "Are you sure that you are going to be able to stand with me on this? Because it means the Farmer Labor Association is supporting a lesbian feminist woman. There's never been an open lesbian elected in the state to any office. Are you sure you're going to be with me?" In the end they decided, and we went for it.

We organized like crazy. Eventually, I decided to run for the House, not the Senate, and we won handily in the end.

TALK ABOUT LOVE

The credit for getting marriage equality passed by the Minnesota Legislature in 2013 goes to an incredible grassroots momentum that was created to try to discuss what same-sex marriage means. Oh my goodness, we came to it in a hard way.

The year before, in 2012, I and everyone else was running for office. In addition to running for office, we had to deal with these two constitutional amendments. One of them was to ban gay marriage in the state of Minnesota, and the other one was to require photo IDs at the polls.

On these two issues, there was a strong connection between labor and civil rights groups, and women's groups, and people of color organizations, and GLBTQ groups, and we just really worked hard. But the way that the folks that were steering the gay marriage amendment approached it was to talk about love, rather than saying this is a civil rights issue. It was an amazing campaign, millions of phone calls. Just a lot of people talking to their families, talking to their friends, talking to their colleagues at work, talking to the people in their faith community. It was an amazing grassroots campaign that happened.

I give our governor, Mark Dayton, a lot of credit for helping us pass this bill. He said, "You put this on my desk, I'm signing it. I want it to pass." He was a very strong supporter. It was an amazing experience.

OUTWORDS interviewed Karen Clark at the Minnesota State Office Building in March 2018. Finding her office was easy; it was the only door in the building decorated with signs like "DIVERSITY MAKES US GREAT" and "WOMEN'S RIGHTS = HUMAN RIGHTS."

RUTH SHACK

PIONEERING LGBTQ ALLY

MIAMI, FLORIDA

> Ruth Shack was born in New York in 1931 and grew up on Long Island. On their honeymoon in 1953, she and her husband, Richard, fell in love with Miami and never left.
>
> In 1976, Ruth won an open seat on the Dade County (now Miami-Dade County) Commission. Soon thereafter, she sponsored a successful county ordinance prohibiting discrimination on the basis of "sexual preference." The following year, the singer and former Miss America Anita Bryant orchestrated a successful campaign to repeal the ordinance and then took her notorious Save Our Children campaign nationwide. The campaign triggered and galvanized gay rights movements all over America. [For more on Anita Bryant, see pp. 27, 237.] In the end, Anita Bryant's victory was Pyrrhic, and Ruth Shack emerged as one of LGBTQ America's most cherished allies.

By the late 1970s, I had been around politics for years, worked for a whole lot of politicians, worked in campaigns, right up front. At that time, several of the Dade County commissioners were removed from the commission in a bogus scandal. The governor appointed a woman who I then ran against, along with eight others. I got into a runoff and then won the election.

In the race for election to the County Commission, three or four men put themselves together as a group and screened candidates. At the time, there was this nondiscrimination ordinance that they wanted to see amended to include sexual preference. I think that was the language. I said, "Absolutely." After I got myself elected, these men came to me and said, "Would you introduce the amendment?" I said, "Certainly." This was no big deal. There was nothing courageous about it. It was the next step.

Six weeks later, there was a public hearing on the ordinance. In the interim, Anita Bryant and her minister and churches, let's say, "opposed the concept" and really came out of the woodwork. Anita had a national name, and the bogus awful "Save Our Children" slogan got international coverage. For the first time, people knew where Dade County was. As virulent and disgusting as the opposition was at that public hearing, five of the nine commissioners held, and the ordinance passed.

The ugly discrimination was no longer played out against the gay community. I became the focal point. Wherever we went, we were threatened. People followed me into the dressing room in Saks Fifth Avenue to tell me how degrading I am, what I've done to their children. To get in an elevator with people who hate you is not wonderful. It's not fun. The elevator just doesn't move fast enough. There were people marching in front of our house. My youngest daughter, who was fifteen turning sixteen, she'd get home and there were death threats on the phone machine.

At the time, it was Richard's and my twenty-fifth wedding anniversary. We took out full-page ads in the *Herald*, with our three daughters behind us, thanking Dade County for twenty-five years of happiness. And someone in an elevator said to me, "Which one of the girls is your lover?"

Anita and her ministry and a bunch of crazies went for a referendum and overturned the ordinance. It was a huge, huge loss.

There is nothing better for organizing than to have opposition. In response to the defeat, it happened with the gay community. There was a sense of pride that we had the words, we had support, and we had passed the ordinance. And then they took it away from us. These were people who we all knew. They were teachers, they were gardeners, they were decorators, they were people we were with every single day. Before the passage, they were still being herded out of bars and into jail in front of cameras. All of a sudden, they were a gay community. I still get goose bumps.

A year after the loss, I had to run for reelection. My opponent was one of the men who had headed up the anti-ordinance campaign. That was the issue that he campaigned on. I never apologized. I never equivocated. I said, "You may disagree with me, but that's the way I feel." People would say to my opponent, "She's a nice lady. We know where she stands. Go home." That's what allowed me to go on a year later to get reelected and to win two more elections after that, because of the way I never apologized, I never equivocated.

In person, Ruth is strong, funny, and frank. Speculating on whether a friend's grandson might turn out to be gay, she said, "I wish him all the luck in the world. I hope he does it with style."

CHARLES SILVERSTEIN

PSYCHOTHERAPIST, AUTHOR OF *THE JOY OF GAY SEX*

NEW YORK, NEW YORK

Charles Silverstein was born in Brooklyn, New York, in 1935. One of his searing child-hood memories was when his family tried to move to Los Angeles in 1946 and was driven out of town for being Jewish.

In 1974, Charles completed his PhD in psychology at Rutgers and opened his psycho-therapy practice, which continues to this day. In the meantime, after struggling against his homosexuality for many years, Charles came out and soon got involved with the Gay Activists Alliance, participating in many of their "zaps" to bring attention to the nascent gay rights revolution. In 1973, Charles played a pivotal role in orchestrating the very public confrontation that would begin to tear down the American Psychiatric Association's definition of homosexuality as a mental illness.

In 1977, Charles co-wrote *The Joy of Gay Sex* with novelist Edmund White. His other published works include *Man to Man: Gay Couples in America*; *Gays, Lesbians, and Their Therapists*; two additional editions of *The Joy of Gay Sex* (with Felice Picano); and *For the Ferryman: A Personal Memoir*, published in 2011. That same year, Charles received a Gold Medal Award for Life Achievement from the American Psychological Association.

CRUISING ON CRUTCHES

Like a lot of people of my generation, I went into psychoanalysis to be cured of my homo-sexuality. I wanted to be cured because I was terribly miserable, and I was in psychoanalysis for seven years and analyzed all this stuff to death. I had sex with some women, which was terribly unfair to them. They thought I was serious, when I was just trying to cure myself.

One day, around 1968, I picked up a sex newspaper, and I started to read the ads, and read all the delicious things that some men wanted to do to other men, and I became overwhelmed with lust. I just could not contain it anymore. So I went down to the Village.

I should mention, I had a broken leg at the time, and I was walking around with crutches. So I didn't know where to go, and I remember hobbling along and there was this luncheonette. So I hobbled in, ordered, and asked the waiter, "Where's the nearest gay bar?" And he said, "Why don't you go to Julius's around the corner?" So I hobbled out, and I went to Julius's. And when I walked in, all eyes turned toward me. Because I was on these crutches with this plaster cast that must've weighed thirty pounds.

I went to the bar, and I struck up a conversation with this fellow whose name was Don. And I said to him, I've got really good pot at home. Why don't you come home with me? I was very ballsy. And he said yes.

We get into my apartment, and I threw down my crutches. And I pushed him onto the couch and then put my leg with the cast over his lap so he couldn't escape. And we went from there.

And that's how I came out. I dropped my analyst, and I joined the Gay Activists Alliance. And that's an organization that many people will tell you, it saved their lives, and I think it did for me.

The Gay Activists Alliance was a radical organization, but it was highly organized in the sense that before a demonstration, or a zap, the publicity committee would make out press releases and send them out to different newspapers. So the newspapers would know where and when our next demonstration was. And it was all to tell the police. We wanted the police to show up, because it's important to have the police. But the most important people were the newspaper photographers, because we had to be very conscious about getting the shit kicked out of us by the police. They wouldn't do that if the photographers were there to take pictures.

About 1992, when hair was in

It was wonderful. I remember we went from a dance, a thousand or so people one Saturday night, and marched down the streets to some politician's house who was head of a committee that was holding up a gay rights bill. We demonstrated at two in the morning, waking up all of his neighbors. And we had what was called the suicide squad. The suicide squad was, police would put up a barrier and the guys in the suicide squad would jump over the barrier. The object was to have police on the other side arrest them. The photographers take their pictures and everybody is happy, and then they let us go. The police show they're doing their job, the newspapers get their pictures, and the gay rights people get publicity in the newspaper, so it was a win-win all around. As much as possible, we tried to do that.

Charles and his lover, William, in 1985 at their home in Napanoch, NY

ZAPPING THE APA

At the Gay Activists Alliance, we viewed psychiatrists as gatekeepers of society's attitudes. So we took it upon ourselves to be a force to eliminate homosexuality as a mental disorder, because if that happened, other changes would automatically follow.

In the early 1970s, there was going to be a meeting of the Association for the Advancement of Behavior Therapy at the New York Hilton. This was a group that used behavioral techniques to cure various things, and one of the things they wanted to cure was being gay.

I presented this to the executive committee of GAA, and I said, "This is really important. We should zap them." So a zap was approved. A bunch of us were going to go into the room where a psychologist from Belfast, Ireland, was speaking about his work curing homosexuality with aversion therapy.

This was the Hilton. The Hilton had their own police force, and they're very nasty. Some gay protesters had gotten beaten up there a year before. I didn't want to get anyone in the room beaten up, particularly not me. So I spoke with friends of mine who were running the meeting, and I said, "Look, this is going to happen whether you like it or not. But we don't want to get beaten up, and you don't want people getting beaten up." And they agreed.

The psychologist's name was Quinn. So I walked into the room and I saw Quinn up front. I went up and introduced myself. "I'm Charles Silverstein, and I'm a graduate student in psychology, and I'm also a gay liberationist." And I told him that we were going to have a demonstration during his lecture. I said, "We're going to let you speak for ten minutes, and then we're going to interrupt." And Dr. Quinn, who was from Belfast where there was all sorts of violence going on, I think he appreciated getting this warning in advance, and he said okay.

I went back to my seat, and we let him speak for ten minutes, and then Ron Gold, who represented the GAA, got up and he interrupted. We had this fierce verbal conflict with the audience, who were pissed off at our doing that. Meantime, my friends from the convention stood at the door, and when the Hilton cops showed up, they stopped them from coming in.

After the GAA zap, a psychiatrist named Robert Spitzer came to us and said that he was on the nomenclature committee of the American Psychiatric Association. Would we like to make a presentation before them about removing homosexuality? Of course, we jumped to that.

We were invited to make a presentation before the nomenclature committee on February 8, 1973. I wrote my speech the night before, with my lover, William, lying in bed right near me. He was a master of language, and he corrected it and made all sorts of changes. The next day, I kissed William good-bye and went uptown. I knew that what I was going to present was right, and we were going to win.

Charles's longtime lover, William, died of AIDS in 1992. In 2017, Charles married Bill Bartelt, but still lives alone in his rambling, book-lined seventh-floor apartment on Manhattan's Upper West Side.

KATHLEEN SAADAT

"THE SOCIAL CONSCIENCE OF OREGON"

PORTLAND, OREGON

Born in Saint Louis, Missouri, and raised in a family committed to justice and education, Kathleen Saadat graduated from Chicago's Farragut High School in 1957 and from Reed College in 1974. In 1976, Kathleen and six others organized Portland's first gay rights march. Later, she helped craft Portland's civil rights ordinance prohibiting discrimination against gay and lesbian people and discrimination based on income. In 1992, she served on the steering committee for the campaign against Ballot Measure 9, which would have effectively defined Oregon gays and lesbians as second-class citizens.

Beyond queer issues, Kathleen has been a constant and vocal advocate for people of color, women, and the economically disenfranchised. She served as executive director of Oregon's Commission on Black Affairs and as director of affirmative action for the state of Oregon, helped plan Portland's International Women's Day celebrations, and was included by *Oregon Business* magazine on its list of "100 Who Lead in Oregon."

The idea of being gay came early in my life. I knew by the time I was seven or six that I was different.

I liked girls. Then I found out I wasn't supposed to talk about it. By talking about it—"Whoa, what's wrong with you?" My cousin said to me, "You're a Do-Funny." I felt so bad and I realized I needed to stop talking about that. Afraid of losing family, friends, connection.

When I talked to my biological mother much later in my life, she said, "Oh, I knew something was different when you were three." I said, "How did you know?" She said, "You quit calling me Mother, and you started calling me Rebecca, and you started telling me what to do as though you were in charge."

I got to college, and I got picked on a lot. I didn't want a boyfriend. I was drinking heavily, and after a year and a half, I dropped out. I was doing well in physics. Doing well in history. I quit and went back to Saint Louis, where I still drank and struggled through this whole identity thing and how could I be straight. Then at some point just saying, "This sucks. I don't want to do this." Just flapping around, all mixed up with whiskey. Scotch usually.

I ended up going to Renard Hospital in Saint Louis, which is a mental health facility.

I was there for a while and learned a lot about myself in terms of a need to be still, and a need to talk more. I didn't talk very much. I didn't tell people what I was feeling very much.

I got better when I came to Oregon. I was thirty years old. I came here with a partner and her five children. Right away, life started to change for me.

THE BIG, BAD, BLACK DYKE

Going into the women's movement in the '70s was quite an experience for me in that I had come from Saint Louis. Saint Louis people are a lot more assertive than Oregon people. I've been in Oregon since 1970, and I still find that there are people that respond to me that way. Part of this is I'm big and I'm black, so

Kathleen speaking at a rally in the 1990s

that intensifies whatever thing it is about me not being nice. 'Cause I'm not nice. I don't need to be nice.

I asked my father, when I was very young, I said, "Why is it that when one of my three brothers gets mad, it's okay, but when I get angry everybody gets really upset?" He had no answer for me.

There was this one community meeting where one woman called me a bitch, and she's sitting across the table from me. I thought, if I get up and go over there and slap her, that's what everybody expects me to do because I'm the big, bad, black dyke. I just sat there and looked at her and said, "Well, that's a personal opinion but not a very good political analysis. Would you like to try again?" Everybody laughed, and she got up and left.

CHOOSING BETWEEN DIFFERENT ASPECTS OF ME

Ballot Measure 9 was a measure put on the ballot by the Oregon Citizens Alliance back in 1992. [For more on Ballot Measure 9, see pp. 189–90.] It would have removed rights from gay and lesbian people. It would have said you couldn't hold certain jobs. It would've also said that people who supported you couldn't hold certain jobs. They would lose their job. There was an inference within that ballot measure that said you would not be able to advocate for yourself to reinstate yourself. You were deprived of the right to even argue the position on some level.

People wanted to form a steering committee to fight this measure. I was elected to the steering committee, along with several other people of color. The message I got from the people there was they wanted people of color in the leadership. My assertion to the committee was that we needed some focus on the black community and other communities of color. I was told directly and indirectly that was not necessary or needed.

Then two people were killed in Salem, about a few blocks from where I lived. One of them was black, and the other one was developmentally delayed. I said, we need to go in the black community, form a group to educate the black community. We got black preachers together to oppose this ballot measure. There were black preachers who supported it, but it was important to have black preachers who opposed it. We did that.

Meanwhile, I'm still working with this larger group that has become more and more hostile toward me. At some point I remember saying, "I understand what the right is doing. I have no idea what you're doing. You scare me more." It had to do with a denial about the existence of people of color in this movement.

I came home lots of nights and just cried. I just cried. Finally, I got the attention of another board member. That started to change it a little bit. I started getting these anonymous postcards. "We're watching." "We know that this is hard for you. Thank you for staying." They were so uplifting, to know that somebody was watching and somebody understood what I was going through.

This was the biggest ethical dilemma I had in my life. I was forced to make a choice between aspects of me. I'm working with a

group that is manifesting racism but is trying to ensure the rights of gay and lesbian people, which includes me. I had to sit down with myself and make a conscious decision to stay.

Kathleen's voice serves for more than activism. She is also a gifted singer, a skill she learned from her grandmother who, according to Kathleen, sang "from morning until dinner time." In 2016, Kathleen's recording of "Love for Sale" was featured on the Pink Martini album Je Dis Oui!

VALDA PROUT

HAIRDRESSER, MOTHER, TRANSGENDER ADVOCATE
WASHINGTON, DC

Born in Boston in 1935, Valda Prout's life has been a long, complex dance between the male identity (and the name Mallory) she was assigned at birth and the female identity and name that are her truth.

After moving to New York at age twenty-four, Valda worked in the stockroom at Gimbels and the records department at Doubleday, and then went to beauty school and worked as a hairstylist at various salons. In her words, she was Mallory by day and Valda by night. "Mallory supported Valda—not the other way around."

In the late 1980s, Valda moved to Washington, DC. Around this time, she met a three-year-old boy named Byron, adopted him, and for the next fifteen years lived as Mallory to avoid causing Byron any trouble at school. After Byron graduated from high school, Valda was free to live entirely as Valda.

When I graduated from high school, I went to New England Conservatory for two years. I studied voice there. The thing was, I had to take piano, harmony, and all that kind of stuff, and I wasn't good at that, so I quit after two years. I had to work and so I got a job at Harvard University working in the mail room. That was a turning point in my life because I met a professor there. He was not a famous professor like Roscoe Pound and Archibald Cox.

This professor, we used to go to the Coop in Harvard Square. He would buy me frappes, sodas, and things like that. He used to tell me how nice-looking I was. I never thought I was a good-looking child because kids used to call me "Big Lips" and "Big Nose" and all that kind of stuff. This professor made me feel beautiful, very handsome. We never had sex or anything like that. At that time, I was innocent, very innocent.

He gave me the most beautiful gift that I have to this day. He took me to New York, and I saw my first play. The play was *West Side Story* with Carol Lawrence and Chita Rivera at the Winter Garden. It was fascinating and I loved it. My professor exposed me to a whole lot, reading and books and things like that. It was wonderful.

Later, I saw Ricardo Montalbán, Ossie Davis. I saw Peggy Lee, Eartha Kitt. Josephine Baker, I saw her three times. Oh, that woman

Valda in 1986

was fabulous. She was in her sixties then. I remember the announcer: "Ladies and gentlemen, Josephine Baker." It was dark. All of a sudden, this light came and there she was. Oh God. We applauded.

Then Marlene Dietrich. She was old at that time, but honey, she was flawless. She had this pink light, and she was in white. She stood there. She didn't move, just sang. See, these women had years of experience behind them. You understand?

SPEAK UP

Eventually, I wanted to get out of Boston. I told my mother I wanted to go live in New York. I only had $2 in my pocket, just $2. I didn't tell my mother that because if I had told her I had $2, she wouldn't have let me go.

In 1956 or '57, I got arrested. They called it loitering, something like that. The cop arrested me and put me not in the paddy wagon, but in the back seat of the car.

He got in the back seat with me. I thought

that was kind of strange. He told me to give him a blowjob. I looked at him, I said, "What?" I said, "Let me tell you something. If you make me suck that dick, I'm going to bite it off and you're going to have to explain to the judge how your dick got into my mouth." That's what I told him. He said, "Get the fuck out of my car."

Let me tell you something. I've been around white people. You people, you know your rights. That came off on me too. I wanted the same rights as you got. I didn't never consider myself a second-class citizen. That cop would never do that to you, because you all speak up. That's what I learned. Speak up. I would get a lawyer in a minute if something goes down in here that I don't like.

CHESTNUT BROWN AND NUT BROWN

Halloween was around the corner, so I decided that I was going to dress up. I got this ponytail and made a beehive out of it. For breasts, I tucked nylons in my blouse, and I had a pencil skirt and whatnot. I looked terrible, but this Spanish guy danced with me. This was 1960.

I had a wonderful time, and that's when I met a lot of the white drag queens. I learned a lot about makeup from them. I got a wig and I got makeup. The only makeup that you could get was chestnut brown and nut brown. You mixed them to get the color you want. That's what you had to do, and that's what I did.

I wasn't a full transgender person yet. I started taking hormones from '65 up to this day. I started developing breasts. As time went on, I started looking better and better and better. I don't take as many hormones now because it takes away your sex life a little bit.

I found being transgender doesn't mean you have to have a vagina. I know a lot of transgender don't have the change. You got to be happy what you are about. If you can't accept yourself, how can people accept you? You know what I'm trying to say?

I said to myself I would never, never have a sex change for somebody. I would have it if I wanted it, because I'm the one have to live with it. You pay all this money to be beautiful, you're going to get old and it ain't going to help you. All that money is gone. You're still an old woman. I am happy being eighty-one. I'm not like I used to look. I accept that.

A LITTLE FINESSE

My ex-boyfriend left a child with me, Byron, who I adopted. During the adoption, my ex-boyfriend and I went to mediation, his lawyer and my lawyer. My ex-boyfriend said about me, "He wears a dress." My lawyer said, "Don't say nothing, Mallory. Don't say nothing." I said nothing.

To make a long story short, I won the case. I'm going to tell you, everything changed. Everything changed when I signed those papers. That was my child. You understand?

One day Byron saw a picture of me in drag. He said, "Who's that picture?" I said, "That's me." He said, "No, that's a lady." I said, "That's me, Byron." That was the last time he ever saw me in drag. That's the last time because I did not want to confuse him. I couldn't take him to school looking like that.

I remember one time I took him to school, and these two boys called me a faggot in front of him. I took the kids by the shirt and marched them to the principal. I said, "They called me a faggot."

I didn't cuss. You don't get no results when you're cussing people out. You have to have a little finesse. They brought the parents in the next day, and we discussed it. I never had an issue again.

I can be nasty when I want to be. But I found if you're nice, you get more done.

Valda stays busy these days attending transgender meetings, visiting with her large group of friends, and staying in touch with her two nieces. She told us she's glad to have lived this long and hopes to live a bit longer. She also said, "The most beautiful gift is death."

If you're looking for a woman at peace with herself, stop by Valda's place.

ABOUT OUTWORDS

OUTWORDS travels America recording professional-quality, on-camera interviews with LGBTQ pioneers and elders—the people who witnessed our history and made it happen.

Our goals are threefold: to ensure that the LGBTQ community's remarkable history is never rewritten or erased; to inspire queer youth and let them know they are part of something much bigger than themselves; and to model inclusivity, integrity, and authenticity to the world at large.

You are invited to share your time and ideas, subscribe to our mailing list, and make a tax-deductible donation.

Website: theoutwordsarchive.org

Instagram: theoutwordsarchive

Facebook: theoutwordsarchive

ACKNOWLEDGMENTS

My dad, Ron Funk, was a journalist. For pretty much my entire childhood, he was the editor of the *Santa Monica Evening Outlook*, our midsize, family-owned newspaper. He was always interested in the stories of individual people—where they came from, how they came to be who they were. My mom, Ann Funk, was a historian. Late in life, she wrote a novel, *Lifeblood*, about one of the first female doctors in the American West. Like my dad, she thrived on people's stories—the forces that shaped them, the choices they made.

My mom developed dementia in her later years, and in February 2015, she passed away. I never had the chance to tell her about OUT-WORDS. Over the next couple of years, as the project began to take shape, my dad told me on numerous occasions, "It's a good project. And your mom would have really loved it." I agreed with him, and that made me feel like Mom was with me, almost watching over my shoulder as I crisscrossed America collecting the interviews that would one day become *The Book of Pride*.

On a bright, warm San Francisco afternoon in May 2017, as I was interviewing the writer Terry Baum (p. 222), Dad laid down for a nap at home in Santa Barbara, California, and passed away.

My parents planted the seeds of OUT-WORDS in me. They did it by falling in love with each other—two people with humanity, curiosity, and creativity—and by always encouraging me to follow my own sense of adventure. They admired people who went against the grain, and that's what OUTWORDS and *The Book of Pride* are all about. Thank you, Mom and Dad, for your lives and your support.

The Book of Pride is a direct result of charitable contributions to OUTWORDS from hundreds of people. I'm grateful to each and every one of them, and in particular to those who have donated $1,000 or more:

Minnie Biggs
California Wellness Foundation
Caron Barrett & Deborah Vial
Alvin Baum
Thomas L. Ford Charitable Trust
Chip Conley Foundation
Steve Crystal & Hillary Seitz
Robert D. Funk
Craig Hartzman & James John
Peter Kallen & Jeffrey Stuhr

Charles D. Urstadt & David Bernard
Aaron Smith & Thomas Moore
Christine F. Purcell
Tabell Family Foundation
Richard Tate & John Hatch
Charles and Elinor Urstadt
Chuck Williams
Mason & Wendy Willrich
Sonni Zambino

OUTWORDS has a tiny, thoughtful, hardworking staff. Thank you to Director of Operations Tom Bliss and to Kevin Birou, Roberto Campos, Sarah Chavez, Larissa Mills, Michelle Patterson, and Molly Underwood. Thanks also to podcast producer Cameron Tenner, and to all our volunteers and interns.

OUTWORDS' erstwhile team of field producers and camera operators have put up with dodgy accommodations, marginal meals, early morning departures and midnight arrivals, sweltering heat, and even a few snowstorms. I thank them all, and in particular Kate Kunath and Natalie Tsui, for helping me to grow this project with clarity and integrity.

Thanks to current and former OUTWORDS board members Richard Tate (chair), Henry Briffel, Ed Campbell, Julie Nemecek, and Sonni Zambino. Thanks to our Leadership Council for their wisdom and guidance. Thanks to Mark Tauber for bringing this book to HarperCollins, and special thanks to editor Sydney Rogers for her infectious enthusiasm and for caring so much about this book and what it represents. Thanks to Nixon Peabody LLP for their pro bono legal support.

I've loved being part of the WeWork Gas Tower community in downtown Los Angeles since January 2017. In May 2018, WeWork honored OUTWORDS with a Creator Award (cash prize, bigger office, smaller rent!). Many thanks to the company and above all, to my WeWork family at Fifth and Grand.

Over the course of my life, two teachers (Ned Spofford and Susan Dodd), two therapists (Greg Byrer and Barry Miller), and two bosses (Carol Fleisher and Read Jackson) saw me and believed in me before I saw and believed in myself. I thank them from the bottom of my heart.

When I met my husband, Jay, at the age of 47, I had never stuck with a relationship for longer than six months. Insightful, passionate, and patient, Jay fashioned a key to unlock my heart. During the life of OUTWORDS, Jay has shown an extraordinary knack for knowing when to question me, and when to simply tell me that he loves me and is proud of me. Thank you, my crown and anchor, for holding me and tending this dream with me.

A final word of appreciation, admiration, and love to the courageous, inventive, beautiful people in *The Book of Pride*, and to whatever higher power chose me to record their stories and share them with the world. It has been the privilege of a lifetime.

In Memoriam:
Ray Hill (1940–2018)
Dick Leitsch (1935–2018)
Donna Red Wing (1950–2018)

PHOTO PERMISSIONS